TIBET THE MYSTERIOUS

The Potala, from the South

TIBET THE MYSTERIOUS

THOMAS H. HOLDICH

WITH ILLUSTRATIONS FROM PHOTOGRAPHS AND MAPS AND WITH MAP IN COLOURS

GYAN

Published by

GYAN

Gyan Publishing House
5, Ansari Road
Daryaganj, New Delhi-110002
Phone: 011-47034999, 9811692060
E-mail: books@gyanbooks.com

Distribution Network
gyanbooks.com
India, USA, Canada, UK, Australia, France

ISBN : 978-81-212-4111-3 (PB)
First Published, 1906

2nd Impression 2020

Printed at: Gyan Press, Delhi.

Tibet The Mysterious
Author: Thomas H. Holdich

TIBET
THE MYSTERIOUS

By COL. SIR THOMAS H. HOLDICH
K. C. M. G., K. C. I. E., C. B.

With illustrations from photographs, and maps and with map in colours

New York · FREDERICK A. STOKES COMPANY · *Publishers*

PREFACE

NO country in the world has exercised a more potent influence on the imaginations of men or presented such fascinating problems for solution to the explorer as Tibet; and this influence has been active amongst all the generations which have exploited the byeways of the earth from the days of Herodotus to those of Younghusband. It may be doubted whether even now the fascination of Tibetan travel is dead. But the glamour of it has undoubtedly faded somewhat since the streets of Lhasa have been trodden by the spurred and booted Englishman and his ruthless hand has exposed the mystic shams of that quaint and squalid city.

With Lhasa, however, this book has little to do. It is intended to illustrate to some extent the sequence of exploration in that great wilderness of stony and inhospitable altitudes which lie far beyond Lhasa, and may serve incidentally as a small tribute to the memory of many great achievements. In compiling a record of adventure so varied as this, no apology is necessary for quoting the works of the best authorities within reach, and the sources of information which have been laid under contribution (Russian, American, Italian, Indian, French, Swedish, and English) are so numerous that I feel it to be impossible to do more than present the reader with a general bibliography of Tibet, and to say that this work owes something to every authority quoted.

For the illustrations I am mainly indebted to Major Ryder, Captain Rawling, Lieutenant Bailey, M. Sibikoff, Mr. Littledale, Mr. John Thomson, the Paris Geographical Society, and to the Royal Geographical Society for the use of their maps.

T. HUNGERFORD HOLDICH.

CONTENTS

CHAPTER VI

CHAPTER VII

CHAPTER VIII

CHAPTER IX

CHAPTER X

ILLUSTRATIONS

TIBET

THE MYSTERIOUS

TIBET THE MYSTERIOUS

CHAPTER I

Early Tales about Tibet — Conformation of Tibetan Plateau and its Mountain Barriers — Routes into Tibet — Northwestern Routes — Leh, Shipki, and Niti Passes — Sikkim Passes — Eastern Routes — Ta-chien-lu — Routes from the North

THROUGH all the ages Tibet has held a paramount position amongst those regions of the world which have been popularly invested with a veil of mystery because they are inaccessible and unknown.

Tibet is so isolated, so lofty, so irresponsive to outside influences, has held herself so far apart from the meddling interference of the busy, commercial world, as to provoke the enterprise of generations of speculative geographers, who, accepting "omne ignotum pro magnifico," have startled the world with small instalments of truth surrounded by wide embroideries of decorative fancy. One of the earliest, if not quite the first, of these Tibetan romances dates from the days of Herodotus, nearly five hundred years before our era. When all the writings of the great "Father of history" can be carefully examined by the light of modern research, it will be found that his general accuracy is indisputable. His knowledge of Asiatic geography and his care in collating such evidence as may be gathered from the earliest of classical "travellers' tales" testifies to the possession by him of considerable analytical faculty and discernment. To one particular tale at any rate he gives a cautious admission of probability, but by no means a cordial assent. It was said that in the extreme northwest of India there existed a race of enormous ants, fierce and powerful, whose peculiar mission in life was the digging out of gold. Traders, mounted on swift camels, occasionally succeeded in seizing the gold which was accumulated in heaps by these excavating ants, and then rode rapidly away, pursued by other ferocious guardians of the soil who slew them if they caught them. Amongst all the ludicrous exaggerations of ancient classical tradition relating to India, this one story evinces a remarkable tenacity of existence. It is repeated in every tale of the East that is told by compilers and adventurers before the days of Herodotus, and is only doubtfully regarded by him as pure fiction. It was not until, in recent years, the trans-Himalayan explorers of the Indian Survey recorded their experiences that any light could be thrown on its origin. These explorers, making their way painfully over the terrific altitudes which intervene between India and western Tibet, reached at length the gold-mining districts which lie beyond the mountains on the great western plains. Here they discovered the Tibetan workman delving for gold after a fashion of his own. The intense cold and the fierce winds of the highlands compelled him to grovel on the ground enfolded in a thick, black blanket, whilst he dug, or scratched, painfully and slowly at the alluvial soil with the end of the first tool available to his hand, which was usually the horn of the Tibetan antelope. To all appearance he was a rough imitation of a huge horned ant grubbing up the auriferous soil and piling it in heaps for subsequent washing. Guarded by immensely powerful dogs (whose ferocity even to this day is a byword amongst travellers in Tibet), he has pursued his unenviable calling from those very early days until now, hardly improving his processes, making but slight impression and shallow indentations in the soil, and probably leaving behind two-thirds of the gold which it contains. Here, then, according to Sir H. Rawlinson, is the solution of the mystery that surrounded that particular tale; and it is but one illustration of the perceptive faculty possessed by Herodotus that he should consider it worthy of record.

Hardly anything of note concerning Tibet occurs in the works of mediæval geographical writers and compilers. The huge, great central upheaval south of the Gobi depression extending along the whole length of the Himalayas (which form its southern buttress or revetment through which the great natural staircases lead upwards to the plateau from the plains), geologically coeval with the Himalayas of the Northwest, but newer by countless ages than those of the East, has ever been a barrier against the ever-recurrent tides of human movement southwards. No mediæval trade routes ever crossed Tibet from the north. Along the length of the intervening plains of Chinese Turkestan they ran westward from China till they touched the central barrier (the Taurus of the Classics), which is the eastern wall of the Pamirs. They then diverged northward, or twisted over the Pamir region to Badakshan and the Oxus, but they ever avoided Tibet. The countless tides of Central Asian emigration (Aryans, Skyths, Mongols, etc.), when they overflowed into India, passed by way of Badakshan and the Hindu Kush — never across Tibet. No Chinese pilgrim seeking knowledge at the fountain-head in northern India ever traced his way across the Tibetan uplands from the plains of western China and Kashgar, although he often selected a straighter route than that of Mongol invaders. Avoiding the central Pamir region and Tibet by crossing the Hindu Kush near its northeastern base by either the Wakjir or Baroghél pass, he entered the valleys of Gilgit and Chitral in order to make his way over routes incredibly rough and difficult to the ancient Gandhara — the seat of all that was most sacred to Buddhism in the extreme northwest of India. The great rolling Tibetan highlands have thus played a most important part in the history of Asiatic migration. They have been the natural buffer-land between Central Asia and India, covering so wide a space of the northern frontiers of India, that the only mountain gateways that have ever been opened from the north into the rich sunlit plains of the peninsula are to be found beyond them, and within the comparatively restricted length of the mountain borderland which stretches between Karachi and the Kohistan of Kabul. Who shall say how much the wealth of India, depending on the accumulation of centuries of patient industry and taken from her own prolific soil, owes to the Tibetan barrier. For countless ages, ere there was added to the world a southern zone of communication represented by the ocean and ocean-going ships, that wealth has been protected by mighty land barriers. For ages, when adventurous and mobile forces bred in the eastern steppes of high Asia, hardened and trained to the exercises of war, found power to traverse the huge continent which contained them, — westward to Europe or southward to Cathay, — and pillage the stores accumulated in the cities of the unwarlike working races of a softer and more genial world, it was only from the west and by very narrow ways that they could touch India. Truly they made good use of their opportunities when they found them, but it is worthy of record that the fiercest and most devastating hordes of all the countless nomads who poured out of Asia from age to age — the Mongols — only made India the scene of their destroying migrations when they could turn the western flank of the Himalayas. They never crossed the Tibetan Chang.

The great corrugated uplands of Tibet, seamed with ridges of high altitude, inhospitable, bleak, and desolate though they be, do not in themselves, however, present any insurmountable difficulty to geographical exploration.

The chief obstacles to Tibetan exploration have ever been the mountain barriers which surround the plateau, rather than the plateau itself. These mountain systems on all sides of Tibet are massed into a series of gigantic walls, the ranges and ridges of which are not fashioned as long spurs reaching out from the highlands and gradually diminishing in altitude till they fade into the plains below, enclosing long sloping valleys which would answer the purpose of ramps or shelving approaches to the heights; but they are folded range after range in gigantic altitudes (higher than the ranges of the plateau), forming a rough but readily recognisable system of parallel flexures flanking the general edge of the central Tibetan upheaval.

Tibet may be described as a huge pear-shaped formation, with the small end of the pear attached to the southeastern corner of the Pamirs at the point where the Kashmir hinterland, from the heights of the giant Muztagh range, looks northward over the sources of the rivers of Chinese (or eastern) Turkestan. The Muztagh range might almost be called the stem of the pear, the narrow end of the pear gradually widening out therefrom being appropriately known as Little Tibet. Little Tibet is politically an outlying province of Kashmir. As the northern side of the pear-shaped formation curves boldly eastward it is represented by the border mountain systems of Kuen Lun, Altyn Tagh, Nan Shan, etc., which, following each other in succession, carry the northern boundary of Tibet to the province of Kansu of China. Where exactly Kansu ends and Tibet begins is a matter rather of conjecture than political certainty; but for the purposes of description we will consider all the country south of the Altyn Tagh and the Nan Shan ranges to be Tibet. To the north of these ranges is the comparatively low-lying region of Chinese Turkestan, with abundant fertility about its western extremity and along the edges at the foot of the mountains, and a sand-strewn desert in its midst, hiding the remains of those cities which have been made known to us by the researches of Sven Hedin and Stein. Throughout the Kuen Lun series of mountain systems there is a certain structural similarity. The main ranges are folded in vast anticlinals parallel to the edge of Tibet and to each other, ridge upon ridge, like a series of walls. It is not to be supposed that the simplicity of this description is readily to be recognised in the mountain masses themselves. There is the usual complexity of subsidiary spurs and more or less isolated massifs, of geological faults, and inconceivably rough foothills, which present to the eye the appearance of mountain features without arrangement and without plan. Nevertheless there is (as there is in the Himalayas) an underlying structural basis which marks them rather as successive walls of the plateau than as direct extensions from it.

The result is extreme irregularity in the main lines of drainage which cut their way through passages transverse to the walls, following the weakest lines of resistance (or, it may be, retaining a primeval course during the upheaval of the mountain masses) till they reach the plains. Not only are the valleys which form the natural approach to Tibet from the north thus liable to narrow restricted gorges and desperately rough intervals where they break across or through a ridge, but they are lengthened inordinately between the plains and the plateau. These main lines of approach (so far as they are known) will be described hereafter.

On the east, at the broad end of the pear-shaped plateau, the mountains of the Kansu border curve round southward (allowing the head-waters of the Hoang Ho of China to pass through them as they curve), and gradually merge into a fairly well-defined north to south range which figures on the map as Sifan. Here, within the limits of Tibet, there occurs the commencement of a most remarkable orographical feature. Range after range striking outwards from the plateau follows the same curving course from southeast to south, bending in orderly procession like the waves of the sea, deepening their valleys and steepening their sides as they proceed southwards, till the whole south-eastern world of Tibet is but a succession of mountain waves whose forest-crested summits gradually reach

Fra Mauro's Map of Tibet, 1459

southwards into Burma. Down the deep troughs of these southeastern valleys of Tibet flow the waters of several of the most important rivers of Asia. The Di chu (or Yang tsi) is the outermost, with a course of eight hundred miles ere it passes the Tibetan frontier. The Mekong, the river of Siam, and the Salwin, one of the two great rivers of Burma, lie within the Yang tsi, and parallel to it. Recent evidence points to the fact that the Irawadi, the next great Burmese river, does not rise far, if at all, within the Tibetan border.

It is the contiguity of these intervening ranges, the difficulty presented by a succession of rugged mountain walls, which proves to be the great barrier between Tibet and China on the east.

But while approach directly from the east is rendered almost impossible by this geographical distribution of ridge and valley, the same distribution rather favours approach from the southeast, *i. e.*, from the province of Yunnan in China, or from Burma. Thus there is a route from Yunnan which takes advantage of the Di chu (Yang tsi) River valley. It is marked by the trade centre of Batang.

In more irregular but still recognisable form the curving structure of the mountain system continues over the intervening space westwards till it determines the bend of the river Brahmaputra, which changes its direction as it flows from Tibet into Assam, and thus rounds off, as it were, the eastern end of the Himalayas. The irregular trans-Brahmaputra hills, through which runs a part of the southern boundary of Tibet, are drained by one or two minor rivers which join the Brahmaputra from the east. They are supposed to be within the sphere of British political influence, but they are practically beyond it, and through their valleys, owing to the fierce and irreconcileable nature of the tribes which people them (Abors, Mishmis, etc.), no right of way to Tibet has ever been established. It may be that eventually it is here that we shall find that open door which, leading upward by paths indicated by geographical structure as the easiest, will reach the cultivated lands of eastern Tibet (and ultimately the plateau) by a route involving no high passes and no long detours. The Brahmaputra marks the natural gateway of the hills. Westward of the Brahmaputra, to the extremest point of the Kashmir stem of the pear-shaped plateau, are interposed the great Himalayan barriers, which are perhaps the most effective barriers of all.

The structural relationship of the Himalayan ranges on the south of Tibet is very similar to that of the mountains on the north. Throughout their whole length, from the great bend of the Indus (where that river leaves the longitudinal valleys of its upper reaches to break transversely across the ridges as it seeks its way to the plains) to the great bend of the Brahmaputra (where that river is forced into a curving deflection from its Tibetan channels), through fifteen hundred miles of mountains, there runs a dominant water-parting, or backbone to the whole system. This is set back from the plains of India at a distance of about one hundred miles. It is on this divide that the magnificent array of highest snow-capped peaks is to be found, from the giants of Kashmir to the groups of pinnacles about Everest and Kanchenjanga. It is the "snowy range" par excellence, as seen from Himalayan hill stations. We are not quite sure what becomes of it through the unexplored regions of Nepal, but it apparently loses its continuity as a district. The general trend or axis of this great curving divide determines the shape of the southern edge of the Tibetan plateau. Infinitely higher than the plateau, it is yet but part of that procession of mountain walls which form its southern support. Northward it overlooks the plateau; southward it overlooks the apparently confused and tangled mass of lower subsidiary ranges which fill up the intervening one hundred miles between itself and the plains of India. But there is no real structural confusion about these minor ridges and ranges. Most of them maintain a parallel formation of ridge and valley to the snowy range. This is very observable in the extreme northwest, and is recognisable throughout the Himalayas in spite of the maze of spurs and offshoots which tend to disguise the fundamental design. North of this range there is a minor (yet still gigantic) subsidiary and parallel wall (enclosing a space of upland waste about thirteen thousand feet above sea level) which overlooks the great troughs where the Indus, the Sutlej, and the Brahmaputra collect their forces. The Sutlej and the Indus flow westward by separate routes to India. The Brahmaputra flows eastward through southern Tibet till it is turned in its course by the eastern walls of the plateau and forced through the Dihang gorges into upper Assam. "On the north of the Himalayan wall rise the Karakoram and Gangri mountains, which form the immediate escarpment of the Tibetan table-land. Behind the Gangris on the north the lake-studded plateau of Tibet spreads itself out at a height averaging fifteen thousand feet. Broadly speaking, the double Himalayan wall rests upon the low-lying plains of India, and descends north into the river trough beyond which rises the Tibetan plateau. Vast glaciers, one of which is known to be sixty miles in length, move their masses of ice downward to the valleys. The higher ranges between India and Tibet are crowned with eternal snow. They rise in a region of unbroken silence like gigantic frosted fortresses, one above another, till their white towers are lost in the sky" (W. W. Hunter).

Yet another river besides the Sutlej, the Karnáli, one of the largest affluents of the Ganges, breaks through the Himalayas between the arms of the Indus and Brahmaputra. The Karnáli is a Nepalese river, and its upper course is therefore but indifferently known. There is no doubt, however, that its sources lie beyond the Himalayas.

The Indus rises on the slopes of Kailas, the sacred mountain, the Elysium or Siva's Paradise of ancient Sanskrit literature. Its long and comparatively straight course from its source at sixteen thousand feet above the sea, through channels running northwest through gigantic mountains, is often comparatively placid. It flows over broad gravel beds, gathering strength as it flows, for five hundred miles ere it plunges into the gorge of Iskardoh, which is said to be fourteen thousand feet in sheer depth. The Sutlej rises on the southern slopes of Kailas. It flows no longer from one of the sacred lakes of Manasarawar, famous in Hindu mythology. Abandoning its ancient cradle in Rakhas-Tal, it now issues from the foothills of Kailas. It cuts its way from birth through a vast accumulation of deposits by a deep gully between precipices of alluvial soil, and finally pierces the Himalayas by a gorge with mountains rising to twenty thousand feet on either side. This is in the region of the famous Shipki pass, where the Tibetan outposts hold the frontier.

The traveller who wishes to traverse the wide desolation of the Tibetan plateau has a considerable choice of routes. From north, south, east, and west explorers and adventurers have tackled the problem of reaching the capital of the country, Lhasa, and with about equal want of success. The northern routes from the plains of Chinese Turkestan which have been exploited by Prjevalski, Sven Hedin, Deasy, Stein, Littledale, Bonvalot, and others are distinctly the most difficult and unpromising, partly because it is necessary to reach the plains of Kashgar before attempting them — and this in itself is no mean performance; partly because these northern routes lead to the wildest and most desolate uplands of all the desolate field which Tibet presents. These are Russian routes, inasmuch as they lead direct from the Russian Asiatic borderland of Chinese Turkestan, and they are long routes, bristling with all the formidable barriers that a bleak and immensely high mountain system can set in their way ere the dreary open steppe is attained at altitudes which are considerably greater than those of southern Tibet. Russia is shut off from the capital of Tibet by natural barriers which are infinitely greater than those which present themselves on the side of India. Geographically, Lhasa, and all of Tibet which holds promise of future civilised development, is within the meshes of the broad network of hinterland communication which is cast from India or from China, and never could be attached to a direct northern system by any but the weakest of geographical ties. There is nevertheless a bond of religious and commercial union between Russia and Tibet which is maintained by a much-traversed route on the northeast, — a long route and an important one, — about which there is more to be said hereafter.

These northern routes will be considered in connection with those explorations which led to their discovery.

From the south Tibet is approached by the Sutlej opening through the Himalayas and by a group of passes leading from Kumaon. There are also routes about which we know little leading direct from Nipal, but the principal (because the most direct and the nearest) group of trans-Himalayan passes into Tibet are those which traverse the valleys of Sikkim and Bhutan.

On the east one or two routes are well known, amongst them one which from prehistoric days has been the main and the best-trodden route from China to Lhasa, *i. e.*, that which cuts the boundary at the frontier station of Ta-chien-lu (Darchendo). This indeed not only connects Pekin with Lhasa, and is historically responsible for the great movement of the Chinese race westward which ended in the conquest of Tibet, but it stretches its length (as will be explained more fully) to Kashmir and India, and must rank as one of the greatest of Asiatic trade routes.

The routes into Tibet from the northwest diverge from Leh, the capital of Ladak, and many a traveller has started from that quaint Buddhist town in search of adventure in the trackless Tibetan plateau land. Ladak is the extreme outlying, uptilted province of Kashmir, and the modern road between Srinagar (the capital of Kashmir) and Leh is a well-laid-out route two hundred and forty miles in length, frequently traversed, but involving some formidable passes. Leaving behind him the sombre shade of the thick pine woods of the Sind valley, the traveller encounters the main orographical line of division between Kashmir and Tibet at the point marked by the well-known Zoji La pass, — a pass which is typical of many other Himalayan passes, where the cutting back of the southern stream at its head has tended to obliterate the steep slopes of the northern side. A sharp ascent of two thousand feet from the south, zigzagging up the face of a precipitous slope, flanking a narrow and steep-sided gorge, leads over the pass to an open and apparently level valley, partly blocked with debris and talus, where it is difficult to determine in which direction the stream runs. Approaching it from the Tibetan side, the great traveller Sven Hedin calls it "the worst pass I have ever seen," although its altitude (not more than eleven thousand five hundred feet) is low compared with many which he must have previously encountered in Tibet. But he crossed it on the 9th of January, when the pass is usually closed by winter snow.

Beyond the Zoji La the road drops into the Indus basin, and is within the limits of Ladak (or Little Tibet), which geographically and climatically belongs rather to Tibet than to Kashmir. Hugging the river banks (but one hundred and fifty feet above it), it passes through some of the grandest of trans-Himalayan scenery. Near Leh the Indus is walled in between tremendous precipices, where it has literally carved a way for itself through the mountains. Its dark green waters flow in tranquil silence through broad reaches, or break up in thundering cataracts where the channel contracts. Occasionally the sunlight finds a way through the deep-shadowed cliffs overhanging its southern banks, and then it strikes the surface into emerald patches, and sends long, slanting shafts into the glistening depths. It is a weird, wild

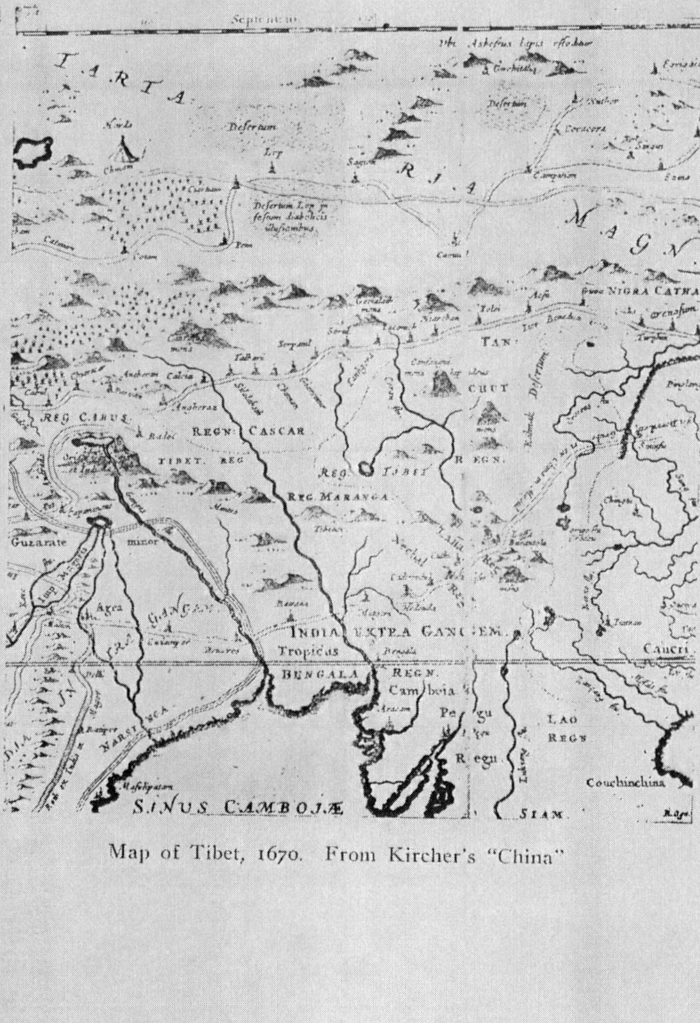

Map of Tibet, 1670. From Kircher's "China"

scene, a fit introduction to a weird and wild country. Yet there are broken spaces of cultivation where apricot and apple orchards hide the dwellings of as cheery hearted a population of mountaineers as is to be found in the wide world. The Ladaki lives to laugh, and, living (as he frequently does) a life in which the carrying of loads seems to be the fundamental object of existence, he nevertheless succeeds in securing for himself a fair share of that happiness which knows no fixed geographical limits.

Leh is the market town, the commercial centre of western Tibet. The town climbs up the side of a hill, as do most Tibetan towns, and the general look of it, flat-topped as to roofs and sloping as to walls, is almost Chinese in effect; but it lacks the grace of Chinese outline. As usual, a monastery dominates the town with high splay-footed walls, perforated by perpendicular rows of windows (or openings) marking successive flats. Red and white against a brown background of rugged hills is the prevaling colour scheme; the air is dry and dusty, with the clear but wintry light of all north Indian highland places. Leh is distinctly Tibetan. There is none of the airy grace of the rickety buildings which overlook the Jehlam at Srinagar. It is substantial, square built, and somewhat heavy — like the Tibetan himself. But it is a busy town, and caravans are constantly coming and going in its market-place.

From Leh into the Tibetan plains there is but one recognised road, and that road crosses the Chang

La (seventeen thousand six hundred feet) within fifty miles of Leh. Still following the right bank of the Indus for a space, amidst scattered evidences of the Buddhist faith (kists covered with stone slabs stretching their length for hundreds of feet along the river side, and repeating with monotonous reiteration the Buddhist formula "Om mane padme hum"), the road diverges suddenly eastward from the village of Sakti, and climbs the Chang La. It is not such a formidable pass as its altitude might lead one to expect, as the snow is usually less here than on the outer Himalayan ranges of similar altitude. The vapour-bearing currents from the southwest lose their moisture on the outer Himalayan heights, where snow is precipitated in vast quantities. Tibet is on the whole remarkably free from snow. The Chang La is occasionally passable all through the winter, but it is precipitous and difficult to climb, — "nothing but blank walls of bare, gray rock," says Sven Hedin. However, he crossed on the 18th of December without any mishap. From the pass the road drops eastward to the Shyok valley (where is Tanksi, with its picturesque monastery of Jova perched on a detached crag), and then rises over the intervening eastern water parting, and drops to the head of the Pangong Lake. Here commences Tibet proper, and from here the recognised caravan roads southeast to Rudok, or by the northern shores of the lake to Gangra, have not always been those selected by adventurous explorers for the purpose of crossing the Tibetan Chang when they designed to leave their tracks on the map of the interior. Here we leave it. Beyond this point the road to Lhasa is an explorers' route, of which we possess but a scanty descriptive outline, although it is one of the great highroads of Asia. From Srinagar to the Tibetan frontier it is the best known of all approaches to Tibet.

Next in order eastward amongst Himalayan approaches are the Shipki and the Niti routes, which are familiar enough to residents in Simla or Naini Tal, but are, nevertheless, but seldom traversed by any of them. Everyone who has visited Simla knows the highroad to Mahasu and Narkanda. The view of the northern mountains from Narkanda, forty miles from Simla, is the most striking view of Himalayan scenery that is to be obtained anywhere near Simla, a town which is not well placed for landscape effects. The sense of astonishment inspired by the magnificent wall of snow-capped mountains towering over the shadowed depths of the Sutlej valley is intensified by the dramatic suddenness with which a sharp bend in the road reveals the vision. So far the great central trade route to Tibet (which this well-engineered road was designed to be) has only carried one along the crests of subsidiary spurs overlooking east and west, long waving lines of green and purple hills spread abroad in infinite variety of light and shade, and chequered with patches of forest and terraced field. The rhododendrons and blue pines and silver oak of Simla have gradually given place to firs and green oak, and long, straight-stemmed pines standing thickly and darkly in the lower depths; but there has been no view of the majesty of eternal snow and glacier till we reach Narkanda.

At Narkanda one suddenly faces a stupendous range, and looks through a vast space of the uplifted mountain side, slung, as it were, midway between unknown depths below and the bright glory of snow outlines clear cut against the azure sky above.

From Narkanda the road dips into the depths of the Sutlej valley, passing under the shadow of gigantic pines, thickly burdened with ferns and moss, till the river itself is touched and the road commences to cling to it. It then follows the Sutlej valley to the main pass on the Tibetan frontier at Shipki, but it is no longer a road of the same class as that which connects Simla with Narkanda. As a Tibetan trade route the road is a failure, but there is a very large local traffic upon it, due to the development of villages and cultivation in the valleys near Simla, which is largely dependent on local means of supply for wood and vegetables. Once in Tibetan territory this route follows the southeasterly course of the Sutlej to its source near the Rakhas-Tal, the westernmost of the twin lakes of Manasarawar. About midway it passes through the Tibetan town of Totling, where there is a monastery, and which is a not unimportant centre of road communications in connection with the gold fields of the west.

Farther east again we find a group of passes connecting Kumaon with Tibet to the north of Almorah, — the Mana, Niti, Milam, Darma (Langpya La), and

Byans (Mangohang La), all forking off from the upper tributaries of the Alaknanda affluent of the Ganges. The Mana (eighteen thousand five hundred feet), which is at the head of the Badrinath stream, leads directly northward to Totling on the Sutlej. The altitudes of the Niti and the Milam are not well determined, but they cannot be much less than that of the Mana on the west. All these passes appear to be over eighteen thousand feet. Across the Milam there is still some traffic in gold-dust and borax, which is brought across the Himalayas on the backs of sheep, which (in spite of certain objections on the part of the lamas at Lhasa) still continue to be beasts of burden in southern Tibet. They travel remarkably well, and keep their condition under circumstances which would prove fatal to the condition of mules. They take back to Tibet cooking-utensils, pots, pans, and earthenware, but naturally no very bulky merchandise can be transported over the rugged mountain tracks in this way.

The Karnáli, or Gogra, River, rising near the sources of the Sutlej and Indus, also affords a trans-Himalayan passage; but it leads through a maze of mountains to the same focus on which the more western routes converge, and has apparently no separate trade outlet of its own on to the Tibetan plateau. All these routes practically centre on the same point, — the twin lakes of Manasarawar in the southern Tibetan district of Nari Khursam, or Hundes, which lie below the sacred peaks of Kailas. The great alluvial plain of Nari Khursam divided by the gorge of the Sutlej

River is a sort of landing in the Tibetan staircase. In its midst Totling is the chief place of importance, as we shall see further on. Beyond it are infinite mazes of mountains still intervening between the landing and the rugged plateau land, but there are no more Himalayas. The farther mountains are but lofty incidents of the great central table-land.

About the passes from Nepal to Lhasa we know exceedingly little, although Nepal was the connecting link of the Tibetan missions with India in the beginning of the eighteenth century. Nepal still maintains a formal recognition of Chinese suzerainty, and from Khatmandu there issues a periodic procession of priests and high military functionaries bearing tribute to Pekin. The procession moves by way of Lhasa, and strikes straight into Tibet. Presumably it crosses the main Himalayas by a pass which was used by an Indian explorer in 1867, who made his way direct from Khatmandu into the valley of the Yeru Tsanpo (Brahmaputra), to the well-known monastery of Tadum. Aided by the disguise of a pigtail and a false bottom to his box of merchandise, this explorer crossed by the No-La (sixteen thousand six hundred feet), at the head of a western affluent of the Gandak River of Nepal, and thence made a most eventful journey through Tibet. It is from such sources that we derive all our geographical knowledge of the most important part of Tibet, *i. e.,* the southern districts which lie immediately north of the Himalayas and are watered by the great Yeru Tsanpo. Doubtless the Gandak affluents draining down the rugged sides of the main range afford opportunities for other passes than that of the No-La. The Kirong, the Jong-ka-jong, and the Kuti, north of Khatmandu, surmount the main Himalayan water-parting at points which can hardly be twenty-five miles south of the Yeru Tsanpo. Nepal has hitherto been a forbidden land to Europeans. Europeans have seen most of Tibet, traversed it from north to south and from east to west; but no European ever made close acquaintance with Nepalese topography until Captain Wood was permitted to fix the position of Mount Everest from points of observation near Khatmandu in 1904. It is impossible to say exactly by what passes the Chinese invaded and conquered that country. It is, however, certain that they must be fairly easy and accessible.

The most significant group of passes leading from India into Tibet is that of Sikkim, connecting the basins of the Tista and of the Ammu Chu (river of Assam) with the valley of the Tsanpo near Lhasa.

Two or three routes into Tibet diverge from our railway base at Siliguri on the eastern frontier. One is carried by the mountain railway line to Darjiling; and from Darjiling as his base the traveller (such travellers as Dr. Waddell, Mr. Douglas Freshfield, and the Bengali pundit, Chandra Das, etc.) descends into the Tista valley, and makes his way by an easily recognisable, but occasionally difficult, route along the Lachen affluent of the Tista and over the Kamba La or Kangra pass (sixteen thousand six hundred feet) to Kamba Jong. Kamba Jong is separated from the trade and religious centre of Shigatze on the Tsanpo by cross-country roads, for the most part no better and no worse than the ordinary unmade country tracks passing through the uncultivated areas of India, but with one or two crossings of mountain passes *en route*. Or, instead of following up the Lachen affluent of the Tista, the traveller may take the Lach-lung affluent to the Donkia pass (eighteen thousand one hundred feet) and strike into the road to Gyangtse. This route, however, involves five or six crossings of intermediate passes before reaching Gyangtse, and although such passes are not formidable, they are obstructive. By far the most direct route to Gyangtse and Lhasa is that which was followed by the Tibetan mission under Colonel Younghusband. From Siliguri a cart road runs by the Tista valley to Kalimpong, just below Darjiling, and thence diverges to the northeast over a series of ascents and descents for forty-two miles to Gnathong (twelve thousand feet), and on to the "smooth and easy" pass called Jelep La, which divides the basin of the Tista (or Sikkim) from the upper basin of the Ammo Chu (or Chumbi), which is Tibet. At this point only Tibet drives a wedge southward into the body of the Himalayas. The valley of the Ammo Chu formerly belonged to Bhutan, but Tibet has recently asserted the right of occupation, and it is here that her troublesome intrusions into British territory necessitated the campaign of 1888, which succeeded in driving the Tibetan rabble over the Jelep La into

Sanlan Sanpo. (Cane Bridge)

Chumbi, from whence they came. Chumbi is said to be a delightful country. It has been called the Engadine of the Himalayas, and it is doubtless a pleasant offset to the wintry regions which lie above and beyond it. Pari, in the upper valley, is a town of about three hundred houses, protected by a fort. According to one authority, it is " abundantly bleak and bare," being four thousand feet higher than the Chumbi town (ten thousand feet), and not far below the Tang La pass, over the principal Himalayan water divide between the Tsanpo and the Ammo Chu. But Hooker describes it as an important trade entrepôt, where tobacco, fruit, and cloth from Bhutan are found, together with vegetables, cattle, and fish. Customs are collected here by Tibetan officials. The Tang La, above Pari (fifteen thousand seven hundred feet), is an exceptionally easy pass for the Himalayas. From it northward there runs a rivulet which, swelling into a stream and finally developing into a full-grown river, flows almost directly northward through an open and gently rounded plain to Gyangtse and the Yeru Tsanpo. There is not a pass to bar the way nor a serious physical obstacle to contend with, as far as Gyangtse. It is, *par excellence,* the great central route across the breadth of southern Tibet,—that part of Tibet which, being within the Brahmaputra basin, is in true geographical affinity with India in spite of the intervening Himalayan wall. The journey from the Indian frontier to Lhasa may be made in a fortnight over fairly good country roads and through tracts which are partially cultivated.

From the north, — from Kashgar or the frontier of Chinese Turkestan to Lhasa, — it is a journey of months across a wild and desolate table-land, the horrors of which have been described to us by Sven Hedin, Bower, Prjevalski, and others, presenting an aspect of Tibet which has little in common with the Tibet of the upper Brahmaputra.

Whilst the gates of Tibet have ever been jealously guarded against European advance from the west or south, and the wild, bleak wind-swept plains and rocky defiles of the northwest, added to the desolation of dreary steppes, stretching in stone-strewn monotony for hundreds of miles, have effectually hindered the progress of trade developments in these directions through all historic times, it has not been the same on the east or the northeast. From the west, in spite of all obstacles, a certain amount of intermittent trade has always filtered through Leh, or over the passes of Kumaon to India, owing chiefly to the fact that gold and borax are easily transportable commodities; but the main trade of Tibet has always run China-wards. Gold, even from the extreme western fields near the Kashmir border, has been carried in far larger quantities to Pekin, over a distance of three thousand miles, than it ever has to Leh, which is hardly three hundred miles from the centre of the western mining districts. The Sikhs, by way of Kashmir, and the Mongols, from the north, have alike attempted the conquest of Tibet with no substantial commercial profit; but the Chinese from the east have swamped the country with most practical results. With a loose and elastic system of administration, which leaves both the spiritual and temporal government of Tibet almost untouched, and interferes not at all with the customs of the people, the Chinese hold on Tibet has yet been of very solid advantage to China. Trade and commerce either follow the flag, or precede it, and most of the material comforts and luxuries of the few centres of semi-civilisation which Tibet possesses are the direct result of Chinese military enterprise. Tea, for instance, of a specially inferior quality, made as much from refuse as from the actual leaf, and cemented with rice water into the form of hard unpromising bricks, is imported in immense quantities from China, and, strange to say, it fully meets the requirements and the taste of a people who do not appreciate Indian tea. Nearly all this eastern trade now flows through the one centre on the eastern frontier called Darchendo in the older maps, or, more correctly, Ta-chien-lu in the newer ones.

From western and southwestern China the approaches to Ta-chien-lu are through a mountainous region by tracks which follow the main courses of the upper affluents of the Yang tsi kiang in the province of Ssu-chuan. From the Min river affluent, which drains a busy and populous centre of Chinese industry, a tributary called the Tung leads upwards to the frontier at Ta-chien-lu; another affluent flowing south, itself a feeder of the Yalung, defines a route which connects Ta-chien-lu with the frontiers of the province of Yunnan. There are no very high passages; no enormous altitudes to be dealt with on these two Chinese roads, which enclose between them a vast mountain tract inhabited by the independent Lolos. They are routes full of the interest of human activity and of magnificent scenery; and about them one of the most fascinating stories of travel ever written has been given to the world from the pen of M. E. Colborne Baber, once secretary to the Chinese legation at Pekin. It is indeed a matter of deep regret that the mysterious visions which haunt the mist-clothed Mount Omi at the junction of the Tung and the Min (to use the Jesuit name for a river which is not known locally as the Min) are found too far from the borders of Tibet to be included with due propriety in the stories of Tibetan exploration. There is no enchanted Omi amidst the bleak desolations of Tibetan highlands. No emanation from the aureole of Buddha, seen as a "golden sun-like disc enclosed in a ring of prismatic colours more closely blended than the rainbow," ever cheers the hearts of the saints at Lhasa. Omi is Chinese, and but serves to emphasise the fact that of all the roads that run to Lhasa, that which approaches from the east is certainly the most fascinating by reason of the glory of its scenery, if it is not also the greatest by reason of its trade.

Ta-chien-lu is a picturesque mountain town, not more than eight thousand four hundred feet above sea level, and it constitutes the doorway into a corner of Tibet which is by far the richest in cultivation, the best in climate, and possibly the most productive in mineral wealth. The town lies "at the western end of a very narrow valley, so narrow indeed that for miles together it has no floor but the path and the torrent, which, after fifteen miles of cataracts, plunges into the Tung at Wa-Ssu-Kou; a mere gorge, in short, between two spurs of the snowy range over which the Che-to road passes." Bower calls Ta-chien-lu a "pestilential spot," but this estimate of its salubrity is probably based more on the well-known want of sanitation which pervades all Asiatic hill towns than on any known condition of climate. Other travellers are more or less reticent. From Ta-chien-lu the great trade route rises to the elevation of thirteen thousand four hundred feet at Litang, between the Di chu and its Tung affluents, ere descending again to Batang, which is in the actual valley of the Di chu (or Kin sha, or Yang tsi). Batang is only eighty-one hundred feet above sea level, and from here the Tibetan highroad, crossing a narrow intervening divide, drops into the valley of the Nam chu, or Mekong River, which it follows to Chiamdo at a high level on the left bank, where "travelling is not difficult" but "the people are given to much thieving." The narrow troughs (rather than valleys) which enclose the waters of the upper Yang tsi, the upper Mekong, and the Giama Nu Chu (which is now believed to be the upper Salwin River) are amongst the most populous and best-developed valleys of eastern Tibet. Their contiguity to the main trade route and their comparatively low elevation combine to render them prosperous, and it is here if anywhere that the future prospect of economic value in regard to mineral wealth appears to be most promising. It is therefore a matter of interest to note that this is a part of Tibet which might be reached from India with comparative facility and without encountering a rigorous climate by other routes than those of China. Following up the Lohit Brahmaputra to the northeast from the head of the valley of Assam, a forest track runs for one hundred and twenty miles to Rima, the capital of the Zayul district. From Rima routes diverge to the northeast and the northwest. Either route must inevitably encounter a high watershed between the basins of the upper Salwin and the Dibang affluent of the Brahmaputra, before descending into the valley of the former river, and it is probable that the passes over this intervening ridge would not be lower than the fifteen thousand feet average of the Tibetan plateau. But the route would not be long, — from eighty to one hundred miles from Rima to the Salwin, and perhaps seventy more to the China route near Batang. This is, however, conjecture, for hitherto the irrepressible hostility of the mountain tribespeople of Upper Assam has proved an insuperable bar to successful exploration. Between the Brahmaputra and the Salwin, across the two hundred miles of intervening mountains, in the hidden depths of which are born the infant streams which swell the waters of the mighty Irawadi, no geographer has ever yet penetrated. It will not always be so. Upper Assam may yet point the way from India to northwestern China.

Setting aside for the present certain routes through Bhutan to Lhasa, we may note that there are yet other ways into Tibet (highways in the literal sense of the word) than those of the west and south and east, and by these other ways adventurers have reached the plateau from the north. By the northeast passage (a passage of primary importance) that grand explorer of Russian nationality, Prjevalski, and his lieutenant Roborovski, penetrated southwards to the sources of the Hoang Ho, the Yellow River of China. That way too came the American Rockhill, and the Frenchman Bonvalot (only a little more to the west). Sven Hedin, prince of Swedish travellers, with Carey and Dalgleish, Stein, Littledale, and Deasy, have all passed the northwestern hills, — so there is no lack of record. Not one of them ever reached Lhasa. Tibetan prejudice against travellers was too much for them. But they all scaled the northern walls of Tibet, and we know that there is not one, but several, recognised passes from the lowlands of Chinese Turkestan to the highlands of the plateau, which even in their rough condition of natural obstructiveness are yet passable for horses and camels. The point to be noted in connection with these northern passes is that they are not, and they never can be, important trade routes. The geographical conformation of the Tibetan plateau itself forbids it. It is not the passes themselves which are the obstacle. It is the great central region of lake-splashed upland — one huge, bleak wilderness of inhospitality — which intervenes between them and the warmer and more genial (comparatively genial) districts of the Brahmaputra basin, wherein are all the great villages and trade centres of Tibet. This is the real obstacle, and has ever been so. No artificial efforts of man will ever contend against the giant distributions of nature in these uplands. The general outline of these distributions will be dealt with later. At present my object is to prove that the outside fringe of the veil of mystery which overhangs Tibet has been lifted on all sides of the plateau. It may well be doubted whether any future explorations will reveal to us more important breaks in the border line of mountain wall than those which we already know. If roads are to be made, we know where they must be made. It concerns us now, geographically, to consider what there is on the plateau when once it is reached; and this we can best do by the light of such revelations as the Tibetan explorers of all nationalities have given us in the records of their wanderings from the earliest ages.

CHAPTER II

Geological Evolution — The Chan Tang and Northern Tibet — Valleys of the Indus and Brahmaputra — The Janglam Trade Route — Eastern Tibet — The Rivers of China and Burma — The Southern Zone — Climate

SO unique is the position of Tibet that a short description of its physical characteristics is almost essential to a comprehension of successive methods of exploration.

It seems probable that the primeval forces which first upheaved this gigantic excrescence on the face of the earth gave it an axis running from west to east, which approximates to the position of the northern water parting or rim of the Indian hydrographic basin.

The plateau elevation culminates on this central line at an altitude of seventeen thousand six hundred feet about the seventy-ninth meridian. From this central line the uplands slope away on all sides — to about thirteen thousand feet towards the east and to eleven thousand in the southern zone, *i. e.*, the basin of the Yero Tsanpo. A secondary axis of upheaval is sometimes recognised in the Kuen Lun mountain system on the northern edge. Modern Indian geologists are disposed to associate the upheaval of Tibet with that of the great trans-Indus table-lands of Baluchistan and

Afghanistan on the west, with the northwestern Himalayas on the south, and the northern Burmese mountains on the east; that is to say, they consider it to be very much more recent than the central portions of the Indian peninsula, or of the Himalayas to the northeast of India. This contention appears to be justified by the discovery of certain forms of fossils indicating the existence of life which has nowhere been found in the great highland steppes of the Asiatic continent, or in the broad expanse of the ancient beds of Central India. In later ages there must have accumulated on these heights a vast superincumbent mass of ice and snow, burying Tibet as effectually as Greenland is buried at the present moment, grinding down the mountain ranges to their present comparatively insignificant level, and spreading the debris of them in vast accumulations of detritus over the face of the table-land.

The next process was the recession of the ice, the gradual withdrawal of glaciers, the formation of lakes, — of lakes innumerable, — which in their turn have, for the most part, dried up and disappeared, leaving traces of their ancient beds behind them, spreading far afield from the present limited dimensions of such relics as remain. There may have been more than one or two glacial epochs, for all we know. There probably have been cycles of accumulation and disappearance; but it seems certain that during all these untold ages the process of gradual upheaval has been continuous, and with the advance of scientific investigation it will probably be proved to be still in action. When man made his first appearance we need not ask, but there can be no reasonable doubt that the Tibetan is the latest survival of the ancient Turko-Mongol stock which once prevailed through all high Asia. The Tibetan came from the northeast in a purely Mongol form, and later from the southeast, — from Burma and Assam in the form of the Tibeto-Burman of modern ethnology, who aforetime occupied a great part of northern India.

The valley of the Brahmaputra, of the Subansiri, and of those eastern affluents of the Brahmaputra which are separated from the sources of the Irawadi only by the narrow Patkoi range, were once the main avenues of approach to Tibet. It is worth noting that the Tibetan himself claims descent from the monkey.

The boundary limits of Tibet and the ways which cross the surrounding borderland of mountains have already been indicated. Within the limits of the recognised Tibetan frontier we have three great physical divisions of vastly elevated plain which it is important to distinguish from each other. There is (1) the great northern plateau flanked by the Kuen Lun and the steppes of Tsaidam, which we know as the Chang tang (the "Northern Plain"). This is the region of highest elevation, too high and too cold for anything but pastoral use, where salt lakes are scattered at intervals amidst vast sterile flats, where grass is scanty and trees are absolutely wanting. It is sparsely inhabited by Mongolian nomads. Intensely cold (yet occasionally baked by more than summer heat under the summer sun), wind-swept, storm-beaten, and barren, it is perhaps the most inhospitable region in the Asiatic world. Its average elevation is about fifteen thousand feet above sea level, and above this again rise the crests of intersecting ridges of rounded outline which seam its surface in every direction, and increase the altitude by two thousand or three thousand feet. Rivers rise in the Chang and flow northward through the Kuen Lun range (and its extensions eastward) to the plains of Chinese Turkestan; the Kiria is perhaps the best known of them. Somewhere on the southern edge of the Chang is the water divide of India. No one has defined its exact geographical position. Some of the gigantic lakes of Central Tibet may possibly be within the Indian basin, but of many of them it is known that they have no outlet. These lake regions form the pasture lands of the Bod-pa nomads.

The Chang is the true Tibetan bulwark of the Indian frontier. It is impassable for large bodies of people, and has proved to be almost impassable for small companies.

The second physical division of Tibet includes the upper valleys of the Indus and Brahmaputra and their affluents, some of which are large rivers, *e. g.*, the Kyichu, on which stands Lhasa. At the parting of the waters where the Indus, the Sutlej, and the Brahmaputra divide to the west and east, southern Tibet is high (fifteen thousand five hundred feet); but for three hundred miles to the northwest (following the

Indus), and for seven hundred miles to the southeast and east (following the Brahmaputra), the level gradually diminishes to about thirteen thousand feet near the Ladak frontier, and eleven thousand feet on the Brahmaputra, south of Lhasa. There is no sudden fall; the descent is gradual, and the great rivers often flow in broad shallow reaches over smooth beds. This is the land of the Bodyul, or settled inhabitants of Tibet. Here are tracts that contain valleys warm enough for cultivation; these the Tibetans call "rong" (a ravine or narrow cleft in a hill), which word is more particularly applicable to the lowest and warmest valleys, which produce crops twice in the year.

"The alluvial beds in the valleys are composed of debris of the surrounding rocks, laid out in horizontal deposits, which in course of time have become furrowed into gigantic ravines, with a succession of narrow terraces forming steps on each flank. It is on the existing lower alluvial beds that cultivation is carried on in plots which are usually well watered and very fertile. The sharp needle peaks which are highest of all and bare of soil, but covered with perpetual snow, are met with most frequently in tracts of rong, and the rounded hills coated with grass to altitudes sometimes exceeding sixteen thousand feet in parts of Chang tang. The forest-clad mountain tracts which are occasionally met with occur chiefly in the rong. The general direction of hill and mountain chains is east and west, but northwest and southwest in western Tibet, where they are most irregular, — northeast and southwest in the province of U, and north and south in eastern Tibet." Thus writes General Walker (late Surveyor-General of India), as the result of observations made chiefly by the native surveyors of his department.

The upper Indus valley contains some notable towns, which are local centres of trade, such as Gartok, Demchok, etc., and is not devoid of the softer beauty of lower Himalayan scenery beneath the stupendous cliffs and crags of the ranges stretching north of Kailas. The Manasarawar lakes and the pasture lands which border them are the western Tibetan shepherds' paradise, — a paradise set amidst a vast stony wilderness. In the valley of the upper Brahmaputra, where the yellow glacial streams pour down from the outer Himalayan wall, or the clear flow of currents from the central lakes join the main stream, there is a gradually increasing extent of cultivation and human habitation. Fine monasteries exist at intervals, great clusters of square-cornered white buildings clinging to the hillsides overlook the valley between Tadum and Shigatze.

Although there is not a town in Tibet that would rank as second class in India, there are imposing collections of stone-built, white-faced houses dominated by ever-prevalent monastic buildings, which are quite equal in the scale of township with the secondary towns of Afghanistan or Baluchistan; and indeed are not unlike the townlets that may be seen clinging to the spurs of the Hindu Kush north of Kabul. Tadum,

Janglache, and Shigatze are the most important towns west of Lhasa.

Throughout the length of this southern region of Tibet there stretches a very remarkable trade route called the Junglam. From Leh it runs west of the Pangong lake to Rudok, the western frontier town of Tibet. Thence it crosses a breadth of the Chang tang lake region till it touches the upper Brahmaputra at its sources on the Mariam La (fifteen thousand five hundred feet), — the meridional water parting between the Indus and the Brahmaputra. Twice it crosses the Yero Tsanpo (upper Brahmaputra) by bridge or ferry, and passing midway through Shigatze is carried by a southerly detour to Gyangtse and Lhasa.

Within this stretch of nine hundred miles there are twenty-five staging places from twenty to seventy miles apart, with accommodation for about two hundred men. The road is generally well defined, loose stones are cleared away in the defiles, and piles of stones with flags on sticks guide the way through the open stretches of table-land. East of Lhasa it runs to Chiamdo (the capital of the Kham province, — a garrison town), to Batang, Litang, and Ta-chien-lu on the Chinese frontier. It is the official post-road between Kashmir and Pekin, traversable at all seasons of the year by mounted men, and is probably the most remarkable (as it is the most elevated) postal highway in the world.

The third great physical division of Tibet comprises the eastern mountains and valleys. From the desolate steppes of Tsaidam on the northeast to the rim of the Brahmaputra basin north of Lhasa, the eastern edge of the great central Chang tang forms an orographical feature which is of vast importance in the physical conformation of eastern Asia. Here arise innumerable rivulets which gather their infant forces together to form the first affluents of the great rivers of China, of Siam, and of Burma. The Hoang Ho (Yellow River) finds its source in the Oring Nor lake (or group of lakes) to the southeast of the great Koko Nor, and curving eastward and northward through the country of the Sifan (the western barbarians of China), till it approaches within one hundred miles of the southeastern corner of the Koko Nor, it takes its way as a full-grown river through northern China to the Pacific. To the west of the sources of the Yellow River rise those of the next great river of China, the Yang tsi kiang. The position of the extremest west of those sources which contribute uninterruptedly to the Di chu (the upper Yang tsi) is not exactly known, but it must be east of the route followed by Sven Hedin in his last adventurous journey into Tibet from the north. It will probably be found about the meridian of 91° east longitude. Flowing southeast, and separated from the upper Hoang Ho by the Baian-Kara-ulla range, it curves southward in about the same meridian (100° East Lon.) that the Hoang Ho curves northward, admitting of the rise of another great river (the Nag-chu) between them. The Nag-chu eventually joins the Yang tsi when the latter finally assumes its eastern

A Typical Peak of South Eastern Tibet

course through the width of China to the Pacific. Next to the Di-chu the Nam-chu (upper Mekong) starts from this same meridional divide, but probably from sources not so far west as the Di-chu, and follows a course which throughout Tibetan territory is almost parallel to that of the Di-chu. Finally a fourth great river, the Salwin, a river of Burma, is represented by the Giama-Nu-Chu, which, gathering together many affluents from the highlands to the northeast of Lhasa, follows a course parallel to the Nam-chu and the Di-chu, curving gradually southward. Parallel to the Giami-Nu-Chu (but separated therefrom by a breadth of from four hundred to five hundred miles of mountains) is the Brahmaputra River, which bends from its easterly course through southern Tibet to pass southeastward through Himalayan gates to the valley of Assam. This broad intervening space belongs to the Brahmaputra basin. Some very important valleys of no great elevation (Poyul, Zayul, etc.) drain into the Brahmaputra within it, being separated by a lofty divide from the narrow valley of the Giama-Nu-Chu, or Salwin, to the east. It is a very remarkable feature in Asiatic orography which thus presents itself. First, the Brahmaputra, maintaining its general characteristic of a wide basin with important affluents converging on to the main stream up to the point where it emerges into the plains of Assam; beyond this, overlooking the sources of these converging affluents, a containing mountain chain, distinct and apart from the Himalayan system, rounding off the heads of shelving valleys which slope westwards to the Brahmaputra, and dominating an eastern structure of enormous parallel mountain folds which enclose between their successive crests the deep troughs of some of the greatest rivers of Asia.

So close set are the successive ridges and ranges which part the Salwin from the Mekong, and the Mekong from the Yang tsi, that, at a point level with the head of the Assam valley, one hundred miles would bridge them all. The Irawadi river of Burma is now supposed to rise to the southeast of this eastern extension of the Brahmaputra basin, amongst the wild hills which lie between the head of the Assam valley and Burma.

In the future of Tibetan commercial policy it is eastern Tibet which will prove to be the most important division, for it is the division of Tibet which contains the greatest present wealth and the greatest promise for the future. Travellers leaving the cold altitudes of the Chang behind them and descending gradually through the long narrow valleys towards the Chinese frontier are never weary of recounting the delightful change of climate and scenery which they encounter. There are magnificent forest-clad slopes beneath the snow-clad crests of the main ridges; there are thousands of well-watered, well-cultivated, and well-populated valleys hidden away amongst the folds of the main chains. The large and better-known valleys, such as Darge on the Di-chu, or Chiamdo on the Nam-chu, are prosperous, populous, and priest-ridden; the lesser-known valleys, such as Poyul and Zayul, are reported to be the centres of Tibetan art and industry. The whole region is full of unexploited mineral wealth, and, like western China, which it so greatly resembles, is bound to prove eventually an important factor in the world's economy. Two great trade routes run through this country, which are sufficiently described elsewhere. One (the Janglam) connects Lhasa with Ta-chien-lu and China; the other follows approximately (in several alternative loops) that line of water division in which the Chinese rivers rise, and connects Lhasa with the Koko Nor and Sining fu in the province of Kansu. Both lead to Pekin eventually, but the most important at present is the Ta-chien-lu route, which absorbs the greater part of the Tibetan trade.

Before describing in detail the progress of recent Tibetan exploration, the reader would do well to recall and fix in his mind the relative position of certain geographical (or strategical) points, which may be called obligatory points for the understanding of the value to be attached to individual lines of research. On the extreme west is Leh, the capital of the farthest outlying province of Kashmir — Ladak.

From Leh the southern valley regions of Tibet can be approached either by passing through Rudok at the southeastern extremity of the Pangong lake or by passing up the affluents of the Indus. It is equally possible to reach the northern Chang from Leh; and thus Leh figures as the principal focus, or point of departure, for those explorers who make Kashmir their base. On the south Tibet is approached more directly either by the Kumaon group of passes, by Nepal, by Sikkim, or by Bhutan, the most direct route to the heart of the southern provinces at Lhasa being by Sikkim and the valley of Chumbi. On the east it is well to note the position of Ta-chien-lu, — the Chinese frontier trading-post. It is by this route that Tibet has been finally conquered, and by this route Tibet now maintains by far the greater part of its trade connections with the outside world. On the northeast the position of Sining fu and the Koko Nor region are of great political importance. This marks the line of route between Manchuria and Lhasa via Mongolia or China, and although the Mahommedan rebellions have temporarily thrown it out of popularity, it is still a great highway of pilgrimage, — the channel by which Lhasa maintains its supremacy in the Buddhist world amongst the far-off peoples of Mongolia and western China. The influence of Lhasa southward terminates abruptly at the Himalayan wall. Northward and northeastward it reaches to the farthest limits of Asiatic civilisation, and it is to four hundred millions of people in the far East what Mecca is to the Mahommedan world of the West. On the north the bleak desolation of the mountain barriers which shut off the lowlands of Chinese Turkestan from the highlands of the Chang tang (as well as the breadth of the Chang tang itself) admits of no base which is ever likely to be of the least importance for

Glacial Lake and Moraine, Source of Zemu, Chathangta Pass

the support of either political, commercial, or military enterprise. It is southern and northeastern Tibet, not northern, with which the world will interest itself hereafter.

The southern zone of Tibet, which includes the true Bod-land, is divided into four provinces; viz., Nari on the west, Kham (otherwise Do Kham) on the east, and in the centre Tsang (adjoining Nari) and U (adjoining Kham), these two provinces being known conjointly as Utsang. A considerable belt of the central country is known as Hor. Nari includes Ladak and Balti, which are now part of Kashmir, but which are frequently spoken of as Little Tibet, as well as the districts of Khorsum and Dokthol, the latter being conterminous with western Nepal, and both being under the Lhasa government.

Nari has only been partially explored by European travellers, the upper valleys of the Sutlej and Indus, the Manasarawar lake region, and the sources of the Brahmaputra and Karnali alone being accessible. Eastwards from Nari, the Dokthol country and the Utsang provinces (economically the most important in high Tibet) were originally explored by the native staff of the Survey of India; they have now been partially surveyed by officers attached to the Younghusband mission, and geographically they may be said to constitute the best-known part of Tibet. There are still, however, some important valleys watered by tributaries of the Brahmaputra flowing from the east into the central channel of the river (where it follows a southerly course to Assam) which are an absolute "terra incognita" so far as their topographical structure is concerned. The valleys of upper Zayul and Poyul are within the pale of Tibetan administration. Lower Zayul is almost certainly outside that pale, and is occupied by independent and barbarous tribes — Maris, Abors, and Mishmis — who acknowledge no authority. The elevation of lower Zayul is not more than four thousand feet, and the climate of these lowlands is so repugnant to the Tibetan highlander that lower Zayul is regarded and utilised as a penal settlement. We are not even absolutely certain that we are correct in uniting the Giama-Nu-Chu with the Salwin. So great an authority as General Walker considers that the body of water contained in the Salwin at the farthest north point to which it has been explored from the Burmese side is not sufficient to warrant the inflow of so large a river as the Giama-Nu-Chu, and that the latter is really an affluent of the Irawadi and not of the Salwin. Native reports however make the Giama-Nu-Chu and the Salwin one and the same river, and this is probably correct. We have at any rate some interesting geographical problems yet to solve in these regions, and they all lie near to our own border.

A prevalent misconception about Tibet is that the climate is so rigorous and the cold so intense that European existence in the country would be sustained with difficulty. It is true that very severe cold is encountered on the lofty passes leading into Tibet, but so far as the southern regions of the plateau are concerned — the valley of the Brahmaputra and the eastern valleys of affluents of the Chinese rivers — no such extreme of temperature is to be feared. The climate is dry, and snow seldom lies long in the plains beyond the Himalayan barrier. Even in winter the streams of the Brahmaputra basin are not always frozen. Two crops a year are raised on the cultivated areas of the lower valleys — such as Shigatze and Gyangtse, or in the Kyichu. Climate and temperature depend more on geographical position than on mere altitude, and the latitude of the Brahmaputra valley is low and its position sheltered. No vast plains of sand stretch their length across its flanks to send scorching blasts across in summer, or the freezing winds of the Turkestan "shamshir" in winter. Under normal circumstances the climate of southern Tibet (at eleven thousand five hundred feet) is delightful in summer, when "the land is covered with vegetation, streams flowing in every valley, and all nature bright, sparkling, and fresh." Even in winter, when snow and frost claim the land as their own, there is general movement throughout the country. It is then that the roads and rivers are rendered passable by ice to the trade caravans of the north and east. At Lhasa the mean temperatue observed by Indian surveyors is thirty-six degrees Fahrenheit in February and March, and sixty-one in June and July. In the eastern valleys the climate is Himalayan in character, and its degrees of salubrity are more or less dependent on altitude. I have been cautious in dealing with map altitudes which have been determined by means of barometrical observations. No such observations are trustworthy at such elevations, and they may very easily be in error by five hundred feet more or less. We now have certain accurately determined trigonometrical results from the observations of Major Ryder, and his assistants with Sir Frank Younghusband's mission in southern Tibet, where it is no longer necessary to depend too closely on the results obtained by native explorers.

CHAPTER III

Short Outline of Tibetan History — Introduction of Buddhism — Struggles with China and Mongol Interference — Growth of Lamaism — Chinese Administration

AN uninterrupted tale of exploration in the wilderness of Tibet, devoid (as Tibetan tales mostly are) of the stirring incidents of personal adventure, would prove but flat and unprofitable reading if they did not lead to a position from which we may form a fair estimate of the present status of Tibetan nationality, and make a rough forecast of the possible future of Tibet in the world of political strategy. But it would take too much space to consider in detail the opinions expressed by each individual traveller and to compare their impressions seriatim. It will be more useful to gather them at once into one collective whole, and to give a short summary of the existing form of government in Tibet and of its evolution, before we follow further the lines of modern exploration. We shall at least incidentally explain the position of some of those Tibetan functionaries with unpronounceable names who are so frequently referred to in the records of Tibetan travel.

The history of Tibet is the history of a country which, like India, has never lately been able to claim an integral nationality amongst the nations of the world. Foreign domination, either in Mongol or Chinese form, is invariably to be recognised, and it need be no matter of surprise to us if Tibetan traditions point to a final domination which is neither Mongol nor Chinese, but European. We are indebted to Prinsep, Kosma de Coros, Schlagentweit, and Sarat Chandra Das for the earliest records which may be called historical, including lists of kings dating from legendary beginnings (about the fifth century B. C.) to the end of the monarchy in 914 A. D. Throughout these legendary beginnings there runs a sort of traditional recognition of a dual form of government for Tibet, spiritual and temporal, — a form of administration akin to that of Rome, and one which finally found expression in Lhasa with the evolution of the Dalai Lama and his regent.

The aboriginal Tibetans appear to have been a savage and warlike people who invaded China and upper Burma with success, and even dictated terms of peace to the Chinese government. It was from China that the first principles of civilisation crept across the mountains to Tibet, coincident with the introduction of Buddhism by the young Chinese wife of the Tibetan King Srong-tsan-gumpo. She was the daughter of the Chinese emperor, and was received in marriage by the king after his successful invasion of China in the year 640 A. D. She found a useful ally in the Nepalese wife of the same monarch, and the two ladies worked together in harmony to lay the foundation of

A Tibetan Lhacham (Tibetan Princess) in Full Dress

one of the mightiest religious institutions that the world has ever seen. King Srong-tsan-gumpo (converted to Buddhism by his wife) founded Lhasa, and Lhasa has ever since been the pivot of Buddhist thought and Buddhist faith for all eastern Asia. It has been as the holy of holies, the dwelling of the ark of the covenant, to one-third of the human race. It is so still. If ever England aspires to be a Buddhist power she must reckon first with Lhasa.

The Buddhism then introduced into Tibet was supported by books and relics collected from India, and two great monasteries (Labrang and Rinpoche) were founded. But Indian Buddhism had long lost the grand simplicity of first principles. This had disappeared with the invasion of the Huns about the beginning of our era. Fa Hian (the Chinese traveller) found the doctrines of the "Great Vehicle" (sometimes called the Skythic form of Buddhism) in full force at Peshawur in the fifth century A. D. "Saints and angels sprang into existence, and grew and flourished till the Buddhist sky was full of them" (says Prof. Rhys Davids). Then the animism of the barbarous Huns was revived, with debasing beliefs in charms and ceremonies. The Tantra system, which was started at Peshawur in the sixth century A. D. was nothing better than witchcraft and sorcery. The Buddhism of Tibet thus partly derived from India did not supplant the older forms of Tibetan demonology till King Kir Song de Tsan reigned over the land (A. D. 740–786). It was then that true religion was acknowledged by ecclesiastical historians to be firmly established, and the Samye monastery was founded to contain the books collected from India. King Kir Song de Tsan is reckoned in Buddhist records to be the most illustrious and the most pious monarch who ever reigned over Tibet. It is worth noting that the son of this king was one of the greatest socialists in history. He enacted that all men should be equal; he compelled the rich to share their riches with the poor; he favoured an absolutely equal distribution of all the comforts and conditions of life. This was indeed the attainment of a high ideal — but it did not answer. In a very short time his people by the natural force of personal idiosyncrasy returned to their former condition of inequality, and after repeating the experiment three times he gave it up. The wise men of Tibet said it was due to a survival of inequality in methods of existence during former lives.

In the early years of the ninth century a severe struggle with China took place, and thereafter, throughout a period of intricate history, struggles with Mongols from the north and with China on the east were periodic. Nothing stands out very clearly after the break up of the Tibetan monarchy into four provincial kingdoms about the end of the tenth century, until the arrival of the celebrated Indian Buddhist Atisha, who settled in the great lamaserai of Thoding in Ngari. He introduced books and education and some of the elements of astronomical science in 1026, and he was probably the first of the great priests whose authority became paramount in the country. He put the whole Tantra system into the background and resorted again to first principles. For three hundred years a purer form of Buddhism maintained its ground, whilst priests and lamas multiplied exceedingly, until the Mogul Emperor Kublai Khan (son of Genghis Khan) invested the high priest of the red-cap sect with sovereign power over the thirteen provinces of U and Tsang (which comprise Tibet proper), together with Kham and Amdo, in 1252. This was a complimentary exchange for the kindly offices of the abbot in crowning him emperor of the widest empire the world has ever seen. For four centuries more the lamas of the Sakya monastery remained spiritual rulers of Tibet, temporal authority being exercised by regents whom they appointed.

Meanwhile a new and powerful sect had arisen in Tibet. Modern lamaism (defined by Prof. Rhys Davids as "the union of ethical and metaphysical ideas with a hierarchal system and temporal sovereignty at Lhasa") may be said to have been founded by the great reformer Tsong kapa (the Luther of Tibet) in 1390. By 1410 there were three huge monasteries and thirty thousand disciples to testify to the activity of the reformation. In all respects Tsong kapa appealed to first principles, following Atisha, and pleading for the re-establishment of ancient customs. It was he who founded the custom of an annual week of fasting and prayer in which churchmen and laymen alike take part, and which is described by the Jesuit missionary Huc. He never disputed the authority of the red-cap Sakya lamas. His sect is known to this day as the "yellow" or "orange" sect, from the colour of the robes its disciples wear. By the middle of the fifteenth century the yellow caps were paramount, and a dual spiritual authority was established over Tibet at Lhasa and Tashilumpo.

When the Mongol dynasty of China ceased, that of the Mings yet further enlarged the authority of the Tibetan rulers and recognised the chief lamas. The failing power of the Mings in China favoured the interference of the Mongols in Tibetan affairs again, and a Tartar invasion occurred in the middle of the seventeenth century, which partially ended the Sakya red-cap rule and established that of the rising yellow caps. The fifth of the grand lamas of the reformed faith appears to have been a man of great strength of character and much diplomatic ability. According to Waddell he made excellent use of the opportunity afforded by the incident of the Tartar irruption, and with the assistance of the Tartar prince wrested the temporal authority out of the hands of the red-caps, and established himself as the first Dalai (or Tale) Lama of Tibet, — practically uniting in his person the offices of high priest and king, although a Tartar prince was nominally installed as king at Lhasa. The word "Dalai" appears to be merely the Mongolian rendering of his name (Vast as the Ocean).

He then set about establishing for himself and his successors a divine origin, based on a book of "revelations" which he "discovered," proving that all grand lamas were incarnations of the Great King Srong-tsan-gumpo, and enforcing his claims and his creed with such strong measures that the Jesuit missionary Grueber calls him "devilish God the Father who puts to death such as refuse to adore him." He however recognised the Grand Lama of Tashilumpo (Shigatze) as the reincarnation of a pseudo-Buddha, second only to himself in spiritual significance, and thus founded the present recognised system of a dual spiritual rule in Tibet. The theory of reincarnation in infant form was not introduced into practice till later, and it was the cause of so much friction between rival sects as to lead to another Tartar invasion in 1717, when Lhasa was taken by storm.

Then the Emperor of China intervened with a powerful army. He ejected the Tartars, established the succession of the Dalai Lama by re-births, and curtailed his power at the same time. Two Ambans (or Ambassadors) were then appointed, with a Chinaman as regent or king. The "king" was murdered by the Dalai Lama in 1727, and the inevitable Chinese reprisals included the transfer of temporal power to a "mayor of the palace," one Miwang, of whom we shall hear more from the Capuchin fathers of the Tibetan missions, whom he befriended for years. A massacre of the Chinese in 1749 led to another punitive expedition (which will be referred to later), and from this time Chinese influence has been paramount in Tibet, until it was discredited by the late war. Latterly the present Dalai Lama, assisted by the young "national" party, has openly defied Chinese authority and has declared himself pro-Russian.

We may note here that the present Dalai Lama is the thirteenth in succession; that he has reached the mature age of thirty (his four predecessors having died or disappeared about the age of eighteen); and that he shows every disposition to follow the dictates of a headstrong will under Russian influence. There is a popular saying in Lhasa, referred to by one of the native explorers of the Indian Survey forty years ago, that the thirteenth Dalai Lama will be the last.

Briefly we may indicate the chief features of present Tibetan administration.

The Ambans appointed by China are responsible for the foreign and military government of the country, leaving civil and religious administration in the hands of the Tibetans. They are appointed for three years only. Subordinate to them at Lhasa and Shigatze are two chief commandants and two paymasters of the Chinese army. These, with three subordinate commanders at Lhasa, Shigatze, and Dingri (on the Nepal frontier), and three non-commissioned officers complete the entire administrative staff of China. It is not a large one. The whole force of Chinese troops in the country does not exceed forty-five hundred men, distributed between Lhasa, Shigatze, and the Nepalese frontier. The chief civil authority in Tibet is invested in the head of the Tibetan hierarchy, — the Dalai

Lama (gyal-rinpoche),— who resides in the far-famed Potala at Lhasa. Nominally equal to him in rank, but in reality secondary in authority, is the Panchen rinpoche, or Grand Lama, who resides at Tashilumpo, near Shigatze; and there is in the far Mongolian distance (directly under Russian influence) a third Grand Lama of Tibet, known as the Bogda (himself an "avatar"), the supreme pontiff of the Lamaistic church, who resides at Urga. This spiritual dignitary is really of older creation than the Dalai Lama, for his office was founded when the Mongol dynasty in China finally disappeared. The authority of the Dalai Lama is unquestioned. His decision is final, and he is only questioned in cases of emergency. His powers are transmitted to a special officer nominated by the Chinese government, who is called by various names. He is the Gyalpo, or regent (when the Dalai Lama is a minor), or Nomokhan (Mongolian),— the "king of the law,"— and he is frequently referred to in books of travel as the "king." He is traditionally selected from the four head lamas of the monasteries of Chomoling, Kondoling, Tangialing, and Chajoling, each one of whom is an "avatar," *i. e.*, he is reincarnated at death in the body of an infant. Equal in rank to the Nomokhan is the Deba Lama of Galdan, the great monastery near Lhasa. But he is not an "avatar." Next to him is the Lama Guru or chaplain of the Dalai Lama, who (like the Deba Lama of Galdan) is the subject of Chinese nomination.

China thus preserves a careful supervision over the

religious element in the Tibetan government. The Nomokhan rules with the help of a council of five ministers representing the financial, judicial, revenue, and home departments, with a lama for ecclesiastical affairs. The four provinces, Nari, U, Tsang, and Kham, are each under a Kablon, or governor, assisted by a competent staff. Outside these provinces are several minor "kings," or Gyalpos, and within them there are four principalities directly under Chinese authority. These are Dyag and Chiamdo on the east, Tashilumpo, and Sakya Kongma to the southwest of Tashilumpo. In the east the principalities of Dargé and Ta-chien-lu (amongst others) are more or less directly under the control of China. The remarkable feature about this form of government is the maintenance of Chinese authority throughout so vast a country with the assistance of so small a military force. China was till lately nominally dominant everywhere, holding the keys of all important positions in Tibet, and regulating all important appointments. Lately the authority of the Amban has been set aside without difficulty when convenient to the Tibetan rulers to dispense with it. Tibet has assumed a new and stronger position of independence since the results of the late Chinese war have discredited the power and prestige of China; and doubtless Chinese diplomacy sometimes finds it convenient to shift the responsibility of action on to Tibetan shoulders whenever such action might jeopardise her friendly relations with foreign powers whom she has reason to respect.

A Tibetan Prince. Dungkhor at Home

Such a government presents unusual difficulties to political negotiation. A nebulous responsibility in the councils of Tibet has hitherto baffled our efforts at establishing a definite basis for the opening of trade and free intercourse with the rich and promising valleys of southern and eastern Tibet. The Tibetan government has throughout all historical negotiations treated the Indian government with the contempt which is always shown by the semi-barbarous and ignorant tribespeople of the Indian frontier towards a power whose reluctance to use force is attributed to weakness. We may perhaps hope for a stronger position in future, but it will depend on some outward and visible sign of our authority at Lhasa.

CHAPTER IV

The First Recorded Mogul Invasion of Tibet — Mirza Haidar's Story — His Geography — Identification of his Route towards Lhasa

ISLAM has never made much impression on Tibet. Sweeping past its northern hills into High Asia, or through the western passes into Hindustan, the banners of Mahomed left Tibet almost unvisited. And yet there has been no lack of determined effort to establish Islamism in these elevated strongholds. We have in the excellent translation by Ney Elias of the Tarikh-i-Rashidi — a history written by one Mirza Haidar, the Mogul cousin of the Turko-Mogul Emperor Baber (who established the Mogul dynasty in India) — a very authentic account of the conquest of Little Tibet (*i. e.*, Ladak) in the sixteenth century A. D., and the extension of that conquest into Kashmir. This may be reckoned the beginning of modern Tibetan exploration, and is well worth a reference in this book for its geographical indications. The history concerns the doings of a branch of the Mogul Khans who separated themselves early in the fourteenth century from the main branch of the Chagatai, which was then the ruling (albeit a declining) power in Transoxiana, and considering the disorder which reigned among the leading families, their constant movements through countries which had no definite boundaries, and the infinite complications resulting from intermarriage, it is a very clear exposition of the events of the times of which it treats, *i. e.*, the commencement of the sixteenth century. Mirza Haidar was but one of the class who made history in those days, — a roving adventurer, or soldier of fortune, exposed to all the vicissitudes of the times. Neither as a writer nor as a soldier was he comparable to his inimitable cousin Baber (afterwards Emperor of India), but he is not altogether unjustified in his claim to be considered a master of verse-making and of epistolary style at a time when literature was the study of every well-bred Mogul gentleman.

Whilst quite a boy he was raised to high position by his kinsman Sultan Said Khan, whom he served for nineteen years as a soldier; commencing in 1527 with a successful expedition against the Kaffirs of Bolor (which then included Hunza, Gilgit, and Chitral). He followed with a less successful incursion into Badakshan; and it was not till 1531 that he undertook his most important service for Sultan Said Khan. This was, first, the invasion of Little Tibet, or Ladak, then of Kashmir and Baltistan, and finally of Tibet proper, — *i. e.*, the Tibet of our modern maps. The excuse for a wanton attack on Ladak was the usual one. There was much paganism in that country, and the Khan, animated by a love of Islam and a desire to carry on holy wars, was anxious to smite the infidel. This was not the first time that Ladak had been invaded by the Mussalman hordes of the north, but we know very little about the earlier records. None of them made much impression; nor did even the successful advance of Mirza Haidar. The Ladaki has fallen, like the Kashmiri, under the Hindu yoke of the Dogra since then, but he still preserves his connection with Lhasa in all religious and social matters.

It is at any rate clear that such northern routes as exist were well enough known in those days. Sultan Said in striking south from Kashgar was apparently inclined to follow the Kiria-Polu route from Khotan, and to cross the western extremity of Tibet to Leh. This indicates that this was a recognised route then, and it is significant that this is the direct route to the western gold-fields of Tibet, which centre to the north of the upper Indus, some three hundred miles to the southeast of Leh. But Mirza Haidar knew what the northern steppes (the Aksai Chin) were like, and dissuaded Sultan Said from attempting to cross a corner of Tibet which has since proved fatal to more than one expedition. The advancing force crossed the Karakorum by the usual trade route between Leh and Kashgar; and it is a matter of surprise that any force (mobile as the Mogul troops undoubtedly were) should have been able to invade Ladak by such an elevated, bleak, inhospitable route as that which stretches its length across that dreary space between the two towns. The invasion was entirely successful. "The talons of Islam seizing the hands of infidelity, the enemy were thrown into disorder and routed. Having deserted the fort, they fled in confusion and dismay, while the Mussalmans gave them chase as far as was possible, so that not one of these bewildered people escaped. Bur Kapa was slain together with all his men; their heads formed a lofty minaret, and the vapour from the brains of the infidels of that country ascended to the heavens." Sultan Said Khan followed his army into the field, but "damgiri" (or mountain sickness) assailed him, and he nearly died on the journey. He recovered sufficiently to lead a part of his army into Baltistan, where he suffered great hardships, and had to retreat first to Ladak and then to Kashmir. But "damgiri" was too much for him on the return route. He died on the Suget pass, and was succeeded by his son. Mirza Haidar meanwhile had advanced into Kashmir by the Sind valley and Zoji La route, and gained some victories. But he could not control his army, and retired without effecting anything important. On the death of the Khan, Mirza Haidar pursued the holy war with much zeal. He even started on a "jehad" to "earn merit" by destroying Lhasa. He advanced into Tibet with two or three columns by the same southeastern route which must, through all time, have been the recognised line of communication between Leh and Lhasa. It is now, as it was then, the great trade route from Kashmir to Pekin. Unfortunately Mirza Haidar is not as sound a geographer as he is historian, although it is true that as a geographer he gives us information which is of some value. It is from his writings, for instance, that we can define the limits of the ancient kingdom of Bolor, which for centuries has been the despair of the geographical compilers. But when dealing with Tibet he is unsatisfactory. He puts the distance between Leh and Lhasa at one hundred and sixty marches. The configuration of mountain and valley and the opportunities for a route through such highlands as those of southern Tibet could not have differed largely then from those which obtain at present. The same physical difficulties faced the traveller of the sixteenth century as would face the traveller of the twentieth. The route must have been determined by the same distribution of mountain ridge and river course, and on that route certain obligatory points exist which must have defined the position of the chief trade and religious centres just as they define them still. Four hundred years have modified or changed the names (Tibetan names are not easily transcribed at any time), but the sites of the principal towns in the valleys of the upper Indus and Brahmaputra cannot have shifted far. The first place of importance reached was called Barmang. Here sheep were captured, and the Champa people (*i. e.*, the settlers in the valley) were plundered of their goods and horses. I can find no trace of Barmang in modern maps, and as there is no mention of a fortress, it is possible that it was no more than what it is described to be, *i. e.*, a suitable pasture land for a halt. The next place is Khardun. I see no reason why this should not be the modern

Khardam, a little to the south of the Manasarawar lakes, near the sources of the Sutlej and Brahmaputra. Next he mentions a place called Luk Liuk or Luk Lanuk (there are other variants of the name) as being half way to Ursang (which is clearly Lhasa, Lhasa being the capital of the Utsang province), and he associates it with a fortress near a great lake one hundred and sixty miles in circumference. Ney Elias identifies this place with Manasarawar on account of the enormous size of the lake, and from the fact that one of the two Manasarawar lakes is called the Tso Lanak. But there are difficulties in the way of accepting this identification. In the first place, we should have to give up Khardam, for Khardam is too close to the lake to coincide with the narrative; and in the next place, we should find ourselves nowhere near to the half-way point between Leh and Lhasa. About such a matter as this Mirza Haidar would be likely to be fairly correct. The length of marches no doubt varied considerably (as they would vary to-day), but the average over a long distance would remain fairly constant. About half way we find the main road approach the Brahmaputra at a point where the monastery of Likeche overlooks the river, nearly opposite Tadum. This more nearly corresponds to Mirza Haidar's description of the castle on the shores of the lake, but raises the objection that it is a river and not a lake which is so commanded. But his estimate of the size of the lake (one hundred and sixty miles in circumference) is so vastly in excess of the size of the Manasarawar lakes (even putting the two together and allowing for the very probable extent of desiccation which has occurred in the last four hundred years) as to throw some doubt on his accuracy in describing it as a lake at all. The river widens greatly at this point, and flows with a broad and placid surface, and it is here navigated by Tibetan boats. Looking east and west it would appear limitless, even as an enormous lake might appear.

Finally he records that with an attenuated force of ninety mounted men (the rest of the horses having died of damgiri) he succeeded in reaching and pillaging a place called Askabrak. There is nothing in modern maps answering to this name, but there is only one place of importance which would give opportunity for the capture of valuable booty anywhere near the position assigned to it by Mirza Haidar (*i. e.*, eight marches from Lhasa), and that place is Shigatze. It is, however, impossible to arrive at any certainty in the identification of this early record of Tibetan invasion. The loss of his horses decided him to return from this point, wherever it may have been, and he retired apparently unmolested, overtaking the remnants of his force on their way back and forming a rendezvous at Guga. There is no difficulty about identifying Guga as Gartok on the upper Indus, about eighteen marches (according to the narrative) from Maryul or Leh. The name Giugh La is still preserved in the pass which crosses the first range north of Gartok on the way to the mining district of Thok Jalung. The expedition failed in its object, but it was not altogether disastrous. There had been but little fighting, and that little had been near the commencement of the raid at Barmang, against a force of three thousand men sent by a "Hindu Rai," who are said to have fought with short knives. This, as Ney Elias points out, appears to have been a Nepalese force armed with kukris (the national weapon of the Gurkha) and not a Tibetan force. But the fight was severe, and Mirza Haidar lost a brave young brother, who was cut to pieces — "so completely that each separate part of his cuirass and coat was in the possession of some infidel." The people of Guga, with true Tibetan complacence, received the broken and battered remains of the frostbitten and starving force with all hospitality. They fed them and kept them, and finally assisted Mirza Haidar to raise a fresh force with which to harry the western districts of their own country. This is the earliest authentic record of any expedition into the southern regions of Tibet which can be said to be productive of geographical information.

CHAPTER V

Eighteenth Century Explorations — Grueber — Capuchin Monks — Their Mission at Lhasa and their Struggles — Jesuit Interference — Desideri — Beligatti — Last of the Mission — Van de Putte — His Residence at Lhasa

IN estimating the position which Lhasa holds as one of the great centres of the religious world, it is necessary to recognise the significance of her religious affinity with Mongolia. The sort of affinity which is based on community of faith bridges over geographical space as nothing else bridges it. Across Mongolia, from Manchuria to the northeastern border of Tibet, there intervenes a good thousand miles of more or less difficult and desert country; but this thousand miles is but a step when the way is a pilgrims' way, and faces are set towards Lhasa as the centre of religious light. No power paramount in Mongolia would experience much difficulty in reaching out its fingers to the indefinite fringe of Tibetan borderland indicated by Tsaidam and the Koko Nor region. The acceptance of such a power by Mongolia would be a spiritual introduction to Tibet, and with such an introduction geographical distances and physical difficulties would be found to disappear with marvellous rapidity.

Mongolia has assimilated Buddhism from a very early period. Mongol power in China was first broken by a Buddhist lama, who founded the Ming dynasty of China in 1355 A. D. Subsequently we find that a noted Mongol chief, Altan Khan, embraced Buddhism about the year 1570, and as the result of his successful raids into Tibet he brought lamaist prisoners to the north, who introduced lamaism to the Tumed branch of his race. He received at his court one Bogda Sodnam Gyamtso Khutuktu, a notable lama of high degree, who is now represented by one of the great leaders of the Buddhist hierarchy who resides at Urga in northern Mongolia under the shadow of the Russian domination. In the beginning of the seventeenth century Mongolia was honoured by the selection of a Dalai Lama from amongst her infants, and by the time that the Ming dynasty was replaced by the Manchu, and the Ordus Mongol tribes were established in the loop of the Hoang Ho River under the suzerainty of China, the power of the Buddhist lama had grown paramount. Probably there is at this time more real honest devotion to the faith of Buddhism amongst the rough and scattered herdsmen of the Mongolian steppes than there is in all Tibet put together. Touch Lhasa, and all Mongolia to the borders of Manchuria will certainly respond.

Mongol expeditions into Tibet from the northeast have been constant through all Asiatic history; but there is little detailed record of them, nor do they add much to our geographical knowledge. Trustworthy narrative of Tibetan exploration (other than military expeditions) commences only with the seventeenth century.

Friar Odoric of Pordenone is said to have reached Lhasa from Cathay in 1328, and there appears to be substantial reason for believing that he really was the first European to cross Tibet of whom we have any record. But authentic information regarding his journey is unobtainable, and we must content ourselves with according him the honour of being first in the Tibetan field. The great Marco Polo never really entered Tibet at all, although he crossed the Pamirs. In the seventeenth century the first great traveller of whom we have authentic record (and whose adventures have been published in at least five European languages) was the Jesuit father Antonio de Andrada. But the story of his travels as we possess it at present is unsatisfactory in many particulars. The letters written in 1626 to his superior, the Jesuit General Mutio Vitelleschi, give but scanty and confused details of a journey which apparently terminated at Tsaparang on the river Sutlej. It is difficult to reconcile the account of his explorations beyond the Manasarawar lake to Rudok, and thence to Cathay and back, either with the topography of the Tibetan highlands, or with the exigencies of time that would be required for such a journey. In spite of his hitherto prominent position as a pioneer in the field of Asiatic geography, Antonio de Andrada must be regarded as but a doubtful authority.

The next recorded exploration in Tibet is that of

the Jesuit fathers Johannes Grueber and Albert de Dorville (which appears to be his correct name, although it is usually written d'Orville) in the years 1661 and 1662. We are indebted to Herr R. Tronnier for an exhaustive examination into the records of this remarkable journey, published in the "Berlin Zeitschrift der Gesellschaft für Erdkunde" for 1904, which has been made with the object of giving the German Jesuit the place to which he appears to be entitled in geographical history. He is clearly the first European who brought back a genuine record of Tibet and its people, and his journey was one of geographical discovery, for it was imposed, not by missionary zeal, but by the necessity of discovering a new route from China, via Lhasa, to Europe. The material from which an account of his travels is constructed are his letters (of which one written from Rome in 1664 is by far the most important), a report by the Jesuit Athanasius Kircher (who published his sketches in his "China Illustrata"), and a long Italian "Relazione" by an unknown author, which appears to be an authentic account taken from the lips of the travellers themselves. De Dorville was a Belgian by birth, who had laboured for some years in the Chinese missionary field at Shansi. Throughout the journey he appears only as the companion of Grueber, to whom alone we are indebted for the astronomical determinations and notes which render this exploration notable in geographical annals. De Dorville died at Agra in 1662, from the effects of the hardships involved in the journey.

Grueber originally occupied the position of mathematical assistant to the Court of Pekin, but after the death of the first emperor of the Manchu dynasty (February, 1661) he was "recalled to receive instructions from the General of the Order at Rome," De Dorville being chosen to accompany him. Macao, which pointed the usual route between Europe and Pekin, was then under blockade by the Dutch, and Grueber was instructed to discover a new route overland. As a matter of fact, he followed a very old one (the same, or nearly the same, which will be described at length in the narrative of the Jesuits Huc and Gabet), — one which has through all historic times connected Pekin with the Chinese frontier town of Sining fu, and which, passing the great blue lake of northeastern Tibet (the Koko Nor), traverses the successive mountain ridges of the Kuen Lun system, and surmounting the Tang-la prominence, drops into the basin of the upper Brahmaputra. It is a long road (with several alternative loops), and a road which bristles with physical difficulties; but it is one of the great pilgrim roads of the world, and it connects, and has always connected, Lhasa more surely with Pekin and Manchuria than any existing route has hitherto linked Lhasa with India. A comparison of existing records shows that Grueber reached Barantola (the Tartar name for Lhasa) in about three months from Sining fu, and that he adopted a westerly route, passing south of the Koko Nor before traversing the ranges bordering Tsaidam. This was then regarded as a "new" route, in contradistinction to an "old" route running more directly southwards from Sining fu via the lacustrine sources of the Hoang Ho River. Recent explorations however tend to prove that there are many routes between Sining fu and Lhasa. Since Huc and Gabet succeeded in reaching Lhasa by much the same route which had been adopted by Grueber, several modern travellers have crossed the ranges south of Tsaidam, and have attempted to reach Lhasa either by the "old" route (via the sources of the Hoang Ho) or by those more westerly routes which either directly traverse the Tang-la divide or flank it on the west. It seems probable that the most direct and the most frequently traversed route is that followed by Huc and Gabet in the winter time, when the affluents of the Mu ussu (or Di-chu) are frozen, and present no serious obstacle. At Lhasa Grueber took observations for latitude (which he places about half a degree too far south), and made sketches which have been reproduced by Kircher. He also set about the discovery of a new route to India. From Lhasa to India was a journey of one or two months (Grueber speaks of one month, but Kircher makes it two, which is the more probable if Agra was the terminus), crossing a high range (Langur) at four days' journey from Lhasa. Herr Tronnier identifies this with the Himalayas generally; but it will probably be safe to assume that it is the range which borders the Yero Tsanpo on the south (now known as the Kambar), on the direct highroad to Gyangtse, or to Nepal via Shigatze.

From Kuti, on the Nepal frontier, they reached the capital, Khatmandu, in eleven days (Tronnier). Here they were well received; and it is one of the most interesting facts about this early connection between Lhasa and India that Nepal, equally with Tibet, was open, not only to European travellers, but to Christian missionaries, who established at Patan (near Khatmandu) a mission which for many years formed a connecting link between Christian centres in Lhasa and India. From Nepal Grueber's journey has been traced by Markham through Molihari (then a Mogul town on the Indian frontier) to Patna, Dinapur, Benares, and Agra, where De Dorville died, aged only thirty-nine years. The two travellers reached Agra in March, 1662 (having crossed the Himalayas at the worst time of the year); and as they started from Pekin in April, 1661, the journey had taken them exactly eleven months, as Grueber himself states. Grueber's observations for latitude in India exhibit a general mean error of about —30′ (or half a degree), and if we attribute this error to a defect in his instrument, and apply a corresponding correction to all his observations, the results are neither discordant nor inaccurate, considering the nature of the instrument he used, — an astrolabe with certain attachments new to the science of those times. Grueber's journey through Tibet must ever be reckoned a remarkable geographical achievement. Now that the general trumpery nature of Lhasa's "mysteries" is fully recognised, it is well to be reminded by his story that two centuries and a half ago there were no mysteries. Tibet (like Nepal) was open to the European equally with the Asiatic traveller.

Grueber finally reached Rome from the Sind frontier of India by way of Makrân, Persia, and Smyrna (which was in itself a journey of remarkable interest), and he subsequently made an attempt to reach China via Asia Minor and Bokhara. This venture was unsuccessful, owing to the disturbed condition of Asia at that period. He died in 1680, at the age of fifty-seven.

The commencement of the eighteenth century witnessed more direct communication between Tibet and Europe than has ever existed either before or since. It seems strange now to recall the fact that for thirty-eight years a Christian mission existed in the very capital itself, maintaining, it is true, but a precarious existence, but never wanting for witnesses to the Christian faith. This Capuchin mission practically died a natural death in the year 1745, when the broken-hearted Orazio della Penna di Billi (the Livingstone of Tibet) breathed his last: although a branch mission near Khatmandu continued in active operation as late as 1768, and only disappeared with the Gurkha revolution. Surely no tale of missionary enterprise which ever was told in this world is more stirring and more pathetic than the story of the Capuchin missions as given to us by the Rev. Graham Sandberg in his recent book, "The Exploration of Tibet."

As early as 1701 Catholic missionaries were on the borders of northeastern Tibet (under the jurisdiction of the Roman Catholic bishop of Pekin), and in touch with certain Christians, who were in all probability remnants of those Nestorian Christian communities of mediæval times which once spread far and wide throughout the highlands of central Asia; but it was not till 1708 that four Capuchin friars started from Nepal (having founded the mission station near Khatmandu) and boldly made their way via Gyangtse to Lhasa. One of the four was Father Orazio della Penna. Here they were well enough received, and they set about their work "humbly and inoffensively," meeting with no great success. But the enterprise was not well supported. The missionaries were reduced almost to starvation, and maintained their existence by writing begging letters to their brethren at various stations. In 1711 the mission was perforce abandoned, and the whole body of Tibetan and Nepalese missionaries were concentrated at the French settlement of Chandernagore in India. Subsequent representations made at Rome, however, by Father Dominico de Fano were successful, and the mission was revived. Twelve priests were allocated to the Tibetan mission, of whom four were to be at Lhasa, two at "Drogugne" in the province of Takpo, two in Nepal, and the rest at Chandernagore and Patna. Once again did Orazio della Penna return to the scene of his former labours. This was early in 1715, and from that time till July, 1733, the solitary little outpost of the great army of Roman Catholic missions maintained its chequered existence, in constant danger from the hostility of the lamas, and the intermittent superstitions of the people, who were ever ready to attribute any disaster that occurred in their city to the devices of the missionaries. Yet it was under the protection of the Gyalpo (Miwang) and of the Grand Lama, who issued permissive decrees in its favour, stamped on yellow satin, with the confirmatory seal of the Celestial Emperor. Ten years after the re-establishment of the mission a little church and mission house were completed, and at the opening ceremony eleven Christians (chiefly natives of Nepal) were present. Della Penna states that the new establishment was even visited by the Grand Lama of Lhasa, and he further asserts that on leaving their house the holy man exclaimed, "Your God is in truth a great God." But the old trouble arising from want of financial support was ever with them, and the Jesuit community was ever against them. In 1729 "starvation once again confronted the workers, of whom two only were left in Tibet, namely, Orazio della Penna and Gioachino da San Anatolia." It appears that the Gyalpo actually offered to provide for them, and suggested that they should charge medical fees for such practice as they had among the people. This suggestion was declined on principle. The missionaries would not receive charity from non-Christians.

Between 1729 and 1733 political troubles supervened, and the enmity of the priestly and magician classes was renewed. Della Penna's health (after twenty years of missionary work in Tibet) began to give away, and he was finally persuaded by his companion to leave Lhasa for Nepal. At Khatmandu he was promptly imprisoned, but he was subsequently released, and for two years more (after being joined by Father Gioachino) he carried on mission work in Nepal under comparatively favourable auspices; for the king, who had first imprisoned him, afterwards gave the missionaries considerable encouragement from political motives. The Capuchin fathers of the so-called "Tibetan mission" had by this time been reduced to three, not one of whom was really fit for active service. Driven to desperation, Orazio della Penna set out for Rome to plead his own cause and outwit the tacit foes of the mission, — the Jesuits. His modest record of work accomplished during twenty-five years of service included the baptism of 2,587 infants, and a small company of Christian converts (Nepalese, Tibetans, and Chinese), numbering about forty in all. It was a scanty harvest, but nevertheless it roused the jealousy of the Jesuit Order, who urged their claim to the Tibetan field on the grounds of priority in exploration. The decision of the Vatican was eventually given against them, but not before the Jesuits had despatched an agent of their own to enquire into the working of the Capuchin missions and to discredit them as far as possible. This agent was Ippolito Desideri, who thus first appears on the field as a Tibetan explorer. Desideri entered Tibet by Ladak, and, as he was something of an observer and a writer, we have some most interesting records from his pen of the nature of the now well-known route to Leh.

It is unfortunate that in the history of geographical exploration we should be so dependent on the records of the few who write rather than of the many who observe. Considering the number of educated Europeans who visited Lhasa in the early years of the eighteenth century, and who knew the Tibetans as no one knows them now, we have strangely little information concerning the country or its people. Desideri was one of the writers. The route from Kashmir (Srinagar) to Leh was that part of his journey which impressed him most. "The greater part of the road is along the flanks of the loftiest and most awful mountains, and in which there is ordinarily not found sufficient space for one man to pass by another." Desideri and his companion (Manoel Freyre) remained eight weeks at Leh, and in August, 1715, resumed their travels eastward. It seems pretty certain that they passed through Tashigang on the Indus, but beyond that their route seems doubtful. It is probable that they passed by the regular Leh-Pekin route over the Mariam La to Shigatze, Gyangtse, and so to Lhasa, which place they reached in March, 1716, seven months after leaving Leh. Naturally there was some little friction at first between the Jesuit Desideri and the Capuchins, whom he had come to report upon; but finally all differences of opinion were smoothed over, and they lived together in one common bond of Christian brotherhood. Desideri prolonged his stay in

Tibet for five years, until he was ordered home by Pope Clement in 1721. Meanwhile he had shown much more geographical enterprise than the worthy Capuchin missionaries, for he had visited many of the most interesting places in southeastern Tibet. When he arrived in Rome he at once drew up the claim of the Jesuits for precedence in Tibet, being opposed by Felice da Montecchio, who advocated the cause of the Capuchins. Finally judgment was given (in 1732) in favour of the latter, and shortly afterwards Desideri died, it is suggested, from chagrin at the result of the decision; but this seems hardly probable, if Desideri's character is to be estimated from his own friendly relations with the Capuchin fathers during his stay at Lhasa.

For seven years (from 1733 to 1740) the Lhasa mission was abandoned, not a Capuchin monk being left in Tibet or (latterly) in Nepal. But the representations made at Rome by that valiant old missionary Della Penna at last had effect, and the Pope himself was interested in the revival of the mission. In 1738 Orazio della Penna and nine Capuchin brethren started for the East, bearing with them presents from the Pope of Rome to the Dalai Lama. Amongst them was Cassiano Beligatti da Macerata, who subsequently proved himself to be the most literary, if not the most capable, member of the whole Tibetan mission. It is from his pen that we get by far the most interesting narrative of the journeys of the Capuchin missionaries, and the most detailed accounts of the manners and customs of the people, albeit we get but little valuable geographical information. The story as told by Sandberg is taken from the "Revista Geografica Italiana," Florence, 1902. The party reached Patna in December, 1739, and there picked up the veteran Gioachino, with whom they continued the journey to Nepal. So little do we know even now of the Nepal approaches, that Beligatti's narrative of one hundred and sixty-four years ago would still be of real geographical value could we only identify the places he mentions *en route*. But this is impossible. At Khatmandu (now the capital of Nepal, then a provincial town) they remained till the rainy season of 1740 had passed, when it is said "the king suffered them to depart," and they started northeastward for Lhasa. Their journey seems to have been painfully slow. It is indeed difficult to account for the time that was taken over its successive stages, unless we assume that the party (now reduced to seven) was occupied with missionary work as they went. There is no difficulty in following their route through Kuti (the frontier town of Nepal, through which all merchandise passes even now) to the valley of Dingri, the great monastery of Sakya Jong, and Gyangtse, which they reached on December 24, 1740, having left Khatmandu on October 1.

Beligatti's description of methods of travel; of the miseries experienced at high elevations; of the obstinacy of the mule drivers; the pig-headedness of the local authorities; the intense cold (it was winter); the want of fuel; and of hospitality on the part of

Tibetans generally, — might apply to the Tibet of to-day. Nothing appears to move in Tibet, and Beligatti's experiences would be those of any modern European who trod the same route now. It is a narrative of more than passing interest, and must have delighted the heart of its discoverer, Signor Magnaghi, who found it in the Biblioteca Comunale at Macerata (Beligatti's native town) a year or two ago.

Beligatti's description of Gyangtse might have been written by the special correspondent with Sir Frank Younghusband's mission; but there is added thereto an account of a certain weird Tibetan ceremony which no member of the late mission ever had the opportunity of witnessing. It was the burning of *il turma* (the *torma* sacrifice) on the fourth or fifth day of the new moon.

From the fusileers who headed the procession, to the cymbal and tambourine beating monks, the "choir master," the medicine man, the dancing Ngaramba ("who danced like lunatics"), the pantomimic hats, the incense-bearers, and the turma itself, we have the whole grotesque show vividly depicted. The turma was a cone of paste tricked out with coloured butter, which was finally deposited on a tripod in front of the temple. Here rites were performed before it, and grain offered to it; hymns were sung, and further invocations and libations poured forth.

Finally it was kicked over by the Ngaramba; the fusileers discharged their blunderbusses, and the ceremony broke up "confusamente e senz' ordine." And yet some of the worthy Catholic fathers have traced points of resemblance between Tibetan ceremony and that of Rome!

On the 27th of December the missionaries started from Gyangtse and trod the now well-known route to Nagartse Jong and the Yero Tsanpo. At Nagartse they tell us of the famous Samding monastery and the Dorje Pagmo, — the abbess who is venerated nearly as much as the Dalai Lama, and is the only Tibetan lady permitted to ride in a palanquin. In Beligatti's time her morals were not beyond reproach, but her sanctity did not seem to be impaired thereby. From Nagartse over the Kamba-la to the Brahmaputra and Lhasa there is nothing new now to be told about the route. They crossed the river in a boat, as the bridge was even then reckoned unsafe, — the boat being navigated by means of a "pulley" attached to a rope stretched across the river, even as our engineers navigated it a short time ago.

At Lhasa the Capuchin fathers resumed their old quarters, which appear to have been preserved. The Capuchin friars were welcomed by all the chief Lhasa officials, including the Gyalpo (king), the Kalons, and the Chinese Amban. It must be remembered that since 1720 Tibet had been formally annexed to China. They were even honoured by an invitation to dine with the king's son, and it is clear that they were on the most friendly terms with many of the leading lamas of the city. Beligatti's narrative is of peculiar interest where he gives us a detailed account of Tibetan religious ceremonies and court functions, and an insight into the inner life of Tibet at least a century and a half earlier than that obtained by the agency of our own native explorers, which were regarded as altogether new to the world when they were first published. The general accuracy of his narrative has been most fully confirmed by these later reports, and it is certainly extraordinary that for so long a period after the final collapse of the Tibetan mission such a veil of ignorance should have again been drawn over Lhasa and its people as that which has lately been disturbed by a mission of a very different nature. Amongst other ceremonies he describes the procession at the Moulam festival (which is officially recognised as a period of prayer lasting twenty-three days, but which is in reality a time of licence and excitement), during which many of the most weird and fantastic performances for which Tibet is famous are rehearsed in fullest pantomime. It commenced on the sixth day of the new year (*i. e.,* 21st of February, 1741), in Beligatti's time, and the Capuchins were enabled to watch the proceedings through their intimacy with "that somewhat disreputable personage," the father of the then Dalai Lama, whose home overlooked the great square where the Central Temple and the Labrang buildings are situated. In short, throughout his narrative the worthy father is much more concerned with the strange processions and the extraordinary antics of the Tibetan priesthood than he is with the records of his own mission — about which he tells us very little indeed. It appears, however, that the veteran Father

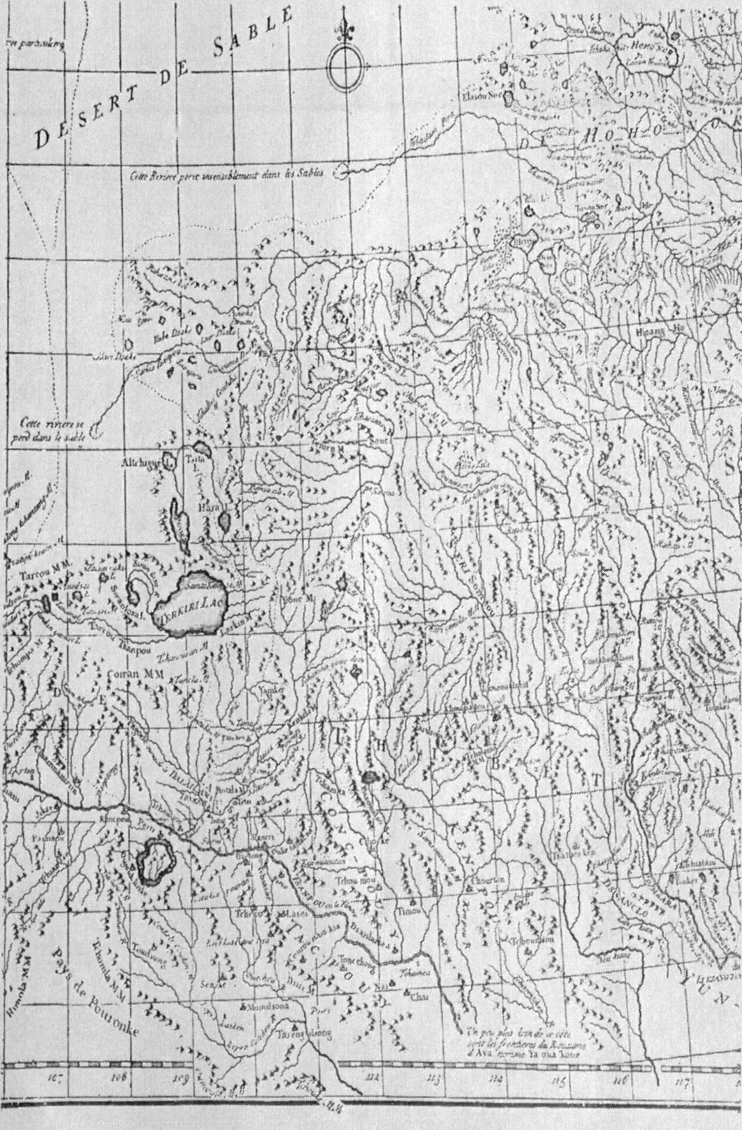

Tibet. From D'Arville's Map of Asia

Gioachino was despatched to Rome in 1741 to report the safe arrival of the mission, and that within four months of their arrival opposition and even persecution commenced. The Tibetan priesthood were naturally antagonistic, and they were alarmed at the favour shown to the mission by the hitherto faithful King Midwang (or Miwang) and others in high places. Finally they invaded the king's palace *en masse* and resorted to threats and invective. This was quite enough for the king, who declared at once against the mission, and caused many of the converts to be flogged. Matters continued to grow worse and worse, until in 1742 three of the fathers (including Beligatti) returned to Nepal. The valiant old Father Prefect Della Penna, although enfeebled by years and labour, still held on at his post; and it was not till April 20, 1745, that he was finally compelled to acknowledge himself beaten, and resolved to abandon the mission. It broke his heart.

"As his hopes departed for ever, so the man already and almost at once began to fade and die. Beholding themselves hedged in on every side, they decided to depart, so much the more as they were assured that the king had ordained that no other missionaries were to be permitted to cross the frontier, and that he worked to make delays till the prefect — already failing through advanced age and the fatigues of thirty-three years of mission work (of which twenty-two had been passed in Tibet) — should be dead, in order that he might then banish the others. Eventually, the king having granted them permission to preach only on condition that they should declare the Tibetan religion to abound in goodness and perfection, they determined to start even at once." The sad little party of three reached the mission hospice at Patan (Khatmandu) in Nepal on the 4th of June. Six weeks later the broken-hearted old chief Della Penna breathed his last. He was sixty-five years old, and he had laboured to the end. He rests in a little Christian cemetery which once existed at Khatmandu, but now is absolutely unrecognisable. Not even the site of it is known. The mission in Nepal lasted till 1768, and disappeared at the time of the Gurkha revolution. Beligatti died in 1785 at Macerata, his birthplace. The old hero Orazio della Penna (like Livingstone) rests in peace on the field of battle.

Geographically we learn little from the investigations of the Capuchin monks. The early outlines of Tibetan geography were filled in, but very indifferently compared to those of early history. Under instruction from the Jesuits the lamas of Tibet acquired a rough idea of map-making and surveying, and they set about after their fashion, providing a general map of the whole country for the Emperor Kang-he of China. Rough and inaccurate as these early maps are, they are of considerable value as first maps. From the data preserved in them D'Anville's Atlas was published in 1733, and they still formed the basis for the mapping of Tibet when Klaproth issued his map in 1824; but there is not much in them beyond rough

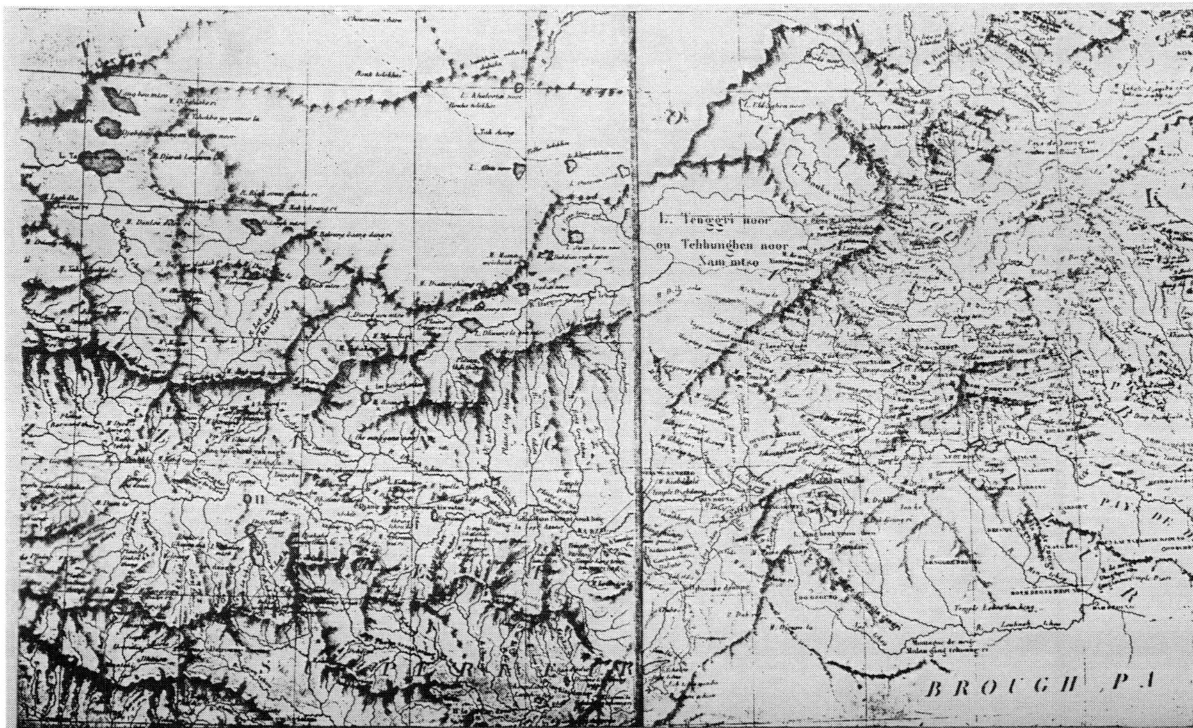

Map of Tibet from Klaproth's Map of Central Asia, 1830

route traverses and the determination of the position of certain towns said to have been fixed by astronomical observations. Such places as Lhasa and Batang are from thirty to sixty miles in error in latitude, and it seems probable that hearsay evidence supplemented by conjecture had a good deal more to do with the construction of these early charts than any more exact process of surveying. Even in D'Anville's map it is difficult to recognise modern names. Lhasa is indicated only by "Pontala" (Potala), the hill on which stands the palace of the Dalai Lama. The Indus is mistaken for the Ganga (Ganges), but the general course of the Tsanpo River and the existence of the Central Lake region are shown clearly enough.

Whilst the Capuchin missions were still in existence, between the years 1723 and 1736 one of the most remarkable journeys in Tibet ever made by any European was made by the Dutchman Samuel Van de Putte, whose father was a vice-admiral of Zealand. He originally left Holland for a three years' tour with a friend, but his love of adventure carried him far beyond his original programme. It carried him with a caravan from Aleppo to Ispahan, and from Ispahan to India. In India he adopted the dress of a native, and extended his tour for several years before he finally crossed the Himalayas into Tibet. We have the evidence of one of the Jesuit fathers that he was an excellent Tibetan scholar and the friend of some of the leading lamas. The tendency of the European to "come to stay" was not at that time fully understood in the East. Not only Tibet, but the frontier countries of India on the northwest, Afghanistan, Persia, and Baluchistan, were equally open to the European adventurer, who obtained something more than mere formal right of way as a foreigner in the country. He was received with courtesy and hospitality. The objection to the incursion of "foreign devils" is comparatively modern. Two hundred years ago the same freedom was accorded to the European to tread the forbidden lands of the East, as we ourselves have ever offered to the Asiatic in the West.

Van de Putte remained in Lhasa apparently as an honoured guest, and when he finally adopted the costume of a mandarin and accompanied a deputation of lamas to the Court of Pekin, he was apparently as well received in China as he had been in Tibet. The route he took was afterwards followed by the Abbé Huc, and will be described further on. On his return to Lhasa he was regarded almost as a saint, on account of the purity of his life. He subsequently recrossed the Himalayas, and reached India in time to be an eye-witness of the sack of Delhi by Nadir Shah. No more thrilling story of travel and adventure could be told than that which would record the experiences of this observant Dutchman, if only there was a story to tell. But unfortunately the accumulation of notes and manuscripts which contained the history of his wanderings was destroyed at his death. He died in Batavia, when on his way home in 1745, and he desired in his will that all his papers (which had been written in a cypher

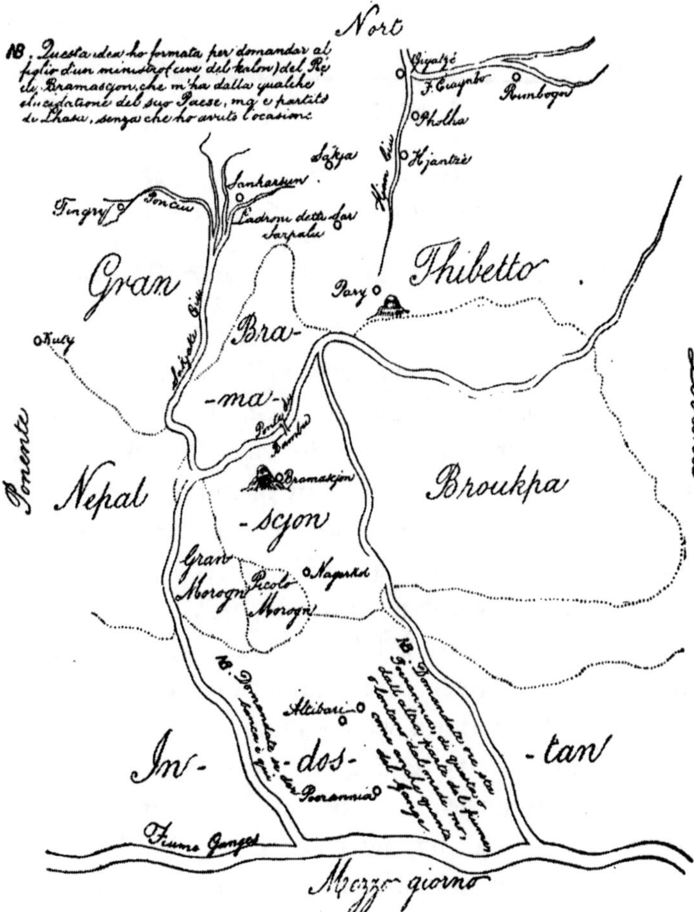

VAN DE PUTTE'S SKETCH MAP FROM THE M.S. IN THE MUSEUM AT MIDDELBURG.

Van der Putte's Sketch Map

CHAPTER VI

Bogle's Mission and Policy of Warren Hastings — Bogle's Route to Shigatze — Description of the Country and of Gyangtse — Reception by the Teshu Lama — Turner despatched by Warren Hastings — His Interview with the Infant Teshu Lama

THE first English mission to Tibet was in 1774, when George Bogle, a Bengal civilian, was deputed by Warren Hastings to visit the capitals of Bhutan and Tibet with a view of opening up friendly relations and promoting trade between Bhutan and India. No happier selection of an envoy could have been made, for Bogle carried out his mission with tact and determination, and established a basis for mutual understanding between India and those countries of her northern borderland which should have been lasting, and should have ended in the establishment of free intercommunication. But the enlightened policy of Warren Hastings has never been popular in India, and this important sphere of British influence has been forgotten for a full century. The seeds of a good understanding which were sown by Bogle never sprang to full maturity, and, indeed, so deeply did the shadow of forgetfulness close over his proceedings that it was with some difficulty, and only by patient reference to journals, official despatches, and private correspondence, that Markham rescued the records from obscurity and published an account of the mission in 1876. From his account we learn that Bogle (accompanied by Dr. Hamilton) followed the same route from India, via Buxa and Punaka (the capital of Bhutan) to Tibet, that was subsequently attempted in 1865 by a British force which failed to penetrate farther than a few marches into the Himalayas.

The Parchu affluent of the Chinchu River leads upwards to the dividing line between Bhutan and Tibet from Paro, the capital of western Bhutan. The pass is certainly not a difficult one, but we have no record of its exact height. From the pass the road drops into the upper valley of the Ammo Chu, leading to Pari (or Pari-jong), where our troops with Younghusband's mission were quartered. This position is abundantly "bare, bleak, and uncomfortable," says Bogle. From Pari (or Phari) fort (14,200 feet) the ascent runs northward to the main water parting where the Tang la (15,700 feet) marks the passage across the backbone of the eastern Himalayas. Bogle says little or nothing about this crossing, which apparently was not formidable enough to attract his attention. Almost overshadowing the pass is the giant Chumulári, a magnificent snow-bound peak, which ever formed the central point of interest in the restricted Bhutanese landscape during the campaign of 1865–66. One of the lines of advance into Bhutan during that campaign followed the route taken by Bogle, above which towers the cloud-wreathed peak of Chumulári.

Bogle's mission to Tibet is of peculiar interest for two reasons: First, because he is one of the few Englishmen who have lived in the country and associated sufficiently long with Tibetans to become an authority on the idiosyncrasies and characteristics of the people. Bogle was an excellent observer, and possessed the rare faculty of adapting himself to the manners and habits of his hosts, as well as the capability of sharing something of their outlook on the world outside Tibet, appreciating their views and to a certain extent sympathising with them. Seldom indeed, in these later days, does any explorer ever study the moral attitude of a strange branch of humanity with such patience, or with the advantage of so close a contact as that possessed by Bogle. To this day, after a hundred and thirty years, he is to us the first and best English authority on the inner social life of the people, — a life which is essentially the same now as it was a hundred and thirty years ago. Secondly, Bogle's route from the head of the Chumbi valley to Gyangtse has become familiar in connection with Colonel Younghusband's mission, for it is the route which that mission followed.

Markham's "Tibet" gives so good a summary of the events and circumstances of Bogle's mission that it is hardly necessary to do more than refer to a few of its main features. The plains of Tibet, over which he passed, after crossing the Tibetan frontier, are described as covered with gravelly sand, producing nothing but some tufts of withered grass which afforded a scanty subsistence to herds of cattle. The slopes of the western hills were perfectly bare; "they appeared like rocks over which the sand and stones had been heaped, leaving here and there the sharp points jutting out. Beyond them could be seen the high mountains in the Demijong country" (the Tibetan name for Sikkim), "among which I fancy is the snowy hill seen from Dinapur and other plains in Bengal. For several days the country bore the same bleak and barren aspect answering to Churchill's description:

> "'Far as the eye can reach no tree is seen,
> Earth clad in russet scorns the lively green.'

The plain cause of this poverty of soil is that God Almighty has so ordered it; but a much more ingenious reason may be drawn from the following circumstances." Bogle then describes the Tibetan method of making their fires and cooking their food with cow-dung gathered from the fields; but whether he considered that the consumption of this material for fuel deprived the fields of their natural manure and so left them barren and unprofitable is not quite clear.

Bogle's journey was taken late in October, and at the elevation of eleven thousand feet there is nothing left of the green of agriculture above the surface so late in the year. "We arrived at Tunno, our next stage, about three o'clock." If Tunno is the same as Turner's Teuna (or Tuna) this was only a twelve to fourteen mile march; and yet Bogle found his servants so tired that they had to be "brought home on peasants' backs." The names of places are not to be depended on over such a length of time as has elapsed since Bogle's and Turner's missions. Moreover, Bogle found the whole country devastated as far as Gyangtse, but he does not say to what this was due. He had to procure "cow-tailed bullocks" for his followers to ride, and thereby offended their Hindu prejudices. By "cow-tailed bullocks" we may presume that the ordinary bullock of the country is indicated in contra-distinction to the bushy-tailed yak. "Our road next day led us along the banks of the lake called Sham chu Pelling. It is fed by a large mineral stream which issues out of the side of a mountain and extends about eighteen miles from north to south. It was half frozen over and well stocked with wild ducks and geese. We also met with some hares and a flock of antelopes, besides a herd of wild animals called "kyang," resembling an ass." "A stream of water falls from the Sham chu into the Calo chu Lake, which extends about ten miles east and west, and another stream runs from it northward." This is the Kalwa-tso of modern maps, near which stands the town of Kalwa Shar. "We kept close to this stream for several days; it falls into the Tsanpu Shigatze, turning many miles on its way." "There are also several bridges on this river, but very different from the wooden ones we met with among the mountains. They are walls, with breaks or openings, to let the water through, which are covered with planks or large flags." All this gives a very fair idea of the nature of the long, narrow curving valley of the Nyang chu, which connects the pass of Tang la (at the head of the Chumbi valley) with Shigatze on the Yeru Tsanpo. It falls gradually and gently to the Tsanpo (upper Brahmaputra), offering no obstacles to the movements of troops. Bare and desolate in the late autumn and winter, it has clearly always been cultivable to some extent in summer, when the green crops which subsequently furnish grain for the mills must give a very different aspect to the scenery. There is indeed nothing more remarkable in the way of contrast than the bare dust-covered yellow plains of the highlands adjoining India in the winter and the almost brilliant effect of luxuriant cultivation in summer. It is the same in Baluchistan as it is in Tibet in spite of the great difference in altitude. Kanmur (Khangmar) is the most important point on the route, for there are good houses at Khangmar with a caravanserai and a temple. Also there were a few willows in Bogle's time which may still survive as the first trees encountered after leaving the Chumbi valley. There is a cross-route to Lhasa from Khangmar which is shorter than the Gyangtse route, but it involves several formidable passes. After passing Khangmar there is a distinct improvement in the character of the country. The altitude falls to thirteen thousand five hundred feet, and the river is made use of for irrigation. The valley widens, evidences of cultivation are abundant, and hot springs burst from the ground some three and a half miles beyond the town. It was here that Bogle lodged in a house "which had lately changed its inhabitants. Of fifteen persons who formerly lived in it every one had died last year of the small-pox." At Dudukpai (possibly the Changra of modern maps) Bogle remarks the cheerful aspect of the village scenery,— willows planted all about, and the people "busy building and stacking their straw and singing at their work." Twenty-four miles from Khangmar is the town of Gyangtse (modern), or Giansu (Bogle and Turner), a large town standing on the right bank of the Nyang chu, in a broad and open valley full of white-walled villages, and commanded by a castle picturesquely clinging to the face and summit of a steep and lofty rock above the river. Gyangtse is about one hundred miles from Phari jong, in the upper Chumbi valley, and can be readily reached in five or six marches. The town climbs the hill slopes, the houses being ranged around the central market-place, and is enclosed within a wall said to be one and a half miles in circumference. Above it towers the famous monastery, the Palkhor Choide, built after the fashion of a pagoda in nine storeys. According to information obtained from Tibetan sources by the Rev. Graham Sandberg, Gyangtse is a trade centre for Tibetan horses, dried and fresh mutton, butter, barley, radishes, and coarse cloths, the staple product of the place. There are Nepalese shops and Chinese restaurants, and accommodation for travellers in the temple. The garrison includes four hundred badly armed

Tibetans and about fifty Chinese troops. Bogle says little about " Giansu," as he did not stay there. He passed through the town on his way farther northward. But Gyangtse is of importance as the junction for the road to Lhasa, which follows a large affluent of the Nyang chu eastward. It is one of the towns which by the treaty lately ratified is open to foreign trade in future.

Bogle duly notes the change of scenery after passing Gyangtse, — numerous villages and cultivation fairly abundant in a light and sandy soil. At Painom, a day's journey farther north, he writes of the valley that it was the most populous he had yet seen, with villages standing very thick. Painom, with its castle rock-crowned and battlemented, he compares to Gyangtse, but considers the position finer. At this point he left the main road to Shigatze, and struck off eastwards by a direct route to the Tsanpo River and the residence of the Teshu Lama near Namling, beyond it. He says little more of the Tsanpo than that at the point where he crossed it was about as wide as the Thames at Putney. He describes the boats as flat-bottomed wooden constructions, oblong in shape, about twenty-five feet in length, with four-foot sides to them. This appears to be the regulation pattern for the larger-sized ferryboats of the Tsanpo, and tallies exactly with the later descriptions given by Indian explorers. From the river he travelled by an easy open road to Namling, near to which place was " Desherigpag," the Teshu Lama's residence.

Bogle did not live in days of scientific exploration, and his records are wanting in geographical exactness. But if he did not excel as a geographer, he has given us a knowledge of Tibetan social life and customs which is as charming as it is original. Instead of the thick-headed obstinacy and pertinacious interference with all freedom of action which we are apt to associate with Tibetan lamaistic methods, Bogle found the people friendly, cheery, easily accessible, good tempered, and always willing to entertain or assist him. Men and women alike — he made friends with them all. At one time he is the official guest of the Teshu Lama, the second great religious dignitary in the land. At another he is entertaining Tibetan girls in his own quarters, or joining the young relatives of the great high priest in hunting the musk deer or shooting partridges, an amusement in which those young people indulged only when they were far enough from the paternal eye. But wherever he is there is always the same friendly interest in all that he heard or saw, and the same rare faculty of observation from the local point of view. Consequently no other writer has given us so useful an insight into the inwardness of Tibetan existence. No native Indian explorer, however shrewd, is capable of entering into the spirit of European enquiry as regards Asiatics. He cannot know or understand what it is that we want to know. He is in fact faced with exactly the same difficulty that besets the European who wishes to explain or describe Europe to the Asiatic.

Tashi Lunpo, from the South

Tibet is an old, old country, wherein the spirit of conservatism still reigns supreme. No European fads or inventions (excepting perhaps those which appertain to firearms) ever disturb the serene assurance of the Tibetan priest, and the priest decides for the people, for Tibet is absolutely priest-ridden. Thus it happens that what Bogle saw and described so many years ago may be accepted as identical with that which the members of our own mission have seen and described to-day, if they are gifted with Bogle's power of perception and enjoy his opportunities.

Next to the Dalai Lama, the Teshu Lama of Teshilumpo (whom Hastings believed to be the chief religious authority) is the ruling high priest in Tibet. Bogle's description of this personage is exceedingly interesting. "On a throne carved and gilt with some cushions above it" sat the lama cross-legged. "He was dressed in a mitre-shaped cap of yellow broadcloth with long bars lined with red satin; a yellow cloth jacket without sleeves, and a satin mantle of the same colour thrown over his shoulders. On one side of him stood his physician with a bundle of perfumed sandal-wood rods burning in his hand, on the other stood his Sopon Chumbo, or cup-bearer." He received Bogle "in the most engaging manner," and thereafter, when two or three official visits had been made and returned, he used to receive him without ceremony, "his head uncovered, dressed only in his large red petticoat, which is worn by all the gylongs" (priests or monks), "red Bulgar boots, a cloth thrown across his shoulders." He threw aside all the "awful part of his character" as "God's vice-regent through all the eastern countries of Asia," and behaved with the greatest freedom and affability. His complexion was fair, he was inclined to be fat, and his age was about forty; and he is described as intelligent, liberal, and humane. But Bogle got no further with his negotiations than the Teshu Lama. At Lhasa the Dalai Lama was an infant, and the temporal power was in the hands of the Greshub Rimboché, who being anxious to secure supreme authority for himself and his family after him, and being entirely adverse to "Fringies" (whom he accuses of being "fond of war, and, after insinuating themselves into a country, raising disturbances and making themselves masters of it"), advised the Teshu Lama to find some method of sending Bogle back, "either on account of the violence of the small-pox or any other pretence." The same authority blocked the way to Turner subsequently, so that no fully accredited trade mission ever really reached Lhasa. Bogle returned from Tibet in June, 1775, with the object of conducting further negotiations at Pekin. Dr. Hamilton, who accompanied him on this first mission, was subsequently appointed to conduct a mission to Bhutan, which country he visited twice, and thus maintained to a certain extent the open door for Tibetan trade.

Warren Hastings determined to keep up the intercourse with Tibet so well inaugurated by Bogle, and in 1779 again appointed him as envoy to Tibet. But news reached India that the Teshu Lama proposed to visit Pekin. He actually made the journey, and sacrificed his life in his efforts to promote a good understanding between China and India, for he died at Pekin of small-pox. Not long after his death his English friend Bogle died at Calcutta.

Warren Hastings, however, persevered in his policy, and with the reappearance of the Teshu Lama in infant form he arranged another mission under Captain Samuel Turner, which started by the old Buxa route through Bhutan in the summer of 1783. Turner's mission added but little to our knowledge of southern Tibet. He followed more or less directly in the footsteps of Bogle, but instead of diverging south of Shigatze to the Tsanpo, he continued his route to Shigatze (or rather to Tashilumpo), where the reincarnated Teshu Lama was conveyed in state from Namling. The chief point of interest in his narrative is that which concerns his interview with the small personage who now represented the Teshu Lama, and the cordial reception which awaited him from the relatives of the late high priest testifying to the popularity and success of Bogle. Markham thus describes his interview with the holy infant, whose regent and adviser were Chanzu Cusho (the brother of the late lama) and Sopon Chumbo, his cup-bearer, both of whom are frequently mentioned by Bogle. The interview took place at Terpaling, about two miles south of the great Tashilumpo monastery. The princely child, then aged eighteen months, was " seated on a throne, with his father and mother standing on his left hand." Having been informed that though unable to speak he could understand, Turner said that the governor-general, on receiving news of his decease in China, was overwhelmed with grief and sorrow, and continued to lament his absence from the world until the cloud that had overcast the happiness of this nation was dispelled by his reappearance; and then, if possible, a greater degree of joy had taken place than he had experienced of grief on receiving the first mournful news. The governor anxiously wished that he might long continue to illumine the world by his presence, and was hopeful that the friendship which formerly subsisted between them would not be demolished, but rather that it might become greater than before; and that by his continuing to show kindness to my countrymen, there might be an extensive communication between his votaries and the dependants of the British nation. The infant looked steadily at the British envoy with the appearance of much attention, and nodded with repeated but slow motions of the head, as though he understood every word. He was silent and sedate; his whole attention was directed to the envoy, and he conducted himself with astonishing dignity and decorum. He was one of the handsomest children Captain Turner had ever seen, and "he grew up to be an able and devout ruler, delighting the Tibetans with his presence for many years, and dying at a good old age." Turner returned to India in the spring of 1874, and the following year India lost Warren Hastings.

After his death diplomatic relations between India and Tibet finally ceased.

It is interesting to note that the first great Church dignitary of Tibet, who, abandoning traditions of sanctified aloofness, descended from Tibetan altitudes to the plains of India in 1905, and there took an active, human interest in the pomps and frivolities of the civilised world, should be the same Teshu Lama of Tashilumpo. According to Lamaistic canons he is literally and actually the embodiment of the same personality who received Bogle with such sympathetic cordiality and good fellowship.

CHAPTER VII

The Conquest of Tibet by China — Remarkable Military Expedition — Its Route into Tibet and the Final Defeat of the Gurkhas near Katmandu — Thomas Manning's Visit to Tibet and Lhasa — His Route through Bhutan — Experiences with Chinese Officials and Interview with the Dalai Lama — His Impressions — Moorcroft's Expedition to Hundes — His probable Residence at Lhasa and his Fate

SUCH was the last official mission to Tibet ere that of Younghusband took the field. It was shortly followed by the occupation of Nepal by the Gurkhas, and during the stormy times which followed on the Himalayan frontier the passes from India became permanently closed.

The final conquest of Tibet by China marked an epoch in Asiatic history, but the story of so remarkable and important an achievement is altogether beyond the scope of this work. Troubles with China did not end, however, with the subjugation of Tibet, and there was at least one Chinese expedition (directed, it is true, rather against Nepal than Tibet) which is of such special interest as illustrating the military possibilities of the eastern and most direct route between Pekin and Lhasa via Ta-chien-lu, that a brief reference to it will probably do more to dissipate the many mistaken notions which exist about

Tibetan invasions than any record of individual exploration.

The murder of the Gyalpo, in 1749 (thirty years after the Chinese conquest), by the Chinese Ambas (or Ambans) led to a general rising and massacre of the Chinese and a final retaliatory expedition from China, which completely restored Chinese ascendancy. The readiness with which such an expedition was organised and led across the Chinese border into the heart of the Bod-yul of Tibet, and its success, is one of the most interesting features in Tibetan history. Mongols, Sikhs, and Gurkhas have alike made the same venture and failed. It still rests with the Chinese to claim the proud position of having reduced by force of arms what may be justly termed the most inaccessible country in the world.

The Capuchin friars left Tibet about 1760, and took refuge in Nepal; and it was about this period that the conquest of Nepal by the hardy mountaineers of the Gurkha tribe was effected. Originally recruited to assist in settling internal disturbances at the capital, they soon made themselves masters of the country by sheer hard fighting and the terror that their frightful atrocities inspired. From the time that the Gurkha Prithi Narayan was installed on the throne of Nepal until now, the gates of that country have been closed to India, and a trade that was once flourishing has been almost annihilated.

In 1792 (after the missions of Bogle and Turner to Tibet) the Gurkhas, inspired by the lust of loot, invaded Tibet. An expedition which numbered eighteen thousand men crossed the Kuti pass (140 miles from Khatmandu) and advanced with great rapidity on Tashilumpo (Shigatze), which was distant another 257 miles. They captured the city and looted the palace. The cowardly Tibetans fled in a panic. The infant Teshu Lama was carried off to Lhasa, and Chinese assistance was at once invoked to repel the invasion. Then followed one of the most remarkable retributions that the world has ever seen. Over the gigantic mountains and snowbound passes of eastern Tibet a force of no less than seventy thousand Chinese was led in two columns by General Sand Fo into the elevated regions of the plateau. The Gurkhas rapidly retreated to a position near their frontier, called Tengri Maidan. Here the first battle was fought, and they were completely defeated. The Kuti post was captured after a second fight, and the Chinese advanced by way of Kirong (on one of the chief rivers of Nepal) to Khatmandu. Their artillery consisted of light field guns made of leather, which fired a few rounds and then burst. The Gurkhas had no guns, and they made their last stand on the river banks at Tadi just above Nayakot, about twenty miles from Khatmandu. To appreciate the position it must be remembered that this unwieldy force of seventy thousand Chinese had marched across one of the most difficult mountain districts in the world for 800 miles from their own frontier before reaching Lhasa. They had then advanced at least another 400 miles over uplands at elevations which were never less than 10,000 feet, involving the passage of many passes higher than Mont Blanc, before meeting the enemy. Practically they were without artillery, and they had in front of them the most tenacious and most valiant foe that ever stood up to fight in Asia, — a foe, too, that was flushed with recent success. It is true that the strength of the Chinese at starting may be reckoned to be vastly greater than that of the Gurkhas in the field against them, and it is improbable that they dispersed that strength by holding positions on the line of advance. It was almost impossible that they should do so. But they must have lost numbers in the passes of the mountains which barred their progress through that 1,200 miles of route from their frontier (2,000 miles at least from the populated district of China), and it could have been little more than an advance guard that faced the Gurkhas on the river Tadi. The Gurkhas, on the other hand, in falling back on their base, were consolidating their strength from day to day, and as they turned with their backs to the river (like terriers against a wall), they were fighting for their women and their homes behind them, and they knew well what defeat would mean. The Chinese wavered. They were massed in front of the Gurkhas, who were between them and Khatmandu, and they were terribly spent with the length and the trials of that long march in the thin atmosphere of the Tibetan highlands. There seemed a chance that the attack would fail at the critical moment. It is under such circumstances as these that great generals prove their right and title to the confidence which their country has bestowed upon them. Sand Fo was a great general, and he rose to the occasion. He turned his leather guns on to the rear of his own wavering troops, and drove them and the Gurkhas in front of them in one comprehensive sweep into the river. The Chinese trampled over friend and foe alike, and they speedily sacked Khatmandu. Oriental methods of treating the vanquished (especially Mongol methods) are usually distinguished by deeds of the most ingenious and repulsive barbarity. Even the Gurkha of to-day is not gentle with a foe. But ingenious as he is in his methods of savage reprisal, he is probably more than equalled by the Chinaman. Khatmandu has never forgotten the lesson that was learned at that blood-stained time. Every five years a deputation proceeds from Nepal through Lhasa to Pekin, and there offers tribute at the foot of the Chinese throne.

Such at least is the story as culled from the lips of an ancient Gurkha official by Mr. Brian Hodgson, and as retold by Sir Clements Markham in his "Tibet." There may be other ways of accounting for the defeat of the valiant Gurkha by the Chinaman of the eighteenth century than those narrated by this ancient Gurkha warrior; but the fact remains, as a marvellous record of Chinese persistency, that Nepal was utterly subjugated by the Chinese at a distance of some 2,000 miles (stretching across a solid barrier of mountains) from their base. It is a useful commentary, first, on the usual statements of Tibetan accessibility, and, secondly, on the usual criticisms applied to the Chinese soldier.

During the progress of the Chinese retaliatory expedition we declined to assist the Gurkhas, and the Chinese had all along been watching with jealous suspicion our attempts to establish diplomatic relations with Tibet. Thus we soon lost all the good effects of the missions of Warren Hastings. The Chinese closed all passes into Tibet to Indian natives, and established military posts along the trans-Himalayan frontier. The Gurkhas despised us. The inevitable result was a war with Nepal (which lasted from 1814 to 1816), the final occupation of Sikkim (after the advance of Ochterlony and the capitulation of the Nepalese), and the opening up of the difficult Sikkim passes into southern Tibet; but the interposition of British authority in Sikkim led to no amicable relations with the Bhutan. We have never been able to effect much with that country. Pemberton's mission in 1838 led to the acquisition of much useful information about the passes; but the unstable condition of the government, the perpetual feud between the Tongso Penlo of the East and the Paro Penlo of the West (the two local governors), and the absence of real authority in the hands of the Deb Rajah and the Dharma Rajah (the two elected chiefs), appears to be chronic, in spite of the fact that the Dharma Rajah is the perpetual incarnation of the Deity. The same uncertainty in the temporal administration existed when in 1865–66 another campaign was undertaken in the interests of peace on the Assam border. Now the passes through Bhutan which were used by Bogle and Turner are no longer open to Englishmen.

It cannot be other than a matter of surprise that at a time when our relations with Nepal and China were about at their worst in the troubled times before the occupation of Sikkim, the one solitary Englishman who has ever reached Lhasa (so far as we know for certain) should have started on an unofficial venture to study China in her most remote dependency,— Tibet. Thomas Manning was an independent gentleman, a friend of Charles Lamb, and an unaccredited traveller, who had been a resident in Canton for a sufficient time to pick up a rudimentary knowledge of Chinese. He had also a certain amount of medical training which (whether rudimentary or otherwise) enabled him to rank as a physician amongst Chinese subjects. In September, 1811, he crossed the north-east frontier by a route to the west of the Buxa route through Bhutan, which had been followed by his predecessors (known as the Laki Duar route), to Paro and Parijong. No European has followed Manning's route either before or since, and it is unfortunate that he has left no record of it which is of the slightest geographical interest. It is indeed much to be regretted that this one English traveller, who, of all the many who have attempted the feat of entering Lhasa, is the only one successful, should be in most essential respects a bad traveller and a worse observer.

Markham has given his diary in extenso in his "Tibet," and it is a monotonous record of small worries and insignificant details which quite block out that larger view of his Tibetan surroundings which it was obviously his intention to present. He gives us little insight into Tibetan character, but incidentally he gives us a far better idea of his own and of that of his Chinese "munshi" (or interpreter), with whom many weary hours must have been passed in the simmering enjoyment of mutual bickering. The munshi was finally retained at Lhasa "in chains" when Manning was permitted to leave, and it is not recorded that a single tear was shed over his fate. Thus he passes as happily from Manning's narrative as he passed from Manning's company. In due time Manning reached the inevitable "take off" for Tibet,— Parijong. There he found the Chinese in some force, and his medical attentions to the general in command and his success with the soldiers ended in an invitation to accompany the general to Lhasa. Of the Chinese soldiers he has much that is good to say, for he remarks on their attention to duty, their civility, and their good behaviour. They might have been "civilians" and not "soldiers." Manning's admiration for their manners is something of a commentary on those of the British soldier of the period,— the Waterloo period,— which evidently furnished his standard of comparison. His complaints of Tibetan horses and Tibetan saddlery have been echoed in other years by other travellers. Evidently the fashion in saddles has lasted for some time, and there seems to be no immediate prospect of a change. Like Bogle and Turner, he was struck with the generally cheerful and well-to-do aspect of the country about Gyangtse after passing through the desolate stretch of elevated plateau, bare of vegetation and swept clean by the wind, which lies northward of the Himalayan water-parting. His route to Gyangtse was the route of the previous missions, but from Gyangtse (where he parted with his Chinese general) he was for some inexplicable reason able to procure an invitation from the regent to visit Lhasa. For a description of the further section of his route between Gyangtse and Lhasa it would be quite useless to refer to Manning's records. It must be taken from those of later explorers (natives of India), who have carefully described this 150 miles of road, and it is of passing interest just now inasmuch as the experiences of the late Tibetan mission include it in their records.

The following account of the route to Lhasa is derived from native sources of information. At first the road is good, but it rapidly merges into a mere country track running through cultivation which is abundant. About eleven miles from Gyangtse it follows the course of a hill torrent running through a steep and narrow valley. Crossing a bridge at Kudung and passing the village of Gyari-dom, the first stage Gobshi (the "Four Gates") is reached at the end of a fifteen-mile march. Gobshi is a comparatively large village, standing amidst poplars and willows and possessing a mill house and a bridge. A stage of nineteen miles connects Gobshi with the post station of Ralung Sampa, where there is a Chinese "stage" master with a large and comfortable rest house for travellers. The track passes through villages at intervals, but involves the passage of a narrow defile and the fording of the river at a point called Shetoi. Monasteries are of course much in evidence along a frequented trade route such as this. From Ralung Sampa to the pretty little village of Dzara is a seventeen-mile march. Near the post-station of Ralung Sampa is the monastery of Ralung Thil, the headquarters of the Red Cap Buddhist sect to which all the people of Bhutan belong. The forward route now involves much steep ground, and the frequent crossing of streams half frozen with slippery blocks of ice, besides the passage of a sixteen-thousand-feet pass — the Kharo la — the highest point between Chumbi and Lhasa. Below the pass, south of it, is a long stony plain scantily supplied with grass, where the black huts of the Dokpa herdsmen are pitched and herds of yak find their living. It is called Womathang, or the "Milky plain." At this elevation glaciers are encountered, and the whole landscape is wind-dried, bleak, and barren. The ascent to the pass is easy, but the eastern descent to Dzara is steep and rapid. Dzara boasts a bad post-house and little besides — no forage and no fuel, but there are scattered grass patches beyond where yak and sheep can graze. The road now runs for six or seven miles through a series of gorges or defiles with a rapidly descending grade till it opens out on the vast stony plain which stretches to Nangartse Jong and the great "Scorpion" Lake — the Yamdok tso. Fifteen miles separate Dzara from Nangartse Jong. Roughly Nangartse may be reckoned at seventy miles from Gyangtse, Lhasa being about eighty miles to the north-east of Nangartse. The route so far presents no very formidable difficulties, although it is often narrow and steep and involves the crossing of the Kharo la. Onward to Lhasa it is a rough country track following the western shores of the Yamdok Lake to about its extreme northern point, and then striking off across the plain that intervenes between the lake and the mountain ridge which overlooks the deep valley of the Tsanpo. All this part of Tibet has been described by the native surveyors who have visited it, and by Manning, as extremely picturesque. Nangartse stands two hundred feet above the blue waters of the Scorpion Lake (the latter being thirteen thousand nine hundred feet above sea), facing the strange mountain forms of the peninsula which, jutting out northward into the lake, spreads itself into the form of a central, circular, and almost insular mountain mass, which itself encloses a minor lake. The deep, dark, mysterious waters of the smaller depression are known to the people as the Dumo tso, or Demon Lake. The great Samding monastery overlooks the weird depths of the Dumo tso from a hill about three miles east of Nangartse Jong. The presiding abbess of this monastery is a very young lady (at present only nine years old), but Dorje Pagmo is the highest lady in the land, and the only one who has a right to be carried in a chair. Spread about Nangartse are fertile flat plains with abundant grass for the crowding herds of yak. There is a fishing population on the lake shores as well as herdsmen, and crudely built boats of hide are used for local purposes of navigation — probably the most elevated navigation in the world. Leaving the northern shores of the lake, the road to Lhasa may cross the low range of hills bordering the Tsanpo valley by either of two passes. The one generally made use of is the Khamba La, but the Nyabso La, not far to the west, is said to be as practicable and fairly easy. The ascent of nine hundred feet from the basin of the lake is not severe, but the northern descent into the deep trough of the Tsanpo is short and sharp (especially near the summit of the pass), although it is engineered in zigzags to reduce the grade. Striking the great Tsanpo River some four or five miles from the foot of the pass, the road to Lhasa now follows the right bank of the river to the historic old suspension bridge of Chaksam Chori near the junction of the Kyichu (the river of Lhasa) with the Tsanpo. The descent from the pass to a level of about eleven thousand feet above sea introduces the traveller (weary with the monotony of sterile altitudes) to quite a new landscape. The route has latterly been picturesque enough, now slanting across plains with patches of good grazing, now striking wide fields of irrigated cultivation, and then again taking to mountain tracks and winding over the face of precipitous slopes with a rushing torrent below; but the grace and beauty of vegetation has been wanting. In the valley of the Tsanpo dense clumps of bush border the river and fill the dells; orchards of peach and walnut trees cluster thickly round the white walls of the villages; wind-swept sand drifts into dunes by the river-side, and low down about the foot of the pass the wild rose blossoms, whilst brambles, fir-trees, and rhododendrons make what show they can.

The ancient suspension bridge which spans the river near the monastery of Penchen Chu Wori is a relic of antiquity and of former trade developments in Tibet, of which it is difficult to obtain a history. Said to have been constructed four hundred and seventy years ago, it certainly did credit to the highland engineers who were responsible for it. Two chains (deeply rusted with age) about four feet apart support a road-way of narrow planking which is supported from them by loops of rope. The extremities of the chains are about seventy feet above the river. In the centre it sags to about fifty feet. No one uses the bridge now-a-days (or has used it for the last twenty years), but the main stays of the bridge, the massive masonry "chortens" within which the chains are anchored to logs built into the masonry, are said to be sound enough, and it is but the roadway which is lacking. The passage of the river is effected by ferries. Two classes of boats of the crudest construction are used.

The lighter leather-covered "coracles" (ko-a) are used for casual passengers, the larger wooden boats (shingi tru) carry horses, cattle, and merchandise. They have been described by one native traveller as "shallow wooden boxes about twenty feet long by eight broad." The junction of the Kyichu (the river of happiness) with the Tsanpo is about three miles east of the ferry. After leaving the Tsanpo, the Lhasa road ascends the valley of the Kyichu affluent, first passing over the marsh lands of the delta where there are scattered villages and townlets belted with willows and poplars. Sand and gravel plains alternate with patches of rich cultivation where peas, beans, and white mustard make a variety in the landscape during the season of flowers, until, beyond the village of Jang toi, the road again takes to the rocky banks of the immediate river-side and runs a chequered course (a part of which is known as the Gaglam, or "path of hindrance") to the historic village of Nethang — the last stage ere reaching Lhasa. Nethang possesses the historical interest of being the place where the great Buddhist missionary from India, Atisha, died. The village stands in a beautiful valley, but is not itself beautiful. "The road passes through a dirty village street flanked by houses of two or three storeys, mostly of a mean and filthy exterior. A large number of pack ponies and donkeys are kept by the inhabitants to be let out by the dozen or so to travellers," says Mr. Sandberg. After Nethang the whole country appears to bloom into luxuriance. Irrigated cultivation rather interferes with the traffic along the route; grass lands, houses, gardens, and fruit orchards are passed in succession for several miles, when once again the stone dusted gravel plain of Tibet is encountered. But here at last is Lhasa in sight. Fourteen miles away the palace of the Dalai lama — the Potala — can be seen glinting in the sun. Crossing an important stone bridge one hundred and eighty feet long over the Thi Chu affluent of the Kyi-chu River at the village of Toilung, and traversing a populous tract of willow-planted cultivation, the great highway between India and Lhasa strikes the first evidence of the existence of the sacred city in the ghastly debris of its slaughter yard, where hundreds of sheep, goats, and yak are daily slain for the consumption of the town. Bones and horns are heaped up by the road-side and around a foul blood-stained tank. Sloping upwards from these repulsive relics are the spurs of the wooded hill on which stands the great Daipang Monastery, which is said to provide accommodation for seventy-seven hundred inmates. Here, doubtless, in the leading monastic establishment of Lhasa are inculcated those Buddhist tenets which prohibit the taking of life. Groves of poplars and walnuts now close in the road which ends at the western gateway of Lhasa.

Such, briefly, is the road onward from Gyangtse to Lhasa untrodden by any Englishman save Manning hitherto, but now familiar to European footsteps. It is not a road which would be written down as "passable for field artillery," but it is not a bad road, and is full of surpassing interest. The view of Lhasa from its western approaches is one which warms even a Bengali heart to enthusiasm. "It was indeed a superb sight, the like of which I never beheld in India," says Chandra Das. It was the Potala, the palace of the great high priest, the Dalai lama, which gladdened his weary eyes. Set up high on an isolated hill, raising its stupendous walls to a height of nine storeys above the summit, crowned with gilded cupolas glinting in the sun, buttressed on the rough crags over which the long lines of countless banner-bedecked staircases climb upward from the plains, a solid red and white embodiment of the strength and might of Buddhist lamahood, the Potala must indeed be a most impressive vision.

At Lhasa Manning was well received by the authorities, though he complains greatly of the want of accommodation in the house in which he was lodged. It must be remembered that his status was purely unofficial. He came with no proposals from the Indian Government to establish either diplomatic or commercial relations. He was simply a travelling European with a knowledge of medicine; and just as the same knowledge has ever and anon led to most important results in the history of the Indian Empire, and the medicine man has been almost invariably the first in a new field, so Manning was now enabled to maintain a tolerable position in the great centre of Buddhism. It was a great opportunity lost to the East India Company's Government. It was also a great opportunity for the acquisition of a knowledge of Tibet and of Tibetan affairs such as never has occurred since the days of Van de Putte, but Manning was not the man to make use of it. Had Masson, for instance, been there instead of Manning, the results would have been very different. He did what he could, however, to make the acquaintance of Tibetan and Chinese dignitaries who might be helpful to him. He polished up a pair of old brass candlesticks which were not his own property (they belonged to the Honourable East India Company), and adding them to two wax candles, some pieces of cloth, and a few silver coins, he made them presentable as an offering to the Grand Lama. He also possessed a bottle of some ancient form of scent (Smith's lavender water) which was added to the offering. The bottle was broken during the process of presentation, and the streamlets of scent imparted a new character to the pervading essence of burnt sandal wood which permeated the sacred presence chamber. But he saw the Grand Lama and made his "katesi," "touching the ground three times with my head to the Grand Lama and once to the Ti-mu-fu." He presented his "clean-shaved head" for the lama to lay his hands upon, and then sat on a cushion not far from the lama's throne to partake of "suchi." "It was most excellent, and I meant to have mended my draught and emptied the cup, but it was whipped away suddenly, before I was aware of it." This was a temporary grievance, but the effect was effaced by his impression of the Grand Lama, which is really interesting. " The lama's beautiful face and manner engrossed almost all my attention. He was at that time about seven years old; had the simple and unaffected manners of a well-educated princely child. His face was, I thought, poetically and affectingly beautiful. He was of a gay and cheerful disposition, his beautiful mouth perpetually unbending into a graceful smile, which illumined his whole countenance. Sometimes, particularly when he had looked at me, his smile almost approached to a gentle laugh. No doubt my grim beard and spectacles somewhat excited his risibility, though I have afterwards, at the New Year's festival, seen him smile and unbend freely, while sitting myself unobserved in a corner, and watching his reception of various persons, and the notice he took of the strange variety of surrounding objects." Manning asked for books respecting the Buddhist religion and the history of Tibet, together with a lama who could instruct him and talk Chinese. His request was only partially complied with, but he received a part of the Buddhist ritual. He adds: " I was extremely affected by this interview with the lama. I could have wept through strangeness of sensation. I was absorbed in reflections when I got home." There is undoubtedly some strange fascination about this child presence which embodies the very spirit of Buddhist mysticism. All who have experienced it speak of it with deep reverence. Something of the spirit of mysterious awe and irresistible attraction which drew the wise men from the East to the foot of the cradle at Bethlehem inspires the modern devotee who toils painfully up the steps and ladders of the Potala to receive the child blessing above. We of the West who honour the wise men should appreciate the devotion of the climbing pilgrim. Manning had not the opportunity of enquiry such as has been given to later visitors to Lhasa, and he tells us little of the life of the people in the sacred city. Incidentally we gather that the Tibetan of Lhasa is hospitable, cheerful, and contented, civil to strangers, appreciative of kindness, and he generally figures as a law-abiding and good citizen.

The manners of the women are affable and friendly, but when Manning writes of "pretty faces" we feel that his long absence from higher civilisation must have quickened his susceptibilities. Beauty of feature is doubtless not altogether incompatible with dirt (the Tibetan men and women never wash their faces), but the final charm of an unsullied complexion must surely be wanting. It is Bogle, I think, who tells of an infant Tibetan which was washed for his benefit, that he might judge of the general complexion of the Tibetan skin, which otherwise there was no possibility of observing. The child screamed and struggled to such a degree as nearly to bring on convulsions, and the experiment was a failure. Manning was not struck with the town, although the palace exceeded his expectations. "There is nothing striking, nothing pleasing in its appearance. The habitations are begrimed with dirt and smut. The avenues are full of dogs, some growling and gnawing bits of hide which lie about in

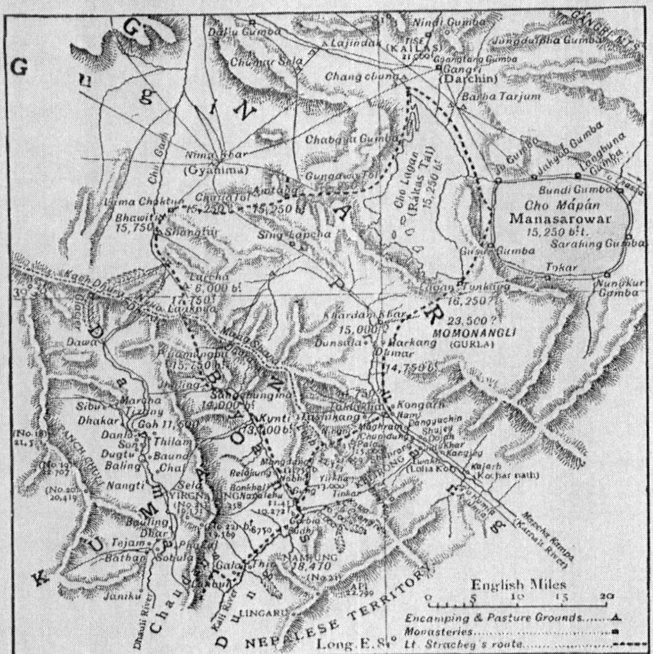

Manasarawar

profusion and emit a charnel-house smell; others limping and looking livid; others ulcerated; others starved and dying, and pecked at by ravens; some dead and preyed upon. In short, everything seems mean and gloomy, and excites the idea of something unreal. Even the mirth and laughter of the inhabitants I thought dreamy and ghostly." Manning left Lhasa on the 19th of April, and reached Kuch Behàr on the 10th of June on his return journey to India.

Almost contemporary with Manning's journey to Lhasa was the first exploration undertaken into Hundes on the southwestern Tibetan border by a civilian of the Indian Civil Service named Moorcroft. He obtained permission to cross the Himalayas by the Niti pass north of Almora, and to visit the Manasarawar Lakes with the object of making a survey of the country at the foot of Kailas, and of procuring samples of the famous wool of which Kashmir shawls are made. After crossing the Shangki (or Niti) pass he travelled for about ten days, till he reached the camping station of Daba on the upper Sutlej. Here he was very well received (Moorcroft being disguised as a merchant), and was allowed to proceed to Gartok on the Indus. Gartok was then but an encampment of black hair tents, a village of herdsmen who here tended enormous flocks of goat and sheep. On the 5th of August he reached Manasarawar, which was then observed to consist of two lakes divided by an elevated isthmus. The eastern lake was fifteen miles long and eleven broad, enclosed by a magnificent entourage of rugged hills. Moorcroft failed to note the connection between the two lakes, the existence of which was subsequently established by the two Stracheys. This journey in itself is only remarkable as an early venture across the Almora passes into Hundes. Many travellers and sportsmen have since followed in Moorcroft's footsteps, but Moorcroft's name is chiefly remarkable for the story told by the Abbé Huc (whose adventures will be narrated elsewhere) of his hearing the name in Lhasa, and of his being told that an Englishman of that name had lived in that city from the years 1826 to 1838; that he was assassinated on his way back to India via Ladak, somewhere in Nari Khorsum. The murderers were caught by the Lhasa people and Moorcroft's property rescued. Amongst his papers were found maps and plans of Lhasa and Tibet. The story is too circumstantial to be ignored. All we know for certain is that Moorcroft made a second journey to Kashgar and Turkestan in company with a German named Trebek, and that in 1825 information was received from Trebek that Moorcroft had died between Balkh and Bukhara. This story was always regarded with suspicion in India, and consequently Huc's information was received as credible from the day that he published it, — all the more so that the Tibetan description of the Englishman who resided in Lhasa and made surveys tallied very fairly well with what we know of Moorcroft.

CHAPTER VIII

The Jesuit Missionaries, Huc and Gabet — Journey from Manchuria to Koko Nor — Notes on Early Christianity in Coria — The Mongolian and Chinese Borderland Frontier Farms — Mongolian Customs — Trade with China — Lamaism in Western Kansu — The Koko Nor and Feast of Flowers at Kunbum

THE chronicles of Tibetan exploration are full of the records of vain attempts to unveil the mysteries surrounding that holy of Buddhist holies, — the city of Lhasa. Geographical literature teems with them. Now that the veil has been easily lifted, and such mystery as there may lie behind it has been exposed to the world at large, it proves somewhat disappointing. The enchantment of speculation has died a natural death, and Lhasa itself, reduced to the level of ordinary experience, will probably soon cease to arouse even the languid public interest which is taken in the world of famous Indian cities. The record of attempts to reach Lhasa is not, however, one of unredeemed failure. We have already referred to two Europeans who have succeeded in their quest, — Van de Putte and Manning. Unfortunately, neither of these two great travellers have told us much of the city wherein the interest of Tibetan exploration has been so long centred. Several native explorers in British or Russian pay have been there and have had their say about the holy city; but the Asiatic mind lacks imagination, and hardly grasps the trend and aim of European enquiry. That which is too familiar to the Asiatic to require comment is often just the point which most usefully illustrates some special characteristic of a people; and when Asiatics deal with the physical aspects of a country, the whole landscape around them is apt to become coloured with the drab tints of their own weary-minded sensations as they toil bravely through the monotonous task which has been committed to their care. Consequently, a very peculiar value is to be attached to the story of those Europeans who, in days later than Van de Putte or Manning, not only reached Lhasa and lived there, but have left a most interesting record of their experiences in a book which is written with vivacity and intelligence and never lacks the interest of personal adventure. M. Huc was a Jesuit missionary, who was appointed about the year 1840 to a Mongolian mission centre which still maintained a precarious existence on the northern borderland of China. He passed through Canton on his way to Pekin during the war which was then progressing between England and China, and whilst the foreigner was yet specially obnoxious to the Chinese nation. A French Lazarist priest "le vénerable Perboyre," was about this time publicly executed at Canton, and it was apparently under his auspices that M. Huc made his first venture in the missionary field. He claims that the Catholic missionaries were the only Europeans who then dared to cross the provinces of China; and he was probably justified in his claim. Christianity on the Mongolian borders of China fifty years ago was but a faint reflex of the widespread form of Christian faith which prevailed throughout so great an extent of High Asia during the middle ages. Without ascribing much value to the mediæval traditions which invested the semi-mystical Prester John with a halo of religious romance and represented him as combining in one person the high offices of priest and king over the vast empire of the Kara Khitai, and at the same time crediting him with untold victories over the invading powers of Islam, there can be no doubt that as late as the middle of the tenth century Nestorian Christianity prevailed in Central Asia to an extent which is hardly realised in the twentieth. Whether or no Gur Khan, emperor of the Kara Khitai in 1150 is to be identified with the mystical Prester John is still a matter of conjecture. Evidences of his Christianity are obscure, but it is an historical fact that the daughter of the last of his race was a Christian, and that she married Kushluk Khan, the king of the great Tartar clan Naiman. There is some ground for supposing that the whole Naiman tribe was once Christian. Traces of the Christian ritual are still to be recognised in the marriage customs of that tribe and amongst the nomadic people of the Pamirs to this day. Christian relics have been unearthed from the ruins of some of the buried cities of Chinese Turkestan, and it seems probable that the Nestorian form of Christian faith, which first spread through Persia. extended eventually right across Central Asia through Tartary to China and Japan, where (we have recently been told) there were more than a million Christians at the period when Japan adopted the form and methods of Chinese civilisation. In the early years of the fourteenth century we find Kuluk Khan treating with favourable consideration John of Montecorvino, the archbishop of Pekin, who was engaged in as fierce a dispute with the Nestorian Christian leaders of his day as that which divided Dominicans and Jesuits three centuries later in China. The first Chinese emperor of the Ming dynasty who defeated the Mongols and drove them back beyond the Great Wall was a Buddhist priest, and from his time onward systematic assaults of Islam and Buddhism combined appear to have prevailed against Asiatic Christianity. We learn little of this from Huc's narrative, but he states that the Pekin mission flourished under the earlier emperors of the Manchu dynasty, and that it was chiefly owing to the precautions of Kia King, the fifth emperor, that the Christians of China were scattered and driven into Mongolian territory. The vicar apostolic of Mongolia fixed his residence at Si-Wang, and it was he who deputed Huc (with one companion, Gabet) to visit Tibet in the interests of Christian missions.

The Catholic community in Mongolia was still holding its own bravely in the middle of the last century, and the story of Huc's parting with his Christian flock when he undertook his perilous enterprise in 1844 is told with pathetic force. Huc had carefully studied the tenets of Buddhism with a view to complete preparation for a theological campaign in Tibet; but it does not appear that he found any lamaistic champion in Tartary who was worthy of his steel. There was a universal tendency to back out of logical argument and to refer him to the headquarters of Buddhism (always "in the West") whenever he endeavoured to push home his advocacy of Christian doctrine with any of the ignorant lamas who professed to be the guides and teachers of the nomadic herdsmen of the Mongolian steppes. To them the great fountain of light was to be found only in Tibet (the West), and they would not admit of any lesser source of doctrinal teaching.

It is noteworthy that the camels of the mission before starting were pastured in the "Kingdom" (royaume) of Naiman (tribal districts are thus indicated by Huc), and its chief pastures were at He-Chung (which appears to be a Tartar and not a Chinese name), about five hundred miles northeast of Pekin and on the southwest borders of Manchuria. Huc's narrative, therefore, first deals with the route connecting Manchuria with the Koko Nor Lake on the extreme northeast borders of Tibet, and then with the recognised highroad to Lhasa from the Koko Nor, which may be described as the main entrance to Tibet from the north, and the only one of importance from any commercial point of view. It is well to the east of the routes taken by Sven Hedin, Bonvalot, and others, but it includes a part at least of that traversed by Rockhill, about whom there will be more to say later on. It is well to remember at this period of our history that whereas the possession of the plains of Chinese Turkestan, and the occupation of Kashgar, Khotan, etc., would assist little or nothing towards a systematic extension of Russian influence into Tibet, owing to the nature of the intervening country, the right of way through Mongolia from Manchuria to Koko Nor and the occupation of that region (which is geographically about as far from Lhasa as is Khotan) might conceivably prove most useful.

The route from Koko Nor to Lhasa is, and has been through all historic ages, a recognised commercial route. This is my excuse, at any rate, for entering rather more fully into Huc's narrative of this preliminary journey through Mongolia from the borders of Manchuria than the limits of this work would otherwise justify.

There were no half measures about Huc. He adopted the dress of the Tibetan lama, the yellow gown and cap, shaving his head and conforming rigidly to all the little social forms and ceremonies which the code of Chinese manners so strictly enforces. He started with his companion Gabet on his adventurous journey, not only prepared to see a strange land and live amongst a strange people, but to live as they lived; to look on the Mongolian world from the point of view afforded by the tent door of the nomad, sharing their sympathies and their prejudices as he shared their dwellings and their food. He piloted the little caravan across the wide steppes on horseback, whilst his fellow missionary Gabet rode a camel, and their one Tartar retainer, mounted on a black mule, led the "baggagers." Owing to his intimate knowledge of the language of the country he was able to make himself at home either in camp or city, and he has consequently illustrated the home life of the border people of Mongolia — Chinese and Tartar alike — as no one else has been able to illustrate it before or since. Starting southwest on the road to Dolan Nor, he struck at once into the desolate plains which stretch away from the foothills of the southern Kinghan Mountains constituting the territory of "Ouniot." According to Huc there was a time (not far distant) when this part of the Chinese borderland was forest-covered, inhabited, and rich in cultivation. About the middle of the seventeenth century the Chinese swarmed into it, destroyed the forests, and spread general devastation through the land, reducing it to its present condition. Deforestation has led to a total change of climate (it is somewhat strange to find a Jesuit missionary of the middle of the last century supporting such a theory), and the terrific "black" storms which now sweep across it unchecked carry periodic destruction with them, filling the air with dust and sand and swamping wide areas with rain flood. Hail storms of extraordinary violence are frequent. We have Huc's testimony to the fact that hail stones weighing two pounds frequently descend on the hard baked earth — such stones as can only be broken in pieces with axes. This is below, and to the east of, the central Kinghan system, which is part of the orographic backbone of Asia. But we beg leave to doubt whether the "black burán" of eastern Mongolia differs essentially from that which is encountered further south on the Chang plains of northern Tibet, which has been so graphically described by Sven Hedin. Desiccation and the resulting deforestation is not the work of man in high Asia. Whatever may be the ultimate cause of the gradual changes in the physical conditions of the continent which have led to these recurrent changes of climate which can be marked by geologic investigations, they belong to a group of natural phenomena which are not even yet fully understood. Throughout Asia such changes are to be noted perhaps more readily than in any other continent; but they are the common heritage of the whole changeable world. Huc had not proceeded far before he mounted the great central plateau spreading southward from the Kinghan, and from this point he commences a daily narrative of his journey, which is full of interest and by no means devoid of humour. The great wide-spreading plains or steppes, the long eternally-winding track (which there was no difficulty whatever in following, for it was often a cart track), the periodic hunt for water, the scattered clusters of nomadic "kibitkas" (or felt tents) which comprise the Tartar villages are all familiar enough to the Central Asian traveller. There is a monotony about Asiatic travellers' tales in this respect which only reflects the monotony of the wearisome grind of each day's toil which they encounter. Even the "black burán," hurling its terrific forces of wind and driven sand upon the devoted little camp, is becoming rather a well-worn experience. Huc, however, introduces an interesting variety into his tale by his description of the Chino-Tartar "auberge" or "sarai," which is to be found at intervals along the Chinese frontier, and in some respects reminds one irresistibly of the Russian steppe post-house. The huge mud-built apartment is reserved for the guests in the centre of the establishment, in the midst of which is the "khang," an admirable arrangement for keeping guests warm and comfortable. The khang is a raised platform, about four feet high, beneath which hot air is introduced from the stoves (*chaudières*) ranged about the apartment. Here the traveller sits; here he takes his meals and smokes his pipe or his opium; and here he spreads his blankets at night and sleeps. It often becomes crowded and noisy, and even to a veteran traveller like the Jesuit missionary it was occasionally difficult to find the needful rest. Nor does it appear that the *ménage* of these caravanserais includes conveniences for cleanliness. There is a gruesome chapter in Huc's narrative devoted to the results of a month's travel without the opportunity of washing his linen. Of all the horrors that can befall the civilised traveller in Asia this he justly reckons to be the most lively and the most intolerable. Uncivilised travellers, however, do not mind it.

The convenience of possessing a tent of their own which they could make use of whenever the laws of hospitality did not enforce their company with fellow-travellers was greatly appreciated by the Abbé. The best of his time was passed in the wilderness, when, free from the wearisome intimacy of the sarai, Huc was left with the wide world of nature around him, listening to those spirits of earth and air which Tartar imagination has conjured from the unknown, or engaged in his own familiar forms of ritual and prayer. But Huc was essentially a man of warm sympathies, a good story-teller, and a good companion; so he never missed an opportunity of attending any Tartar function which might afford him food for amusement or for reflection, even though his efforts to distribute a few ideas of the grace and beauty of the Christian faith amongst his companions generally met with no response. He was present once at a singular operation which aimed at casting the devil out of a man; this was new to him, and had the merit of being perfectly successful. Every form of sickness in Tartary is attributed to some special "Tchutgour," or demon, who fosters it. Consequently the only medical practitioners in Mongolia are the lamas. They prescribe medicines or remedies, always composed of vegetable matter pulverised and made up into the form of a pill. Mineral specifics count for nothing with the lama medicine man, and if vegetable ingredients fail, that also is not of much consequence. The name of the remedy is then written on paper, rolled up and mashed with saliva, and administered in the same form as a veritable dose, with precisely the same effect. After medical treatment prayers are said, strictly conformable to the quality of the devil to be exorcised. If the sick man is a poor man, the "Tchutgour" obviously is of no great account; he is but a "diablotin," and a simple exorcism is usually sufficient for him. But if the sick man is rich, "les choses vont tout différemment." The devil is of a certainty powerful and terrible, a bad spirit worthy of great consideration. It is not decent that he should make his exit as if he were a mere "diablotin"; he is supplied with good clothes, a hat, boots, and, withal, a young and vigorous horse to ride; and it may happen (in the case of a very rich patient) that the devil maintains a troop of servitors, all of whom must be supplied with mounts. The ceremony of exorcism finally commences. Many lamas are invited, and prayers are continued for seven or eight days without intermission until such time as the lamas are assured that the devil has disappeared, — that is to say, until they have exhausted the resources of the family on which they live. If "au bout du compte" the man dies, that only shows how well the prayers have been recited. It is true that the sick man is dead; but he will lose nothing by that. He will transmigrate into a better state with a yet larger fortune at his command. Huc was present at a ceremony where the devil was actually represented by a dummy (" mannequin "), which was set upright in the family tent. After a frightful musical orgie and much lamaistic ritual, with prayers and incantations and terrific din, ending with a wild dance of the entire assembly round the tent, the chief lama set fire to the "mannequin," who was then seized by "les hommes noirs" (*i. e.*, the lay members of the assembly), and carried out into the prairie to burn. The lamas meanwhile sat in the tent and chanted their prayers gravely and solemnly. When the brave destroyers of the "mannequin" returned, the chants ceased and gave way to joyous congratulations. The family formed a procession, — the "hommes noirs" first, then the sick man supported by two relatives, then eight or ten lamas, — and they all marched to the sound of their "épouvantable musique" as far as a neighbouring tent, where the sick man was to remain for some days. After this bizarre treatment, says Huc, the sick man was entirely cured. The devil was the devil of intermittent fever, and he returned no more.

Incidentally we learn something of the natural aspects of the country through which the missionaries passed, but we do not gain much in the way of geographical information. It was not all desolate wilderness that spread itself between the intermittent cities of the route. We hear of wild roses and gooseberries, and, when once the plateau land had been reached, of wide forest reserves especially sacred to the imperial chase. As they ascended to the uplands of the southern Kinghan they almost touched the sources of the "Chara Muren," — the river we know as the Liao Ho, which flows into the Liao Tung gulf to the west of Port Arthur. Brigands, of course, kept them in constant fear for their lives and property, but the brigand of the Chinese border is far in advance of his *confrère* on the Tibetan side. His politeness would do credit to the old school of British highwaymen, who were nothing if not gentlemen in their methods of robbery and murder. There is much said about the genuine feeling of kindly hospitality which is invariably shown by Tartar nomads to strangers. The two missionaries were never at a loss for food and shelter so long as a nomadic village was in sight. Invariably treated with respect and consideration, they naturally bestowed their sympathies on the simple-minded folk of the field rather than on the long-headed and far-reaching Chinese townsmen, who made an easy prey of the Tartar nomad whenever the two met on commercial grounds. Many a tale has Huc to tell of the ingenuity of the heathen Chinee in extracting money from the pockets of the slow-witted Tartar, who appears to be equally robbed by the Chinese dealer and his own priest. "Catching a Tartar" is a phrase which apparently carries a different significance in the East to that which it bears in the West; but it does so happen now and then that the Chinaman overreaches himself, and the Tartar maintains his European reputation. Huc's description of the Chinese frontier towns of Dolon Nor (Tolon Nor in map) and Kuku Khoto, which he passed *en route* to Tibet, is full of the lively interest of personal adventure. Narrow disreputable streets, so full of pitfalls and clogged with mud as to make the passage of camels through them a process of probable shipwreck and disaster; a crowded township full of the lowest class of Chinese traders, who were, however, distinguished for a most remarkable code of slimy politeness; fifth-class restaurants and overflowing pawnshops surrounded by a sea of insanitary filth, — combined to produce an impression which required the wild, free sweep of the black burán of the open plains to wash out of the mind and memory. Between the two towns the travellers crossed the great Russian port and caravan road to Pekin which links the capital city of China with the southern shores of Lake Baikal. It is about 900 miles from Pekin to the Russian frontier, and would involve rather more than 1,000 miles of line to connect the two by rail. Of that 1,000 miles some 250 or 300 would run amongst the mountains which frame in the Baikal depression. The rest would be more or less of a surface line across the Mongolian steppes. After passing Kuku Khoto, our travellers adopted the direct route to Sining-fu and the Koko Nor, which crosses the great northern bend of the Hoang Ho (Yellow River), and this proved to be the most serious of the difficulties which they encountered. The Hoang Ho was in flood, and days were spent in floundering through the flood-ridden plains on either bank of the river before the actual crossing was effected.

But this was only rendered necessary by the limit of time and expenditure which the missionaries had imposed on themselves for the maintenance of their adventure, and which precluded the lengthy detour which would have been entailed by rounding the northern loop of the Hoango Ho. On the whole the route was evidently a well-trodden and comparatively easy commercial road. Immense caravans were met with strings of camels extending for miles in length. Carts, too, were a feature of the road traffic; no formidable passes were encountered; and it may be accepted that the road from Pekin to Sining on the Tibetan frontier is a fairly practicable one for all classes of conveyance. The one great obstacle is the Hoang Ho, and that may possibly be turned or navigated.

There is so much direct analogy between the nomad peoples north and south of the Tibetan border that a comparison between their methods of life and means of subsistence would reveal no great difference. Chinese brick tea is the universal drink, and whether it finds its way by Ta-chien-lu direct across the eastern Tibetan border, or through the frontier Chinese towns into the Mongolian plains, it appears to be precisely of the same quality. Huc describes the brick tea of Kuku Khoto in almost the same terms as Little describes that of Ta-chien-lu (Darchendo). It is made up of big leaves and twigs, the refuse, in fact, of the tea industry. It is hardened into cakes or bricks by the liberal use of rice water, and is finally prepared for consumption with butter and salt. Neither Bhutia,

Tibetan, or Tartar will use any other, and no effort to introduce the tea of civilisation into these vast tea-consuming areas has had the slightest success so far. The Tartars, however, seem to prefer milk to butter with their tea. There is no accounting for the taste induced by education and custom. The Russian prefers lime-juice or jam; the Persian takes his tea with so much sugar as to render it nauseous to Europeans. The habitations of Tartar and Tibetan nomads is the same in all essential particulars, as we may find in Turkman villages on the Oxus, or in Kirghiz encampments on the Pamirs. It is common to all the wandering peoples of Asia, and the construction is the same whether it is called "kibitka," "yurt," or "aul." The felt rugs stretched over the circular lattice framework with the rounded roof and the upper aperture for the chimney, the division of the interior to screen off the apartment of the women folk; the domestic implements, reeking of butter and mutton grease, the antiquated arms, and the pungent smoke, are to be found in all of them; and in all of them that nameless essence of rancid grease and unwashed humanity, which Huc calls the "odeur empyreumatique," permeating the interior with an atmosphere that can be felt. The atmospheric oppression of a late second-class metropolitan railway carriage sometimes conjured up a faint reminiscence of it.

The extraordinary influence of Lhasa as the centre of the Buddhist faith over the whole of eastern Asia was brought home to the missionaries wherever they set their feet, or announced their prose.ytising purpose. All enlightenment was to be found in the West. All lamas with any pretensions to influence amongst the tribespeople or the townsfolk were educated in Tibet. From Tibet came the law and the gospel of Buddhism, and there can be no doubt that political influence in Lhasa meant then (as it probably means now) political strength in all the councils of the far East. There was more than the extension of the Christian faith to be attained in Lhasa by the missionaries. There was an outside knowledge of the world to be carried to the inner recesses of the holy places of the great Buddhist hierarchy, which might open their eyes to the advantage of secular alliance with the powers of the West. In Lhasa was to be found the key which might unlock many doors at present shut to the Christian missionary, through which might drift the first ripples of Catholic temporal ascendancy, along with Catholic spiritual enlightenment.

Mongolia is permeated with lamaistic influence and superstition. The easy life led by the priest is doubtless a great inducement to join the religious brotherhood, and the whole country is consequently as completely overridden by the priest as is Tibet itself. Huc describes the Mongolian lama, whether of the red or the yellow sect, as belonging to one or other of three very distinct types. The "home" lamas (lama *à domicile*), after taking a degree in one of the lamaserais which abound in all the central towns, seldom definitely fix themselves as permanent residents therein. They return home, preferring the smaller field of labour which offers itself in the scattered colonies of the prairies or steppes. There they live a life which is more free and independent than that of the Buddhist universities. Sometimes they live in the bosom of their own families, occupied, like other Tartars, in sheep farming. They prefer the life of the nomad to the rules of the monastery and the daily repetition of prayers. These lamas are no more religious (says Huc) than the red or yellow garments which they wear. A second class of lama neither remain in the lamaserais nor with their families. They are vagabonds on the face of the earth. They live like birds, which roost nowhere in particular. Impelled by some secret nomadic instinct, they start on their travels for the simple sake of moving, to traverse the road, to change their scenery. They travel from lamaserai to lamaserai, stopping *en route* at all the pastoral tents they meet, ever assured of the welcome accorded by the rule of Tartar hospitality. They walk in without ceremony and seat themselves by the fire, and whilst they drink the tea which is offered them, they recount with vast pride the number of districts they have visited. If they wish to stay the night, they just stretch themselves out like dogs in a handy corner, and sleep soundly till morning. At dawn, before starting on their vagabond voyage, they take count of the weather and the prospect, turning their heads from side to side "comme pour interroger les vents." Then they start, without definite aim or object, with their heads

General Group of Lamas

stretched forward, their eyes on the ground, a long stick in their hands, and a deerskin wallet on their backs; when they are tired they repose under the shadow of a rock, on the crest of a hill, at the bottom of a ravine, or anywhere else that appeals to their fancy. When night surprises them on their pilgrimage they sleep beneath the sky, which is, they say, but the roof of the world's tent. The vagabond lama visits all eastern Asia, China, Mongolia, and the Tartar steppes, Koko Nor, Tibet, India (not many reach India), and Turkestan. There is hardly a river which they have not crossed, a mountain they have not climbed, a grand lama before whom they have not prostrated themselves, nor a people amongst whom they have not lived and whose manners and customs they do not know. They are never afraid, they cannot lose themselves, as the place they reach is always for them the objective of their day's journey. Like the wandering Jew "qui marche et marche toujours," they seem to be impelled by some of that divine force which gives impulse to the solar system, and keeps the planets ever moving through infinite space.

The third class of lama is composed of those who live in community. A lamaserai is a collection of small dwellings centring on a Buddhist temple. They vary in style and quality, but the lama of the lamaserai is almost always of a superior stamp to the vagabond or the tent dweller. He is given to study and to prayer, and lives a life of regularity if not of asceticism, modified, however, by many comforts. He has his cow and his horse, and is generally a sheep owner. Most lamaserais are endowed either locally by the royalties of the district, or else by the imperial treasury. At certain seasons the revenues thus paid in to the establishment are distributed amongst the lamas according to their standing in the hierarchy. But no lama is ever rich. His money is spent as soon as he gets it. He will visit the nearest Chinese town, and swagger in fine clothes so long as his money or his stock will last. After a month or two his money will be gone and his fine clothes will be found in what M. Huc frequently refers to as the Mont-de-Piété. This appears to be perhaps the most flourishing commercial establishment of all Chinese frontier towns. It is the equivalent of the pawnshop. The fine clothes remain there, however, and the lama returns neither sadder nor wiser to his habitual disregard of the first principles of economy.

It is always an interesting question what proportion of the entire male population of Mongolia and Tibet are lamas by profession. Huc estimates their proportion at one-third, but it is a little doubtful whether he includes both men and women in the term "population." Probably he means men only; but considering that in nearly every Tartar family all the sons, with the exception of the eldest, are lamas, this proportion seems small. There is no question of inclination about it. The parents of the family decide for the children, and the latter gradually accustom themselves to their vocation, and usually end by acquiring a certain "exalta-

Cliff Temple where Huc Sojourned

tion religieuse," which seals them by choice to the priesthood.

In the discussion of questions such as this, the testimony of an earnest-minded missionary, of whatever persuasion, is most valuable. It is indeed in the presentation of a comprehensive idea of the social life of the people, whether priests or laymen, that the records of this traveller are of unique value. No subsequent traveller has enjoyed similar opportunities for studying the idiosyncrasies of the eastern Asiatic from a standpoint of such intimacy; neither has any European since his time been received into the inner sanctuary of Buddhism, and there examined the fundamental doctrines of a creed which has influenced so vast a proportion of humanity.

The journey of the missionaries through the western regions of the Kansu province from the Yellow River to Sining fu (the great commercial centre and frontier town of China, east of the Koko Nor Lake), presented almost more difficulties from the excess of cultivation than of desert. It was frequently difficult to find a passable track through the mazes of the cultivated fields which spread around towns, villages, and hamlets, riddled and intersected with the network of an ingenious system of irrigation. Precisely the same difficulty occurs in the cultivated villages of Persia and Afghanistan to this day. Now and then the travellers hit upon a good road for a certain distance, as, for instance, after passing the old town of Ninghia, when, for a time at any rate, the road was found to be excellent, until, after crossing the great wall, they gradually drifted into more deserted tracts ere they encountered the sandhills of Alechan. So far as the route through Kansu to the Koko Nor is concerned, there is obviously nothing in it to prevent the movement of a considerable force. It is on the whole cultivated, well supplied, and flat. Between the Yellow River and the Koko Nor the great wall is crossed three times. The Abbé Huc is careful to explain that between the great wall, as seen near Pekin, and the great wall of these outlying western provinces of China, there is a very great difference. Built (or commenced) about the year 214 A. D., it is supposed to have taken ten years to build, and it was doubtless a gigantic work from whatever point of view it is examined. But the solid masonry construction of Pekin is not found in the far West, where it is not always a solid masonry, and frequently nothing but mud.

Where our travellers first crossed it after leaving the Yellow River it was in ruins. They were on one of the great Asiatic trade routes which runs westward from China through Tsaidam in northeastern Tibet to Chaklik and Lob Nor, and thence passes to Khotan — which is probably the Ili referred to by Huc as the bourne from whence no Chinese exile returns. Something of the nature of the widespread pest of brigandage which prevails all through high Tibet and the borderland of China may be gathered from a curious experience of these two missionaries. They were given their choice of inns or sarais in which to put up for the night, the difference between these various "hotels" being chiefly in their cost. There were inns where they "fought" and inns where they did not fight. The latter were the cheaper of the two classes. Here they received travellers hospitably, but no guarantee for security. If the brigands came, so much the worse for the resident travellers if they could not defend themselves. At inns where they fought there was no satisfactory guarantee either; but the defence of the position against brigands was not left to the travellers only. The people of the inn undertook to make the best fight that they could under the circumstances; but travellers must of course pay for the possibility of such a casual engagement being rendered necessary, and the hotels were dear in consequence. Huc describes the people of western Kansu as being far more Tartar, or Tibetan, in their social characteristics than Chinese. He calls them religious and hospitable, but inquisitive. They could not divine the nationality of the Frenchman. They knew that they were not "diables marins" (English), because they had neither red hair nor blue eyes, and, moreover, they could ride, — and it was well known that the sea devils could do nothing of the sort. All the same, Huc encountered a "Buddha vivant" who could talk English and Russian, and was apparently much grieved at his want of knowledge of French. The reverend Abbé is nothing if not a loyal Frenchman, and a profound hater of the English and all their ways. The pleasure of his ultimate voyage to his sunny home in France was much marred by the prevailing evidence of British occupation, which seemed to him to stretch from the English Channel to India — as indeed it really did.

Huc observed a slight alteration in the method of warming the kang, or central platform, of the houses in western Kansu from the Tartar fashion of the steppes. The kang in one form or another seems to be an institution which is indigenous to all high Asia. An analogous method of warming the actual floor (not a raised platform) by flues is to be found in Korea. A method which is but another variation is common in Afghanistan, where a "charpoy" or raised dais on legs is placed in the centre of the room with a brazier of live charcoal beneath. The guests sit round it, and a "rasai" or felt rug is then spread over the table and carried across the legs of the sitters around. If it is properly tucked in, it is astonishing what a power of heat this "thermal bath" arrangement is capable of evolving. In western Kansu the kang, instead of receiving currents of hot air beneath derived from the stoves used for cooking, has the heat generator placed directly beneath its boards, where a judicious admixture of "*fumier*" (powdered horse-dung?) and live charcoal is so spread about and arranged as to start the warming process from all points at once.

Sining fu is described as an immense town with but few inhabitants, but the surroundings appear to be fertile, cultivated, and picturesque, with villages, hills, and streams forming a distinctly Chinese landscape rather than a Tibetan one. Not far to the south is the

The Potala in the XVII. Century

great lamaserai of Kunbum, and here our missionaries made the first stand for their faith and endeavoured to start a Christian propaganda. Three months were passed in Kunbum ere moving farther on the way to Tibet, and it is doubtful if this would not have served the good Abbé as a permanent resting-place and a centre for the diffusion of Christian teaching and enlightenment, but for the dress regulations of the monastery, with which the reverend pilgrims were unable to comply. Some of the religious customs of the lamahood are graphically described by Huc, and are well worth a reference. The great Kunbum monastery is a borderland feature of Tibet, situated on the wild mountains which lie southeast of the Koko Nor Lake, the summits of which overlook the upper tributaries of the Hoang Ho. Here are gathered pilgrims in countless numbers from every part of Buddhist Asia. There is not a day in all the year unmarked by the advent or departure of strangers from Tartary or Tibet. The monastery is chiefly famous for the religious festivals which are held three or four times during the year, which are celebrated with such pomp and solemnity that not even Lhasa itself can boast of such impressive Buddhist functions. Amongst them that which is called the "feast of flowers," which takes place on the fifteenth day of the first month, is most famous. For weeks beforehand the influx of pious pilgrims commences, and for days nothing is heard but discussions apropos to the fête. The ravishing beauty of the flowers is the theme of every tongue. The council of the "Beaux Arts" (it is a little doubtful to what council the Abbé refers here) pronounced them on that particular year to be superior to any which had preceded them; and the Abbé himself awaited with impatience the explanation of this magnificent exhibition of flowers in an all but flowerless land. The explanation was simple. Such flowers as there were were made of butter, and the whole exhibition was but a sort of waxwork show in which butter took the place of wax. Six lamas distinguished for their artistic skill were employed in the preparation of this quaint museum of art, which included representations of men and things in as nearly a natural form as they could be made to assume. One master mind, or chief, directed the artists who manipulated the raw material into the desired form. He further superintended the subsequent colour effects which were as important as those of design. On the day of the fête enormous crowds assembled. The grave and serious air of religious existence which usually surrounded the monastery, enveloping it with an atmosphere of saintly grace and mystery disappeared, and a little host of tents sprung up around on the mountain slopes. On the fourteenth day the usual pilgrimage around the monastery took place. The great crowd of slowly moving pilgrims, prostrating themselves at each pace they took, and repeating the Buddhist formula with each prostration, affected the Abbé greatly. He saw amongst them Tartars moving with firm and heavy mien, but applying themselves withal to the most strict performance of this religious duty; "longues chevelures," or the bandits, who trod freely and proudly with full equipment of arms and a savage air of devotion which was strangely in contrast with Mongol mysticism; and the Sitan pilgrims of Amdo who took matters with a general air of being too much accustomed to such performances to be particular as to details, together with not a few Chinese merchants of Khata, who "thought nothing of Buddha, but a good deal of a passing reputation for godliness which might assist in the disposal of their wares." The good Abbé did not take kindly to the heathen Chinee, and has but little good to say of him apart from his own beloved missionary field. But he was immensely struck with the fashion of the women of Amdo, who wore caps, or little pointed hats, altogether of the style which in France (in his time) were known as "chapeaux à la trois pour cent," and who allowed their hair to fall in ringlets rather than divide it into the dual pigtail which is the common Tartar and Tibetan fashion. On the 15th the crowd of peregrinating devotees was not so great. All thoughts were centred on the approaching fête. At night-time it took place. The "flowers" were arranged in the open air in front of the temples of the lamaserai. They were illuminated brilliantly with lamps artistically arranged in yellow or red copper vases distributed amongst them in fanciful designs, and the Abbé declares that it could not have been better done in Paris. The flowers ("fleurs") struck him with astonishment. The artistic efforts of the lamas had resulted in the production of works of art such as could hardly have been anticipated in a country where nature lends little aid to the imagination. They consisted chiefly of bas reliefs of colossal size, representing incidents in the history of Buddhism. The figures were living and animated in expression, the pose natural, and the draperies arranged with grace and ease. It was even possible to distinguish the nature of the material thus represented in butter, especially the furs and skins, which the Abbé declares to have been so well reproduced that it was necessary to touch them in order to feel assured that they were not real. The figure of Buddha, where it appeared, was full of majestic grace and beauty, represented with Caucasian features true to the accepted type which historically declares him to have been light in colour, with a pink and white complexion, wide open eyes, prominent nose, and long undulating wavy hair. All other figures were Tartar or Mongolian in type, but it was easy to distinguish Tibetan, Tartar, Chinese, or Si-fan (eastern Tibetan nomads) by their peculiarities of feature, and to differentiate between them. Hindus and Negros were also represented and attracted much attention from the crowd. The representations of human types were surrounded with decorative designs which included animals and flowers; the whole exhibition being remarkable for fidelity of expression and colour.

Whilst we must make allowances for the impression produced on the mind of the Abbé, which might be due to his long separation from civilised centres of art, and the savage and wild nature of his surroundings, we possess quite sufficient evidence of the artistic capabilities of the Tibetans in their quaint and original works in copper and bronze to assure us that the instinct for design is very highly developed amongst them. Rougher and more crude than that of China, there is nevertheless a strength and a breadth in the quality of Tibetan design which places it in a position unique amongst Oriental art work; and we need not discount the vivid description of the Abbé too severely. We must remember, too, that he had no opportunity of judging the quality of Buddhist design from the famous examples which exist in India. He had never visited the Peshawar valley, Benares, or Sanchi, and consequently he was unprepared for the developments which certainly were derived in the first instance from India. The one feature of this singular exhibition which seems altogether unaccountable is the introduction of a variety of natural colour. Tibetans are colourists without doubt, but their scale is limited. Red and yellow, black and white, pretty nearly complete the list of primary colour effects which they employ, and in what way these could be modified and intermingled so as to produce anything approaching to the natural beauty of floral colouration in such a material as butter it is hard to imagine. However, we must accept the reverend traveller's description of the exhibition with such reservations as we find necessary for our own faith in his general truthfulness, and we shall find far less difficulty in realising his sensations as the fête proceeded. A theatrical representation (all in butter) in front of one of the temples did not amuse him; it struck him as incongruous; but the arrival of the Grand Lama of Kunbum, preceded by a vast concourse of priests and much noise of trumpets and "cinques marines," interested him greatly. The Grand Lama was middle-aged, fat, and common looking, but his clothes were superb. He carried a yellow mitre on his head, a long "baton" in the form of a cross in his right hand, and his shoulders were covered with a mantle of violet "taffetas," which rendered his whole appearance singularly like that of a Roman Catholic bishop. Huc does not fail to remark maliciously that as this Grand Lama surveyed the dignified and well-proportioned figures of the butter Buddhas, he must have been struck with his own modern degeneracy from the original type. When he had made his tour of the butter exhibition, he returned to his palace. With the exception of the Tartars (always the most devout and religious-minded of Central Asiatic communities) few in the crowd paid much attention to his movements; but his departure was the signal for the commencement of one of those orgies, or carnivals, for which Tibet is famous all over the world. Out of the howling and gesticulating crowd the Abbé and his companions were extracted by their faithful attendant with some difficulty, glad enough to escape from the risk attending further developments. They returned to their lodgings, and by the following morning nothing remained of the "fête de fleurs" except a vast quantity of butter, massed in a neighbouring ravine, where it had been thrown to feed the ravens. With the butter images the pilgrim crowd too dispersed, scattered into the wilds of the Chinese borderland and the Tartar steppes, and probably also on the road to Lhasa, which was shortly to be followed by the missionaries.

The Abbé has much to say about the beauty of the great blue lake, the Koko Nor, and its magnificent pasturages, and he relates the tradition of its first appearance in the region which it now occupies, which, by the light of Sven Hedin's recent investigations in the Lop Nor basin, is of considerable geographical interest. It is too long to narrate here, but it recognises the fact of migratory or moving lakes, and makes Koko Nor one of them. Further, it connects the appearance of Koko Nor on the land surface with the building of Lhasa. For many years it was found to be impossible to construct buildings on the site of the present city which did not collapse as soon as they were completed. Their foundations gave way and the buildings disappeared. When, however, the great secret of an underground sea which swallowed up the buildings was at last revealed by accident to the Lama of Oui, the escape of that sea by an underground channel to the site of Koko Nor was the immediate result. Vast areas of prairie land were inundated, and the luckless individual who gave away the secret was the first to perish in the flood. It is a curious tradition when collated with the known fact of the present migrations of Lake Lop Nor; and it possibly points to a geographical fact that the Koko Nor is of comparatively recent origin. The Koko Nor was originally known to the Chinese as Si-Hai (western sea), but they now call it Sing-Hai (blue lake). In Huc's time (*i. e.*, fifty years ago) it was said to be one hundred leagues in circumference, but it is probably desiccating and diminishing, like all other Tibetan lakes. Its waters are salt as the sea, and subject (Huc again) to tides like the sea. This now is known to be the normal condition of all great bodies of water, but the phenomenon is not precisely the same as that of ocean tides, nor is it due to the same causes. A rocky and barren island in the Koko Nor is the perpetual home of some twenty lamas, who live a life of silent contemplation and cannot be reached from the mainland excepting at those periods when the lake is covered with ice. South of Koko Nor is the district of Amdo, occupied by nomadic pastoral Tibetan tribes, — and here the cultivated and luxuriant fringe of western China comes to an end. Amdo is a region of wild and savage mountain scenery, the typical scenery of northern Tibet, and from this point onward to Lhasa Huc has a new and very different tale to tell of the varied adventures of the two plucky missionaries, who, after a vain effort to establish Christianity in Kunbum, moved southwards to Lhasa.

CHAPTER IX

Huc and Gabet (continued) — From the Koko Nor to Lhasa — Rockhill and Prjevalski in Northeastern Tibet — Rockhill's Second Journey towards Lhasa and in the Eastern Valleys of Tibet

LEAVING Kunbum after a three months' residence, where the missionaries found themselves unable to comply with the regulations of the lamaserai in the matter of dress, but were otherwise under no sort of compulsion, they took up their quarters temporarily at Tchogorton (not marked in any modern map), which cannot be far from Kunbum, as it is called, the country residence of the Faculté de medicin, and a single day's march was sufficient to bring them there. As, however, it was necessary to cross a mountain and descend into a wide valley, it is probable that Messrs. Huc and Gabet were still in the mountains south of Koko Nor. It was the month of May, but there was little appearance of spring about the valley. The lamas' homes were situated at the foot of a barren hill, but shaded by trees which were the resort of thousands of crows. Little irrigation rivulets meandered through the flats, and in the distance were the black tents of the Si-fan with troops of goats around. On the summit of a rocky hill adjacent, lived five " religieux contemplatifs," like eagles in an inaccessible nest. Some of them had excavated their own caves in the rocks; some had built for themselves cells of wood, "fixed to the hillside like swallows' nests." These saintly hermits, living a life of eternal contemplation apart from the world, were frequently encountered, and exercised the mind of the Abbé considerably. What was it that engaged their thoughts? What were they eternally contemplating? He complains with some bitterness that they none of them seemed to know. They lived that life because they had read in their books that saintliness was acquired thereby; just as certain well-intentioned Chinese Buddhists live near the summit of a mountain pass in order to acquire merit by feeding passers-by, or even as certain Alpine monks exercise the rites of hospitality to much the same purpose. For the rest, they were a quiet, sensible, peaceable folk "nullement farouche," and often rendered assistance to the missionaries. Their stay at Tchogorton was not for long. Lhasa was the first objective, and between them and Lhasa lay nearly one thousand miles of most difficult and most inhospitable country. We must, however, concede that the route followed by the missionaries is probably the best of all the northern routes to Lhasa. Littledale, Sven Hedin, Bonvalot, Rockhill, Prjevalski, and others have crossed the Tibetan border from the north, but always in small parties, with a light company and little impedimenta. The two Jesuit missionaries accompanied a huge caravan which they encountered on its way back from Pekin (as we shall see), and although, for some part of the distance at any rate, they must have been pointing the way for Prjevalski and Sven Hedin to follow subsequently, it is not clear that they were actually on the same route as those travellers. It is improbable that a large caravan of Tibetans accustomed to pass between Lhasa and Pekin would have taken any but the most favourable road.

From the month of May till late in September the travellers rested near the Tchogorton Monastery, and during that time collected much valuable information about the country of the Si-fan (eastern Tibetans) and its climate. Snow fell more or less to the middle of June, when it gradually gave way to mists and rain. Later in August the hills and plains lost the effect of barren desolation which usually distinguishes them, and freshened up with an abundant vegetation. Then the medical faculty spread abroad for the collection of medicinal plants. Huc thinks that the Tibetan lamas really possess valuable secrets in the healing art which might be well worth investigation; and indeed it seems probable that in a country where the drugs of Europe are not to be had, necessity has long ere this taught the people the value of such simple remedies as lie to their hands in the glens of the mountains and on the banks of their streams.

Late in September came the news that the Tibetan ambassador had arrived on the frontier, and was busy making up his caravan for the forward journey to Lhasa. This was Huc's opportunity. It was obviously late in the year for such a journey in such altitudes, but the very fact that Tibetans face the mountainous North at all seasons of the year leads to the inference that it is regarded as an open road, and that in favourable seasons it may present no very formidable difficulties.

Huc made a four days' march from Tchogorton to Koko Nor, where he picked up some useful ethnographical information in the tents of the Mongol nomads. All Tibet is infested with brigands, but nowhere do they flourish with such vigour as amongst the Si-fan Tibetans in the neighbourhood of Koko Nor; there they are known under the generic name of Kolo, and they still keep the whole country in terror of their depredations. As an ethnographical designation, Huc maintains that the well-known name "Kalmuk," applied to certain Tartar or Mongolian tribes, is unrecognised in high Asia. He failed to identify any people under that name. He found, however, a small subdivision of the great Kolo fraternity (Tibetan in origin) called Kolo-Kalmuk, who possess no lands of their own. They are a comparatively insignificant section of the Kolo hordes. If this is so, the name Kalmuk has certainly attained a significance in geographical records which it is not entitled to bear.

For about a month the missionaries remained with the Tartar shepherds of the Koko Nor plains, shifting camp from time to time for fear of brigands. It was not till the end of October that the ambassador arrived, and with him a number of Mongolian caravans which had seized this opportunity of making the journey to Lhasa in force. Once every three years a political mission visits Pekin from Lhasa and returns. At one time this mission was annual, but the annual embassy was abandoned after the Grand Lama who filled the post of ambassador had once been stolen, and once been slain, by the brigands *en route*. Now the mission moves in force, and of late years has passed along its way in peace; but it is always the brigands — never the passes or the rivers — that are the terror of the pilgrims of the Tibetan embassy. The company which the missionaries joined for the journey to Lhasa must have been sufficiently remarkable. Huc estimates the number of men composing it at two thousand, with fifteen thousand yaks, twelve thousand horses, and as many camels. The "Tchanak Kampo" (or ambassador) travelled in a litter carried between two mules. The mounted men were all well armed, and prepared to defend this unwieldy assemblage from the Kolo brigands. The time of the year was late autumn, verging on winter, and the road to Lhasa was intersected with ranges of vast altitude, and with immense stretches of plateau land devoid of vegetation, scoured by terrific winds, and petrified by intense cold and biting frost. Yet there seems to have been no hesitation in taking the road, and it is tolerably clear that whether this is or is not the same route which was followed by Prjevalski, it is a well known and very much trodden route. On the 15th of November they left the magnificent pasture land of Koko Nor and passed into the windswept valley of Tsaidam. The pastoral country extended northwest from Koko Nor for about eleven days' march, during which they crossed the Puhain Gol (Buhain Gol), flowing from the Nan Shan mountains on the north, and subsequently the Toulain Gol — both shallow rivers, but covered with ice. After passing the latter river they struck southwards into Tsaidam, and at once the promised charm of an ideal march through a land of plenty and luxury was rudely destroyed. Thenceforward they had the typical characteristics of northern Tibet before them, — arid, boundless wastes of stony upland, streaked with yet more barren rocks and ridges which occasionally rise to the eminence of mountain ranges and bar their southern tracts with inconceivably rough and difficult passes. They were to the west of Koko Nor, and almost due north of Lhasa, having made a considerable detour to avoid crossing the range immediately south of Koko Nor. Huc, at any rate, says nothing of crossing any pass into Tsaidam. The Tsaidam valley is not high (8,000 to 10,000 feet) but it is inconceivably bleak and inhospitable, and is only occupied by rough Mongol nomads who talk a guttural language which the Abbé could not understand.

Only two days were occupied in crossing the valley ere encountering the pestilential heights of Bourhan Bota. The Burkhan Buddha range (to give it its modern name) is a portion only of the mountain "system" which parts the lower steppelands of

Tsaidam from the great upland flats of the Tibetan plateau. The system stretches itself northwest to a junction with the Altyn Tagh mountains, and, like them, is the flanking revetment of a plateau rather than a distinct anticlinal formation. Huc has a story about poisonous gases which hang about the northern slopes on a windless day, which are said to deprive travellers of the power of motion. Animals are said to be equally affected with men. Great precautions were taken against their influence. The thin cloud films which cling to the mountain sides were declared to be gaseous emanations of this poisonous character, and great was the discussion, and very varied were the oracular indications of the most trusted prophets amongst the lamas as to what the end might be should this gigantic caravan face the danger so visibly displayed before them. However, the auguries were of the usually vague nature, and they all acted as they thought best. The two missionaries crossed without mishap, and those who waited for the clouds to disappear were equally fortunate. Huc seems to be persuaded that it is really carbonic acid gas which forms these emanations. A day or two after crossing the Burkhan the travellers encountered the Chuga, — a range which is obviously the modern Shuga, of which the pass would be about seventeen thousand feet, — and there their troubles commenced. Deep snow, intense cold, and the impossibility of finding fuel enough for the cooking required by such a host of people were but a part of their daily miseries.

M. Gabet lost his nose and ears from frostbite, and subsequently became so desperately affected by the severity of the cold that his life was despaired of. The everlasting prevalence of gales of wind in such a temperature was the one feature which made the cold so unendurable. This country, according to Huc, was the border of Tibet proper, and from this point, accordingly, all the Mongol and Tartar escort returned. Winter was well advanced now, and the demons of snow, wind, and cold were set loose on the caravan with a fury which seemed to increase from day to day. The Abbé describes this part of Tibet as "le pays le plus affreux qu'on puisse imaginer." The animals died first, and were left on the road where they fell; then men began to drop out, and there is a gruesome tale of a lama found sitting frozen on a rock by the wayside. Early in December they reached the foothills of the Bayen Kharat (Baian Kara ula), which separates the sources of the Hoang Ho, or Yellow River, from those of the Di chu, or Yang tsi. Huc says that he crossed this range not far from the sources of the Hoang Ho, which was on his left about two days' journey. This would be in about 94° 30′ east longitude (by Walker's map), and he was then close to the route followed subsequently by Wellby, running north of the range and parallel to it, if, by "source of the Hoang Ho," he refers to its remotest source in the mountains.

The subsequent account of a lake from which water was procured in abundance appears to support this view, and it is the most obviously direct route southward to Lhasa. Here the climatic conditions were somewhat better, and, being now on a well-trodden pilgrim route following the Di chu valley, plenty of the usual fuel in the shape of "argols" was found. Crossing the Di chu (or Mur ussu, as it is called near its source), an extraordinary spectacle presented itself. A herd of yak had endeavoured to pass the river whilst it was in the process of freezing, and had been frozen in, — caught in the grip of the ice and retained there with just their heads above the river surface. They appeared as if they were still swimming, but they must have been frozen for a considerable time.

After leaving the Di chu valley the caravan broke up into troops for the convenience of camping, and the missionaries having camels (which are much faster over a road than yaks) proceeded ahead with the first party moving. The next two or three weeks brought but the repetition of their previous experiences of the intense misery of an ice-cold, northerly gale perpetually acting on their half-frozen bodies. More than forty of the party died of cold ere they crossed the plateau commencing at Tangla. The ascent to these mountains is described by Huc as a gradual rise, step by step, over successive ridges which formed a vast amphitheatre; and it lasted six days. It was about this part of their route that they encountered Kolo brigands for the first time, but there was an apparent bond of union between certain of their own party and the brigand company which saved them from disaster.

The brigands indeed seemed to have behaved with all the courtly grace and consideration which we usually associate with the best traditions of the early British highwayman. For twelve days the party was occupied in crossing the plateau of Tangla, which Huc believed to be the highest part of Tibet. The altitude is generally about 16,000 feet above sea, the pass itself being about 16,400. This is geographically the most important water divide of Tibet. From the Tangla mountain crest northern affluents wind their way to the Mur ussu, — the upper Yang tsi. From the plateau land southward meandering streams collect to form the head of the Giama Nu Chu, which we believe to be identical with the Salwin River of Burma; and somewhere between the two, a little further to the east, are born the infant sources of the Mekong. Rising and falling between 15,000 and 16,000 feet, the mountain uplands from which these rivers flow extend with a general falling grade to its southern edge. In spite of its altitude, the crossing of this wide expanse of upland did not prove to be nearly as trying as the previous experiences further north. The air was still and the atmosphere clear. M. Gabet rapidly recovered (contrary to the prognostications of the lamahood), and, excepting for a continuance of intense cold (it was now the depth of winter), and the absence of fodder for the animals, the journey would have been endurable. The winter snow was hard frozen under foot, and the stiff spikes of such yellow herbage as existed, incapable of nourishment, cracked between the teeth of the famished baggage animals. The track became bordered by the skeletons of mules and camels, whilst monstrous eagles followed the caravan, picking up a ghastly livelihood from the debris. The scenery is described as magnificent, — line upon line of snow-white pinnacles stretching southward and westward under a bright sun and the clear blue sky of the still winter days. After twelve days on the plateau the descent is described as "long, brusque, and rapid," like the "descent of a gigantic ladder;" but it is difficult to understand how any descent of such a nature could have lasted through four days without arriving somewhere near sea level. They did, of course, reach much lower ground, and Huc speaks of the camp being pitched in a wide plain with such a spread of pasture land that the dry winter grass caught fire, and the conflagration was with difficulty arrested without doing serious damage to the Tibetan encampment pitched near by. There were sheep here in abundance, and hot sulphur springs, which sent clouds of white steam into the still air. Several days were next passed in traversing "a series of valleys" before arriving at the edge of the Na Ptchu (? Nu Chu or Salwin) River, where they encountered the first Tibetan town and the homes of settlers instead of the tents of nomads. It is a little difficult to place Na Ptchu, but it is apparently six days' march (and exceedingly rough marching) from Lhasa. This would bring it about thirty miles to the east of the lake Tengri Nor, on about the same line of latitude; but as Tengri Nor is more than 15,000 feet above sea level, the good Abbé must clearly be a little wrong in his general estimate of descent from the Tangla plateau. It is quite possible that the head of the Nu Chu lies as far south as this point. South of "Na Ptchu" the road is described as so rocky and difficult that camels had to be exchanged for donkeys. Snow and ice seemed to have gradually disappeared. Five days' march from Na Ptchu, at Pampou (which, on account of its contiguity to Lhasa, is generally looked upon as its suburb), there was apparently no snow, and only the edges of the stream and canals were fringed with ice. This at the end of January.

Pampou is a well cultivated plain, with neat white-washed farmhouses standing about at intervals, well shaded with trees, on the terraced hillsides. But it cannot stand at less than 12,000 feet above sea level, and the absence of rigorous cold at such an elevation in January proves that Lhasa is abnormally situated as regards temperature. The valley of the Tsanpo (or upper Brahmaputra) is obviously much warmer than any known region in the same latitude, and at the same altitude in the Himalayas. Indeed we know it to be so from the testimony of subsequent travellers. The people were friendly and hospitable, and appeared to possess that charm of happy-mindedness which is a distinguishing characteristic of most Tibetans. But one more pass remained to be surmounted before reaching Lhasa, and (according to Huc) it was as bad as the worst they had encountered. On the 29th

W. W. Rockhill

A. E. Carey

of January, 1846, our two travellers, after paying some little needful attentions to their toilet, descended from this intervening pass into the valley of the Kyi chu, and there at their feet lay Lhasa, — the mystical, the inaccessible, — unknown to Europeans, hidden from the south in the folds of the northern mountains. Girt around with thick groves of trees, its spreading vista of white flat-roofed houses dominated by the gilded spires of its many temples, and the majestic influence of its crowning glory the great palace of the Potala, impressed the good missionaries deeply; and one can easily imagine the devout feelings with which they received the welcome of their Mongol friends who had preceded them to prepare a place for them.

Here for a time we must take leave of these Jesuit fathers, for their record of experiences in the city of Lhasa must be co-ordinated with that of other later visitors who have had perhaps even better opportunities for recording impressions than they. Lhasa, after all, but represented the end of one stage on the most remarkable journey made by any traveller of the period. From Lhasa through Tibet to China we may follow them again; but across the wide regions of Central China to Nankin, Canton, and Pekin, or by their devious tracks along the eastern coast through many thousands of miles by sea and land, they wander too far from Tibet to keep touch with our purpose.

Meanwhile it may be useful to note what other subsequent travellers have to say about the great highways between Manchuria (or Pekin) and Lhasa, for it is probably the best-trodden route of any which end in the Tibetan capital excepting the more direct Chinese route via Ta-chien-lu and Batang. We shall see subsequently that it is the only route from the north that can bring Russia into practical communication with southern Tibet. The possession of Manchuria would undoubtedly carry with it a possibility of commercial enterprise along that line; it is therefore a matter of rather exceptional interest to examine its possibilities by the light of explorations subsequent to those of the Jesuit missionaries.

Two travellers only can be said to have added much to our knowledge of the eastern edge of the Tibetan plateau; one an American — Rockhill; the other a Russian — Prjevalski. The latter was the first great practical geographer to teach us the real nature of the orography of northern Tibet. It was Prjevalski who first discovered the connection existing between the Nan Shan mountain range to the north of Koko Nor and the Altyn Tagh, which latter range forms an intermediate link in the great buttress of the Tibetan plateau which thus stretches from the Muztagh or Karakoram mountains to the frontiers of China in one unbroken line of vast elevation parting the Tibetan uplands from the Turkestan lowlands. During his journey of 1879–80 Prjevalski explored southward from Saitu (or Sha-chan), — the well-known Chinese frontier station on the eastern edge of Chinese Turkestan, — crossing the Altyn Tagh at the point of junction with the Nan Shan, and then skirted along the eastern limits of the Tsaidam depression till he hit off the head of the Baian gol River about the same point to the southwest of Koko Nor that presented itself to the Abbé and his pilgrim company. But he did not immediately cross the Burkhan Buddha and the Shuga ranges by the pilgrim route. He bore away westward along the foot of the Burkhan Buddha by the defile of the Nomokhan gol, and crossing the Burkhan and Shuga mountains on comparatively easy terms by a pass 15,200 feet, entered a remarkable valley seventy miles long, which formed a natural causeway between two ranges. He crossed the range to the south (which he calls Marco Polo range, but which appears to be a mountain extension westwards of the Baian Kara ula) and reached the elevated plateau land wherein the great Yang tsi (under various names — the best known of which are Mur ussu and Di chu) takes its rise. He crossed the most northerly affluent of the Yang tsi somewhere midway between Huc's route and Rockhill's, and pursued a southwesterly course towards the Koko Shili (another branch westwards of the Baian Kara ula) which lay like a wall in front of him. Crossing the Koko Shili, which rises about 1,500 feet above the plain (16,000 feet above sea) with difficulty, and without a guide, Prjevalski found himself on a plain 15,000 feet above sea, studded with lakelets set in a sandy soil which supported a scanty vegetation including both alpine and steppe floral forms. The Dumburé was the next range presenting itself, which must have been crossed close to the pilgrim route, but was found to be flanked by half-frozen marshes which presented great difficulty to the travellers. At the foot of the southern slopes of the Dumburé they hit off the pilgrim route of Huc and must have crossed the main affluent of the Yang tsi almost at the same point. The Mur ussu was then only two and a half feet deep, with ice which would not bear the weight of a loaded animal. Here sickness and privation had begun to tell severely on the party, and the baggage had to be decreased on account of the loss of animals; but still, with the great swelling upland of the Tangla before them, they determined to push on. The Tangla upheaval is only 2,000 feet above the level of the Mur ussu on the north, or of the Sang chu (Giama Nu Chu — Salwin) on the south, yet the ascent was eighty miles long, and the descent fifty. "Thus," says Delmar Morgan, "the Tangla might be easily crossed by a railroad." If the Tangla stood alone perhaps it might. Huc, however, describes the descent as sharp and severe. The Tangla is the crowning orographical feature of eastern Tibet. East and west of the pilgrim route it concentrates into well-defined masses of great elevation crowned with perpetual snow. The route across it, followed by the pilgrims, is a natural depression which is not found elsewhere. Rockhill's route southward turned the range by a detour far to the west. On the fifth day of their descent from the Tangla the Russian party reached the Sang chu (14,700 feet), where they encountered the first black tents of nomadic Tibetans, and two marches further, at the village of Nat chu, they were met by Lhasa officials (170 miles from the capital) and compelled to turn back. Here, then, we have a very fair confirmation of the story of the Abbé's wanderings, but we have in addition an immense amount of scientific information which it was not in the Abbé's power to collect.

The flora and fauna of northern Tibet are described with scientific accuracy by Prjevalski. We find a poor vegetation contrasted with a most unusual number of herbivorous animals. There are no trees in northern Tibet, and only three kinds of bush, including the willow. There are three or four sorts of grass, but they are all of them scanty, and it appeared marvellous that the enormous herds of wild yak, antelope, and asses should be able to find the sustenance necessary for their existence in such regions. There are also two species of wild sheep, and a deer which is found only on the mountains. Prjevalski's description of the general character and scenery of northern Tibet differs but little from such generalisations as may be gathered from Huc. The great expanse of elevated salt marsh and clay flats which constitute the Tsaidam "depression," swept by perhaps the most persistent and awful winds in the world; the gigantic table-lands 13,000 to 15,000 feet above sea and the stupendous mountain ranges which streak them, not relatively lofty, perhaps, but entirely alpine in character; the utter loneliness, the weary desolation of it all; the intense cold even in summer, and the prevalence of storms of terrific violence in spring, — all these things place northern Tibet outside the category of possible theatres for military expeditions involving the march of armies, or even for the rapid advance of commercial development. We know that in spite of all these physical difficulties trade between Pekin and Lhasa is a busy and flourishing institution; but it can maintain only a chequered existence so far as northern Tibet is concerned. We must look to the East for further avenues of commercial traffic with China. Bad as they may be, they would seem to be better than this Manchurian route from the northeast. Before following the venerable Abbé eastward from Lhasa, however, it will be convenient to turn to the records of another great traveller from the northeast, who combined the vigorous determination of a born explorer with the ripe knowledge of an Oriental scholar. Rockhill is very much more than a scientific adventurer. His knowledge of the Chinese and Tibetan languages places him almost in a line with Huc as an authority at first hand on the subject of the religion and literature of the country. No other European has, of course, enjoyed the opportunity of the Jesuit missionaries for that social intercourse and intimate relationship with the priestly peoples of western China and Tibet which must make them for ever the best possible exponents of all that concerns the inwardness of Tibeto-Chinese existence. They stand in relation to the Mongolian, Tartar, and Tibetan as Burton stood to the Arab, — the interpreters of native philosophy of life and its surroundings to the European mind. If they fail somewhat as students of geography they stand unrivalled as students of humanity; and not even Rockhill, with the learning of an Orientalist and the discriminating eye of the geographer combined, can tell us so much of the Tibetan as Huc, though he may tell us much more of Tibet.

On his second journey to Tibet Rockhill left Pekin in December, and practically followed the route taken by the missionaries forty-six years earlier to the Chinese frontier at Sining fu, east of Koko Nor. He passed through Kalgan to Kweihwa and maintains the general accuracy of Huc's description of that town. The inhabitants (all Chinese) are "about as rascally and depraved a lot as I have ever seen in China. The town is dirty and ill built." The trade between Kweihwa and Chinese Turkestan is described as insignificant. Crossing the Yellow River at Dugei (important on account of its soda works) he found himself amongst the Jimgar Mongols, the easternmost of the seven Ordos tribes. The Ordos country is now settled by Chinese from Shensi, who rent the land from the Mongols. Recrossing the Yellow River, he traversed the desert sandy waste of Alashan, where "travel is rendered difficult by the innumerable holes dug over the face of the country by licorice diggers," varied by spaces of "soft sand, irrigation ditches, willow brush, and alkaline bog." Perpetually sweeping over all was the everlasting wind. He made a short halt at Ning-hsia-fu to engage carts to Lanchan. This city has been identified as the Egrigaia of Marco Polo, and is a great centre for rug (or "camlet") making. The plains beyond, for a distance of 175 miles, consisted of drifting sand alternating with alkaline marshes and patches of mixed loess and gravel. "Chinese enterprise has converted this unpromising plain into one of the most fertile districts of the province." Wheat and rice and fruit in abundance, with all manner of vegetables, are sold in the "bustling villages." Passing through Lanchan, Rockhill adhered to a former route of his through the Hisho valley to Hsining (Sining-fu), from which place he made for Lasar (Kunbum), where the Jesuit missionaries had remained so long, and where there were exceptionally good opportunities for making preparations for the journey onward into Tibet. So far Rockhill only confirms the Abbé's story. So far there appears to be no essential difficulty about this Chinese frontier route from Pekin. It is Tibetan altitudes which form the real obstacle to communication with Lhasa. Before starting on the difficult and dangerous quest of Lhasa, Rockhill (like Prjevalski) crossed the Nan Shan range and visited the valley of the Hoang Ho, or Yellow River, which at this point is barely fifty miles south of the Koko Nor. Here he made an interesting discovery. He found a colony of Kargan Tibetans who had mostly become converted to Islam by the contiguity of a tribe of Salar Turkmans who had no written tradition of their migration into China, but maintained that their advent dated from about the middle of the fourteenth century.

There are some forty thousand of them at present, and they live distinctly cleaner and more enterprising lives than their Buddhist compatriots. South of the river the mountains were covered with a forest growth of pines, juniper, birch, and cypress, and here was an agricultural Tibetan people (Rongwa), living in log cabins surrounded with cultivated patches in the midst of the forest clearings. They irrigated their fields much after Swiss fashion by means of troughs made out of pine logs, and turned their prayer wheels by an ingenious application of heated air from the cooking stove. They were chiefly of the Binbo religion, and offerings to their great god Shenrab were generally to be found in one corner or another of their dwellings. Over the flat-roofed houses, "tied to long poles, white flags wave, printed with prayers and charms to ward off danger; and below the house, in a log hutch built over the brook, a big prayer barrel is kept turning ever by the water as it dashes by."

It was not till the middle of March that Rockhill's preparations were complete for his journey southward. The springtime of the year is certainly better for travel over such vast altitudes as are presented by Central Tibet than the winter months, when the Jesuit missionaries made their venture in company with the Pekin ambassador's suite and his escort. But the snow time is usually in the early spring, just as it is in the Himalayas, or in eastern Tibet between Lhasa and the Chinese frontier at Ta-chien-lu. From midsummer to late autumn the best opportunities occur for travel between the Pamirs and China. To one item of equipment for his venture Rockhill failed to give proper attention, — viz., shoes for the baggage animals, and he was severely handicapped in consequence. Not a remnant of his transport reached the journey's end.

Once more crossing the Koko Nor range, Rockhill struck almost due west across the basin of the Wayen (Baian). The country is an "undulating plateau, bounded by low hills running east and west. To the southwest, in the direction of the Yellow River, we could see, a hundred miles away, snow-clad peaks rising above the bare reddish maze of the mountains. Not a tree, not a shrub anywhere; here and there a black tent and a little flock of sheep huddling together to escape the fierce, incessant west wind. This is the country of the Panaka or Panakasum, who, coming from the south of the Yellow River, have within the last fifty years dispossessed the Mongol owners of the land, driving them back towards the bogs and desert wastes of the Tsaidam. It is a magnificent pasture land, but poorly watered except at the foot of the mountains." "From the Wayan Nor we could see the mountains which mark the famous Gork gold-fields, from which the Yellow River and the 'Three days' desert' separated us. Discovered in 1888, they yielded to the Chinese who flocked to them over ten thousand ounces of gold in less than two years; but now they are abandoned, the primitive methods of the gold washers being only remunerative with the richest gravel." Passing through the valley of the Huyuyang River (which may possibly be an affluent of the Hoang Ho), Rockhill struck southwest for the Wahon La Pass, over the mountains separating the basin of the Huyuyang from the Tsaidam basin. This (late in March) proved to be an exceptionally difficult snow-covered pass. It was apparently not the same as that crossed by Huc's company, who took a more northerly route from the Koko Nor into Tsaidam. Both authorities agree about the richness of the pasturage found in the undulating uplands south of Koko Nor and east of Tsaidam.

From the Wahon La he dropped into an affluent of the Yellow River called Tsahan Ossu, which flows "through the mountains from Tsaidam on the northeast." Four days' march along this valley brought him to the head of a small southern feeder of the Tsahan Ossu, and he mentions a pass (Koko-Kutul — it is strange to find the Persian word "Kutul" or "Kotal" so far east) where were cedars and junipers and a fine grass valley. He remained in the valley of the Baian Gol, at Shang, till the end of April, before resuming his journey to Tsaidam. Shang is not far from the spot where Huc crossed the Baian Gol, before ascending the Burkhan Buddha range.

Once in the Tsaidam basin Rockhill continued to follow the northern flank of the mountains which are known under various local names (Burkhan Buddha, Ho Shili, Tokai, etc.), but which form the northern ridge of the Kuen Lun extension eastward. He crossed the routes of Huc and Prjevalski, where they strike southwards over these mountains, taking a more westerly pass, which followed the Naichi Gol.

He reached the Naichi Gol on the 11th of May, after a horrible journey through the morass and shifting sands which flank the mountains (where, however, he found excellent grass), and made his final dispositions for entering Tibet. The Naichi Gol turns the western flank of the Burkhan Buddha and Shuga ranges (which unite a little to the east of it), and this certainly would appear to present an easier route than that of the pilgrims' highroad to Lhasa, which negotiates both these ranges at points of formidable altitudes, but which, on the other hand, avoids the terrible Tsaidam swamps. Rockhill crossed the range at the head of the Naichi Gol some thirty miles west of Prjevalski's and Carey's route, and from this point across the intervening lateral valley to the Koko Shili range; across the next lateral valley to the Dungbure range; and again from the Dungbure range over the elevated steppes of the upper Yang tsi (Mur ussu or Di chu) to within sight of the Tangla upheaval. Rockhill was not far west of the routes of Prjevalski, Carey, Sven Hedin, or of the pilgrims of Huc's adventures, whose route was, and is, the recognised highroad to Lhasa. Once south of the mountain system which represents the Kuen Lun extension, the successive ranges encountered on the route southward, *i. e.*, the Koko Shili, the Dungbure, and other lateral ranges running more or less east and west between the Kuen

Lun extension (represented by Huc's Burkham Bola and Shuga ranges) and the great Tangla upland, are but natural divisions between the various affluents of the upper Yang tsi. This is the great feeding-ground of the Yang tsi, which, taking its rise so far west and flowing southeast, still leaves room to the east of its sources for those of the Yellow River, which are shut off from it by the Baian Kara ula range, and which also start on their way to the southeast. The Baian Kara ula gradually merges into a wild mass of inaccessible and untraversable mountains dividing the two rivers so effectually that they never approach each other again between the highlands of Tibet and the Pacific Ocean. All this region, including the Tangla Upland, represent the great transverse water parting of Tibet, dividing the eastern region of great rivers from the central region of inland lakes, and connecting the Kuen Lun on the north with southern Tibet (or the valley of the Brahmaputra) on the south. Apart from its altitude, its wild desolation, and its inhospitable character, it does not appear to present great physical difficulties to travel. Travellers have crossed it (or rather followed its strike) where they will, and have always crossed it successfully. They have rarely trodden in each other's footsteps, nor accepted the verdict of the inhabitants as to the most practicable highroad to Lhasa. The physical obstacles of the route have never barred the way to Lhasa.

Rockhill's experiences in the month of June were not very dissimilar to those of Huc in December.

"Grazing was better here than in the north, but the weather was bad, the wind so violent, the snowstorms so frequent and severe, that we could make but little headway." "Throughout the journey across this high plateau I was surprised to find so few snowpeaks. No chain except the Dangla rose much above the snow line, which my observations fixed at about seventeen thousand feet above sea level, nor do I believe that I saw on the whole journey through Tibet a single glacier, though there was much nevé on the Dangla and other chains further south." About the head of the Mur ussu (*the* river) the country was mostly of limestone formation, the grazing good, and game plentiful. There were even primroses here and there. "Until we reached the tents of the Namru Tibetans in July, it changed in no appreciable way. The soil was sandy or alkaline, or limestone, or granitic formation, but for ever our route was over low hills or down broad valleys with just enough grass to keep our animals from dying, and fuel so scarce that we could barely find enough yak droppings to make our kettle boil." Keeping westerly along the base of the Dangla, Rockhill reached the great central plateau known as "Naktsang," and here he considered that he had reached the true boundaries of Tibet. North of this he calls the land a "no-man's land," the home of the Golok (Kolo of Huc) and kindred brigand tribes.

About two days' march north of the Tengri Nor Lake, and the same distance west of the Amdo tso, Rockhill's route southwards (and his provisions also) came to an end. He had been starving for two or three days when he first fell in with Tibetan tents and encountered signs of inhabited country. He was here clearly very close to Bonvalot's route from the north, if not actually on it; but he could get no farther south. By the same marvellous system of intelligence which invariably keeps the Lhasa officials well informed of the approach of travellers from the north, and which frustrated the intentions of Bonvalot, Littledale, Sven Hedin, and others, the movements of the American had all been recorded, and there was a guard on the northern passes awaiting his arrival. The usual negotiations with obstinate Tibetan officials ended in the usual way. Rockhill was told to go back on his own footsteps and retrace his way to the north. The utmost concession that he was able to obtain was permission to work his way out of Tibet eastwards instead of northwards, and to make his exit by the better known trade route of Chiamdo and Ta-chien-lu. This, however, from the geographical point of view, was not altogether a disadvantage. We know pretty well what lay between Rockhill and Lhasa, and we are by no means without good records of Lhasa itself, but we knew nothing of that province which appears to be under special Chinese jurisdiction, called Jyade, and we should have continued to know nothing but for Rockhill's detour through it on the way to China.

First striking northeast back again towards the Dangla (or Tangla), he turned southeast from the foot of those uplands, and followed the main valley of the

Giama Nu Chu (Salwin) basin, by a route running north of that river, through a rough and mountainous country, till he reached eastward the meridian of 96° E. L. He then crossed from the upper Salwin basin into that of the Nam chu (or upper Mekong) by a track which appears to be the main trade route from Lhasa followed by Huc, and which joins Rockhill's route in the upper Salwin valley, and so reached the neighbourhood of Chiamdo on the upper Mekong. He did not see Chiamdo, — he was held off by officious local magistrates and compelled to pursue his journey to the Tibetan frontier at Ta-chien-lu by the regular Lhasa route, the road which possesses Chinese posts and rest houses at intervals. Whilst in Namru discussing future movements with the Lhasa authorities he was well treated. "I had been supplied daily with every delicacy of the Tibetan cuisine — sour milk, clotted cream, tsamba, mutton, and buttered tea — which our long fast prevented us for days from enjoying; and the Deba had made me many presents, amongst others a good saddle pony; and now I left with an escort of ten soldiers, resplendent in purple gowns, high, wide-brimmed, summer hats, and all their many silver-mounted arms and accoutrements." The incessant rain (July) acting on soft gravelly soil and bog rendered all the first part of their journey distressingly uncomfortable and difficult, and solid ground was not met with till the party crossed the regular Lhasa route from Kunbum (which was followed by Huc) near Nagchuka. Rockhill's Tibetan escort had returned to

Lhasa, as he was now under direct Chinese jurisdiction in the province of Jyade. This Chinese province extends from east to west over two hundred miles and more of country, "with a probable breadth of sixty or seventy miles, touching, to the north, the Dangla and its eastern branches, and, to the south, bordering on Lhasa governed provinces." "Its people have from the oldest times preferred the Binbo religion (a form of devil worship or Shamanism which has at one time or another prevailed over most of Asia), — a creed not tolerated in the kingdom of Lhasa, which tried for a long time to crush it out of these regions." The incessant warfare between the two ended in the formation of a special province by the Chinese, which included all the Binbo principalities. Thirty-six chiefs are appointed by the Chinese Amban at Lhasa, and they govern the various clans under their own hereditary chiefs. Jyade is all pasture land (13,500 feet), and the people, though poor, are a happy-hearted race. Binbo lamaserais are neither large nor numerous, and the lamas of this faith are liberal in their views. Rockhill says that the importance of this form of lamaism has not been hitherto suspected. All along the eastern borderland of Tibet, in Jyade, and in all the southern provinces of Tibet, not under the direct rule of Lhasa, its lamaserais may be found. So it seems that this faith obtains in two-thirds of Tibet, and that it is popular with at least a fifth of the Tibetan-speaking tribes. "In dress and in their mode of living the Jyade differ in no appreciable way from most of the Tibetan tribes leading a semi-pastoral life." "The clothes of both sexes consist in a single gown with a high collar; in winter of sheepskin, in summer of "pulo" (native cloth); violet for the men, blue for the women. Sometimes they also wear a light shirt of silk (buré) with a high red collar. Boots with cloth tops fastened below the knee by broad garters complete this picturesque though rather clumsy dress. The women wear their hair in a great number of little plaits, falling over the shoulders like a cloak and reaching below the waist. Down the middle of the back is fixed a broad band of red, green, and other coloured stuffs, on which they sew any ornamental knick-knack they may own." So far-reaching is fashion in the Asiatic highlands that women may be seen very similarly dressed sitting in rows at the annual fair at Sipi, near Simla, waiting for matrimonial engagements. Their clumsy ornaments of silver and turquoise are a source of much competition amongst the smarter ladies of Simla society. The valley of the Upper Salwin was "fairly well peopled. We passed, every mile or two, clusters of tents, near which were herds of Yak and little flocks of sheep and goats." Here, on August 18th, at a village on the Zechu (one of the northern affluents of the upper Salwin), Rockhill found himself to be on Bower's route by the unmistakable evidence of a receipt for forage which had been given to the head man of the village by that traveller on December, 1891. Here, too, Rockhill gathered some interesting information about the wild country immediately to the south, lying between the upper Salwin and the Brahmaputra, near its bend. Poyul is an absolutely unexplored part of Tibet, yet it appears to be one of the richest. The mountains of northern Poyul are inhabited by a lawless race of herdsmen, but southern Poyul is said to be warm and fertile, and to offer such attractions that a number of Chinese soldiers deserted to this district in former times and settled there, with the result that there is now a thriving trade in blankets, baskets, silver and ironwork, red pepper, and remarkably fine wheat flour. As will be seen from more modern reports, there can be little doubt that the basin of the Brahmaputra about its great bend southward from Tibet is full of most promising country. Poyul is practically independent.

As the elevation of the upper Salwin (the Giama Nu Chu) lowered, the scenery changed from Tibetan to Himalayan, and gradually became strikingly beautiful. Crossing into the Tsechu valley (an affluent of the Salwin), Rockhill reached Riwoche, with its beautiful temple and "picturesque situation, at the foot of steep forest-covered mountains, between which winds the broad, swift river, here spanned by a substantial bridge of huge pine logs," and in two days more (August 24) reached a Chinese post station. Avoiding Chiamdo (under compulsion), he followed the Chinese trade route to Batang; at first over steep and high mountains, then down a "valley covered with most beautiful pine-trees, their branches draped in long cobweb-like moss of light yellow and bright orange;" with pheasants in the underwood, and bears, leopards, and wolves in the forests above; following next a valley of great beauty, in which "I found nearly every variety of tree and wild fruit known to Tibet, — cedars, junipers, cypress, pines, and maples, plum and apple trees, cherry and apricot, raspberries, both the orange and red varieties, strawberries, and currants." This part of the journey was full of Himalayan characteristics. At Batang Rockhill found but little trade, — only two small Chinese firms doing business. The bulk of the trade is in the Lamas' hands, who prefer the pawnbroker's business and lend money to the Chinese soldiers. This is exactly what Bower says of them. He learnt with astonishment that the bulk of the Lhasa-Chinese trade from Ta-chien-lu followed the route through Horba and Darge countries, which he had explored in 1889, instead of the more direct Chiamdo road; but it appears that there were serious war operations in progress at Litang (between Batang and Ta-chien-lu) which might have diverted the trade for a time. The northern route, however, possesses material advantages over the Chinese post road in spite of its circuitous character. The latter first rises from Ta-chien-lu (8,300 feet) over the divide separating the Ssechu from the Nagchu (14,700 feet), then drops to Nagchuka (8,400 feet), next rises to the Litang uplands (13,400 feet), drops to Batang (8,150) on the Di chu, crosses the divide (about 14,000 feet) into the valley of the Chiamdo

(Nam chu, or Mekong), which it ascends to Chiamdo, and then, rising and falling over many successive ridges and spurs (described subsequently in Huc's narrative), it reaches Lhasa by a comparatively straight route, south of that taken by Rockhill through Jayade. This is the Jung-lam, or official road, from Lhasa to China, along which Chinese posts are maintained at intervals. It is said to be about nine hundred and fifty miles long, but it is probably more. The former (or Chang lam) also passes by the valley of the Di chu, but it strikes off to the north-west from Ta-chien-lu, and following up a succession of valleys (trending from N. W. to S. E.), it clearly involves gradients of much less severity before it finally drops into the Di chu valley in the district of Darge, at least three hundred miles above Batang. Darge is reputed to be one of the richest and most populous valleys in all Tibet, containing towns where all the best jewellery, saddlery, guns, and swords are manufactured. Passing through the important centre of Jyekundo, the Chang lam turns westward across the Chang tang highlands for three hundred miles, till it strikes into the southern pilgrim route from Koko Nor followed by Huc. Very little is known about this part of the route. Jyekundo has been visited by several travellers from the north (including Rock-hill and Miss Taylor), and it was near Jyekundo that the luckless De Rhins was murdered; but between Jyekundo and the pilgrim route is an unexplored section of the Hor country, from which innumerable tributaries of the great rivers (the Yellow River, the Yang tsi, the Mekong, and Salwin) take their rise. Its altitude cannot be much less than that of the Tangla, farther west. It is said that official obstructions to trade are less heavy by this route, and that there is good pasturage throughout, but the fact that such a detour northwards should be preferred to the Junglam says much for the difficult character of the latter.

CHAPTER X

Huc and Gabet on the Post Road to China and in Eastern Tibet — Approaches to the East from the Koko Nor and its Geographical Connection with Assam — De Rhins and Grenard — Needham and Krishna — The Brahmaputra Valley and the Passes through Bhutan — Kinthup's Explorations and Reports — The Methods of Native Explorers — — Chandra Das — Nain Sing's Early Journeys

FOR an account in detail of the official road (the Junglam) between Lhasa and the Chinese frontier at Ta-chien-lu, we are still dependent on the Abbé Huc if we wish for European authority. The Abbé left Lhasa under compulsion, but it was a retreat with honour, and a very different experience from that of his northern travels. He had no tent to pitch, no baggage animals to tend and guard, — no difficulty but that of keeping on good terms with his fellow-travellers. Chief of the party was a Chinese mandarin of great magnificence, haughty and insolent in the presence of Tibetans, but most insignificant when faced with an official superior, who was entitled " Pacification des royaumes." He had the good sense to look well after his European fellow-travellers who had been specially confided to his care, and, on the whole, he fulfilled his trust satisfactorily.

Some of the most interesting pages of Huc's narrative deal with the manners of the Chinese in intercourse with the Tibetans, and the social spirit of fraternity which prevailed amongst the latter. The little touches of human sympathy, the humour and the shrewd perception which underlie the story told in the book, show the Abbé to have been a man of warm feelings and good heart, — one who thoroughly appreciated the value of good fellowship and mutual understanding between fellow-travellers of whatever degree. He only hardens when he has anything to say about England. The English were to him as to the Chinese, — "marine devils," capable of no good thing. From no other writer on Tibetan life do we get so much insight into Tibetan character and the mutual relations between themselves and their conquerors. The rest of the company was composed of escort, and returning traders taking advantage of the official journey to China; with them all the missionaries were on equally good terms.

The river of Lhasa, the Kyichu, flows from the east and the valley of it affords the best opportunity for a route eastward. For a couple of days travelling was easy and pleasant, following the well-cultivated riverain, but for the next five or six days Huc describes the Junglam as passing through a labyrinth of mountains. It then strikes the upper course of "the same" river (this is, I think, doubtful) as it turns north to avoid the bend of the Brahmaputra (Tsanpo), which here makes a loop northward ere finally sinking southeast to the head of the Assam valley.

The Junglam at this point cannot be more than fifty miles or so from the Brahmaputra, which would certainly appear to offer the greatest facilities for a road eastward, but which probably lies enclosed amongst a rugged wilderness of impassable mountains. Crossing the Loumma Ri Mountain (Gia la in Walker's map) by an easy pass which did not oblige them to dismount from their horses, they arrived at Chiamdo, which is described by Huc as a "vast agglomeration of houses," where were to be found Bhutanese traders and a fair surrounding of cultivation, with a wretchedly bad bridge over the local river. For the next four or five days they were wandering over apparently deserted mountains, but as the "oulah" (the enforced supply of baggage animals) was always forthcoming from stage to stage, Huc considers that there were populous villages concealed amongst the folds of the hills, which were not visible. Of a place which he calls Atdra (where there is a small lake) he records that this is the favourite haunt of the Tibetan "licorne" or unicorn, an animal in which, apparently, he possesses considerable faith. He gives it the local name of "serou," however, — a name which is well enough known in many parts of the Himalayas, and indicates a species of mountain goat (*Nemorhaedus bubalina*). It chiefly inhabits the precipitous wooded mountains of the central ranges of the Himalaya between Kashmir and Sikkim, and is always found in thick forests. It stands about three feet two inches in height, and weighs about two hundred pounds. The horns (two) are short, roundish, ringed more than half way, tapering, and curved backwards, with points inclining outwards, and measuring about ten inches. This generally answers to Huc's description of the "licorne," with the exception, of course, of the remarkable feature indicated by a single horn.

They crossed the watershed of Lha-ri (the "spirit" mountain, which can only be the Tola la of the Indian explorers, 17,400 feet) with some difficulty, owing to the depth of snow. The passage of it affords the Abbé an opportunity for some thrilling details. He was apparently much surprised to find a glacier on the northern flank of the mountain, at the foot of which was the town of Lha-ri. The travellers had no sooner accomplished the feat of crossing the pass of the great spirit mountain than they were faced with another pass, called by Huc Chor Koa la. This must be the Archa-La of Walker's map. However, it proved to be less formidable than the previous pass, but the general altitude of the route from this point was extremely great. There is a legend of a mutiny of Chinese troops at the top of the Archa-La, where they successfully threatened their officers with instant destruction unless they were promised more pay. The legend, at any rate, indicates that it is over this most remarkable military route that the Chinese armies have passed to and fro. Probably there is no other military route in the world to compare to it for altitude. The passage of the Alps by Napoleon, or of the Andes by San Martin, was child's play compared to it. For some days they followed a comparatively level road over these huge elevations (which almost overlook the valley of the Brahmaputra) until the descent into the valley of a southerly affluent of the Giama Nu Chu was before them. The horrors of this descent seem to have impressed the pious missionary more than any which preceded it. He dare not dismount, so "nous recommandâmes notre âmes à Dieu," and feeling "une sueur glacée ruisseler de tous nos membres," arrived at the bottom safely, without, apparently, the loss of a single baggage animal. From Alan-to (? Alachiago), at the foot of the pass, to the village of Lang-tsi-Koung was but a day's march over the slopes of a pine-clad valley. There they were face to face with a new peril. The passage of the Tanda watershed was before them, and it was pronounced by experts to be impassable from the depth of snow which covered it. Huc would have been very well content to remain where he was in the town of Lang-tsi-Koung, where the quaintness of the habitations, and of the people interested him greatly. He could occupy himself with "prayers, chess, and promenade." But an official mission to China was not to be delayed by such a trifle as snow. Spring was now well advanced; Lhasa had been left in March amidst the usual spring downpour, and probably the dreaded Tanda was about as deep under snow as it could well be at any time of the year. A month or so of delay would have improved their prospects of crossing. The Tanda is probably the pass entered in Walker's map as Nub Gang La, the second name being derived from the explorations of native surveyors.

However, by making use of the yaks to force a passage through the snow for three days previous to their start, the mission accomplished the passage of the pass without any greater difficulty than was caused by its formidable altitude. We have no authentic data for its height, but it is probably not less than seventeen thousand feet. Between the Tanda pass and the Chinese post of Barilang the route runs through a plain of sufficient magnitude to be called locally the "widest in Tibet." There was, however, yet another pass to be surmounted, which Huc calls the Dchak-La. It did not prove to be formidable, and probably only crossed a southern spur flanking the Giama Nu Chu, which valley the party was now following. The road was now fairly good as far as Chobando (Shobando of Walker's map). Two long and difficult days' journey from Shobando brought them to the banks of the Suk-chu (? Giama Nu Chu — Salwin), which was crossed without accident in spite of the bridge having broken down. They were then confronted with the famous Wa-ho plateau, which, according to Walker, marks the divide between the Giama Nu Chu and an affluent of the same river from the north. On the summit of the Wa-ho is a lake, and by the borders of it dwells the spirit of the mountain in the form of a gigantic toad which is seldom seen but very frequently heard. Strict silence in crossing this plateau is enjoined. A word hastily spoken may bring destruction on travellers, who will instantly be engulfed in snow. Possibly there is something in the legend. It is a pass which is evidently dangerous from the presence of avalanches, and it is possible that (as the story states) the reverberation of a cannon-shot inadvertently fired might tend to loosen a hanging mass of snow, and bring it on to the heads of passers-by.

The dreary desolation of the snow-covered plateau is well described by Huc. There was not a tree, not the trace of animal existence, not a sign in all the whole expanse except the line of straight black poles set up to guide the traveller. Twenty hours of continuous marching on a clear bright day, without wind, brought them to the eastern foot of the plateau, and to the port of Ngenda-Tchai. Three "detestable" stages further, "penibles et irritantes," on account of numerous Tibetan bridges of frail construction, brought them to Chiamdo, "on the Kiang Tang Chu," where we can leave them, for the rest of the route has been described sufficiently. It is, however, clear that the last three days' march was along the course of a river, and that the Wa-ho was the last pass surmounted. This, however, creates a map difficulty, as it would indicate that the Wa-ho mountain, or plateau, divided the Giama-Nu Chu (Salwin) from the river of Chiamdo (which is the Mekong) and not from an affluent of its own (as indicated in Walker's map), which would involve another "divide" before reaching the Chiamdo valley. It is, however, to be noted that the lower course of this affluent and its junction with the main river is only shown in dotted lines. This means that it is doubtful. So it may possibly join the Mekong and not the Salwin. It is also to be noted that there is a pass called the Dja La (suspiciously like the Dchak La of Huc), marked in Walker's map far to the north of Shobando. It is impossible, however, to bring this pass within Huc's itinerary. It clearly belongs to a more northerly route.

Before parting with such an enterprising, devoted, entertaining, and (on the whole) truthful explorer as the Jesuit missionary, it is as well to reckon up what he has told us of the Junglam (the great official highroad between Lhasa and China), so far as that section of it is concerned which links Chiamdo with Lhasa. Huc makes the distance 750 miles. This is, of course, an exaggeration. Measured directly, it hardly amounts to 500, and by the same measurement the onward route to Ta-chien-lu amounts to another 400. Taking Walker's estimate of 930 miles (derived from the route reports of native surveyors) as fairly approximate for the total length of the Junglam from Lhasa to the Chinese frontier, it is probably about 550 miles in length, including all divergences. Huc describes at least six formidable passes, any one of which must be considerably higher than Mt. Blanc. Between Chiamdo and Ta-chien-lu there are at least five more of equal difficulty, besides a multitude of

Jules Leon Dutreuil De Rhins

local "divides" of a less formidable nature. By the light of such geographical evidence as this, added to the information which we possess of the wide wastes of inhospitable highland which prevail at intervals along the route, the extraordinary military feat of the conquest of Tibet by a force of seventy thousand Chinese in 1720 (a force which included guns) becomes little short of miraculous. No military march in history encountered such altitudes. The retreat of the Greeks under Xenophon from Persia; the advance of Alexander to India over the northern passes, and his subsequent retreat from India through the Makran defiles, are all marvellous records far surpassing those of modern times; but they will not bear examination when placed in comparison with this Chinese exploit. Even Mirza Haidar's extraordinary achievement when he advanced on Lhasa from the west, pales before it. It is true that the Chinese guns were made of leather, that they burst easily, and that they were more useful when applied as persuasives to the rear of the Chinese army than as destructives to the front of the foe; they were in fact archaic mountains guns; but that hardly detracts much from the astonishing feat of endurance, of resistless, patient determination which must have animated that Yellow Mongol host setting forth on its gigantic enterprise. It brings home to us a lesson in Mongol persistency which is useful. It explains something of the impetus which moved Mongol irruptions in the middle ages, and, at this late period of the world's history, it appears to be recrudescent in Japan.

Further than this, it brings a strong geographical light to bear on the political problems which beset Tibetan national existence. Bad as are the approaches to Lhasa from China on the east, and northeast, they are even surpassed in difficulties by those directly from the north, or from the west, as we shall see. It is only from the south — from Chumbi, and from India — that Lhasa is easily reachable. Only one formidable pass (the Tangla), which is high, bleak, windswept, and occasionally dangerous (but which is not steep), separates the Chumbi valley from the Tibetan highlands. Between the Tangla and Gyangtse, there is no formidable divide to cross, and the routes which we have already described, one of which was followed by the late mission to Lhasa, include two difficult passes only between Gyangtse and Lhasa.

Amongst those travellers who have contributed valuable additions to our knowledge of eastern Tibetan geography, the luckless Frenchman Dutreuil De Rhins takes a prominent place by reason of the excellent topography which, with the able assistance of M. Fernand Grenard, he was able to secure. The hurried journey of his compatriot Bonvalot, who was accompanied by Prince Henri d'Orléans, resulted in no very satisfactory additions to the map of Tibet. No persistent effort was made to secure good observations, or to keep a record such as would certainly indicate the direction of their route, or the precise position of their halting-places; but their success in crossing Tibet was undoubted, and it inspired De Rhins to attempt a similar enterprise. De Rhins and Grenard left Cherchen in Chinese Turkestan on the 1st of September, 1893, and struck across a new and unexplored pass through the Akka Tagh. Then commenced the dreary monotony of northern Tibetan travel through wide desolate valleys, with blue lakes scattered at intervals; across stormy uplands and rocky snow-bound passes with the same forbidding aspect of desolation, and the same eternal silence around them, that have left so deep an impression on the minds of all who have faced the desolation of the Chang wilderness. It is this monotonous tone of weary desolation which leaves so little to tell of the features of northern Tibet. For hundreds of miles there is no change, no life, no movement but for the furious rushing wind. The mournfulness and the melancholy of it seem to permeate the story of every explorer who writes. Three months of this uninviting experience brought the travellers to the Tengri Nor, and here they were but a week's march from Lhasa. After Bonvalot, they were the first Europeans to touch the shores of this lake since the days of Huc. Here the usual Lhasa deputation met them with the usual apologies and excuses for stopping their further route. There was no incivility. There was but the usual shifting of responsibility from the shoulders of the Chinese members of the mission to those of the "barbarous" Tibetans, and from the Tibetans back again to the obstructive and stiff-necked Chinese. Either Tibetan envoys or Chinese would have been equally delighted to welcome the foreigners at Lhasa, but for the impossible attitude assumed by the other, so they said. It was but a sample of Tibetan policy in larger matters than those affecting the progress of an exploring party. So they turned northward as Bower, Littledale, Rockhill, and Bonvalot had to turn, and set their faces for the Chinese frontier at Sining fu. As far as Nagchu they were but following the usual Mongol pilgrim and caravan route, which was traversed previously by Huc, although they separated and reached that point by different roads in order to embrace a wider field of observation. From Nagchu (which they reached on the 27th of January, 1894, and where they remained until early in March) they left the direct pilgrim road and struck into the northern trade route between Lhasa and Batang, eastward. This apparently was unintentional, for they subsequently made a long (and as it proved a fatal) detour in order to regain the direct road to Sining; but it was then that they made what was, from the geographical point of view, the most interesting discoveries of their journey. After crossing four most formidable ranges and losing the last of their camels in the snow-blocked passes, they reached the most southerly affluent of the Yang tsi kiang near its source. They were then in territory inhabited by Tibetans of the Bon religion, who were more or less hostile to the lamahood of Lhasa and professed themselves to be friendly to travellers on that account. On the 8th of April they crossed the Dzanag-lung-mung pass, and found themselves in the region of the sources of the

Mekong River, never previously explored. It was a great achievement, this determination of the sources of the great river of Siam, and it sent them on their way rejoicing in the assurance that they had made a new and important geographical discovery. Here they joined a small fraternity of lamas on their way to the Tashigompa monastery. This position is not fixed on our maps, but it is said to be fifteen days' march from the central town of Jyekundo. On the 16th of April they reached the monastery at the junction of the Lung-mung stream with the Dza-chu, where a fair was being held which had attracted great crowds from the surrounding country. After thoroughly exploring the Dza-chu affluent of the Mekong, they surmounted a dividing watershed (17,500 feet), and dropped into the valley of another affluent of the same river — the Dze-chu — and again devoted themselves to the examination of the river to a point where it divided the mountains by a terrific gorge, and could be no more followed. Once more resuming their route to Jyekundo they reached that large straggling village in the basin of the Di chu (Yang tsi kiang), on the 22d of May.

Here their troubles began. A turbulent and hostile population, lay and clerical, made themselves most objectionable to the French visitors. Stones were thrown about, and it was evident that nothing but the most tactful determination would prevent a tragedy. Rockhill had once been obliged to take a hurried departure from Jyekundo in the middle of the night, and it is clear the Jyekundo is a place to be avoided by those who wish to journey in peace through the heart of eastern Tibet. Unfortunately it is a most important centre for supplies and transport, and is not easily passed by. It is doubtful whether De Rhins possessed the requisite combination of tact and firmness which has carried other Tibetan explorers so far afield. It is true that he obtained all that was absolutely necessary to enable him to make a start northward for Sining, and that he succeeded in making one day's march from Jyekundo in safety. The dawn of next day heralded disaster. The rain poured down in torrents. The travellers lost their way, and finally hit off a wayside village named Thom Bundo, where they secured a very rough shelter under the roof of a surly Tibetan, who was at first but little inclined to receive them. On June 3 the weather cleared and a bright sunshine tempted them once again on to the rough and dangerous mountain paths which lead northward to the Chinese frontier. There had been trouble the previous day, owing to the theft of two of the baggage animals, and there were ominous signs of the coming tragedy in the air even before they started. It appears that the route ran for some distance, skirting the side of a stream on the opposite banks of which a straggling line of low-roofed houses and walls afforded cover for a flanking fire on the party as it advanced. It was not long before the shooting commenced. Tibetans are as a rule such amazingly bad marksmen that it can only be accounted as a most

N. M. Prjevalski

unlucky accident that De Rhins should have fallen a victim to them. He was severely wounded in the groin. Grenard's attempts to rescue him and to induce a parley with the Tibetans were fruitless. It was as much as he could do to save himself. He improvised a litter for De Rhins, but the instant the march was resumed the firing recommenced, and the baggage animals fell one by one before it. Grenard was himself struck down as the villagers rushed upon the party, but he was not injured, and he was able finally to reach the boundary of the Thom Bundo district, where his pursuers left him, content, apparently, with having ejected him. Luckily he had previously made friends with a Chinese government official in the neighbouring demesne of Labug Gompa, and with him he ultimately found refuge. From Labug he endeavoured to recover the body of his friend, together with some of his baggage and animals. But all demands were met with a flat refusal from the Thom Bundo villagers to surrender anything, and it was not till his cook turned up that he learnt that the end of the tragedy had been the casting of De Rhins' body into the Di-chu stream. So passed away one of the pluckiest of the many French explorers who have done so much to make Tibetan geography. Grenard returned to Europe with the results of the joint work of the expedition; and amongst the many additions to Tibetan topography which have been placed before the public none excel these French maps as specimens of effective cartography.

It was in northeastern Tibet in 1898 that the Dutch missionary Rijnhart met with a fate similar to that of De Rhins. This brave missionary conceived it possible to reach Lhasa with his wife and child from the Chinese frontier by passing east of the Koko Nor without any suitable escort. The little party did actually reach the Dza-chu affluent of the Mekong. Here it is believed that Rijnhart was murdered by nomads, from whom he requested food and assistance. At any rate, he never returned from their tents. His wife, who was a lady doctor, subsequently accomplished a march of three hundred and fifty miles to Ta-chien-lu, the frontier town of Sechuan, all alone, and finally wrote an interesting account of her travels. Expeditions of this nature, however, do not throw much new light on the geography of Tibet.

The scientific expeditions of the assistants of the great explorer Prjevalski, however, which were carried out after his death, notably those of Roborovski, have indeed added immense material value to our general knowledge of the topographical conformation, geology, botany, etc., of the northeastern frontier of the plateau. Russian explorers were, in fact, continuously busy along the Tibetan frontier between the years 1889 and 1894, but their explorations seldom overlapped the northern borderland southward. Prjevalski alone attempted to penetrate to Lhasa. The Koko Nor steppes, Tsaidam, and the ranges north and south of the great blue lake, have been most thoroughly mapped by Russian surveyors, and the Russian

Captain Kozlof

government undoubtedly possess accurate geographical maps of all these regions. This great no-man's land lying cornered between Mongolia, Tibet, and China possesses a future value in the political distribution of Asia which is neither overlooked nor underestimated by Russia. The record of Russian activity in eastern Tibet would not be complete without some reference to their latest efforts in the cause of geographical discovery which have recently led the gallant explorer Koslov to a point within measurable distance of the Assam frontier. Starting from Urga (from which place it will be remembered that the Dalai lama retired during the British occupation of Lhasa) he crossed the Mongolian steppes to Sining fu and the Koko Nor. Then, crossing the Koko Nor range by Wellby's route, he struck southward to the sources of the Hoang Ho and into the Darge valley (the valley of the Di chu). About the parallel of 32° north latitude he left the Di chu and crossed into the valley of the upper Mekong (Nam chu or Chiamdo chu) and thus opened up the direct route to Batang and the eastern Tibetan valleys generally, reaching the eastern edge of Brahmaputra basin at a point barely two hundred and fifty miles from the Assamese frontier. He must have touched the trade route between Lhasa and Ta-chien-lu. This appears to be the most southern exploration effected by any Russian explorer, but it is significant, indicating that it is the rich eastern and southeastern valleys of Tibet that are really the Russian objective, and that there is no great difficulty in reaching them from the Koko Nor. The Koko Nor region, at present regarded as an insignificant geographical feature — a sort of waste hinterland to Tibet proper — and the home of the worst robbers in Asia, will some day rise to importance as the subject of political controversy — is it Tibetan, or is it Mongolian?

We have enough before us in these records to indicate the general character of eastern Tibet, and to guide us to some conclusions as to the possible future development of those long curving valleys of the great rivers of China, Siam, and Burma, which constitute its main features. Undoubtedly much of the wealth of Tibet lies in them, — wealth which is not only represented by somewhat crude but original arts and manufactures, but by immense mineral value. The possibility of gold production will be dealt with elsewhere. Here we only wish to point out the bearing of the geographical features which we are considering on Tibetan policy. One important feature to note is that the geographical remoteness and inaccessibility of Lhasa is not repeated in the case of the towns and villages of eastern Tibet. There is no vast difficulty in approaching these eastern valleys from the Koko Nor region, itself closely adjoining the Kansu province of China. About the Sipan country, which embraces the sources of the Hoang Ho, we do not know very much; it appears to be a wild wilderness of mountains; but the route from the Koko Nor district to the head of the Hoang Ho and hence southward into the valley of Yang tsi (Di chu) about Jyekundo has been fre-

Rai Bahadur Kishen Singh, Milamwal. (Krishna)

quently traversed, and from Jyekundo at once the whole series of southeastern valleys, gradually stretching southwards, populated, rich, and often beautiful, is open to the explorer through Tibetan territory. Geographical difficulties no longer stand in the way. Eastern Tibet is accessible from the Koko Nor, and the Koko Nor is easily accessible from China, and (more remotely) from Manchuria. The occupation of Manchuria would give Russia a predominant influence over all western China, and would inevitably lead to the gradual absorption and occupation of that no-man's land in the northeast of Tibet which borders the Koko Nor.

The Koko Nor can be approached through Mongolia as readily as through China. Already Russian concessions are said to be granted in western China, — in Sechuan, — closely bordering Tibet; and Russian interest is undoubtedly much alive in that quarter. It seems probable therefore that political relations between Russia and Tibet would lead much more definitely to developments in the valleys of the East than to any direct commercial relations with Lhasa. Lhasa is out of reach from the north; but eastern Tibet is well within reach, and from the politico-geographical point of view there is a wide world of difference between them. Some 700 or 800 miles of difficult, yet traversable country separates the central villages of eastern Tibet from the Koko Nor pasture lands. And over this 700 or 800 miles the foot of the European has trod, if not frequently, at least sufficiently often to test the general character of the intervening highlands, and to prove the possibility of establishing a right of way. Only 200 or 300 miles (possibly less) separate British Indian territory from the lower reaches (and therefore the richer and more productive reaches) of these same valleys, and over that 200 miles no foot of European has ever trod at all. The valley of the main Brahmaputra stream leads directly up to that region of Poyul which is described by Rockhill as such a land of promise. The shorter valley of the Dihang taps the same country on the south. The Lohit stretches upward and eastward, pointing the direct route to Batang from the head of the Assam valley, and indicates the most direct route to Sechuan and the upper Yang tsi basin. Some of its shorter affluents drain Zayul and other valleys which lie east of the Brahmaputra bend and run parallel to it, about which we know only what native explorers have told us. This is all close to our frontier; but we have never properly exploited it, and it is not surprising that our enterprise, when balanced in the scale with that of Russia, should be found so wanting as to induce the theory amongst our frontier neighbours that we are afraid to venture. Possibly our improved relations with Tibet may lead to exploration of the Brahmaputra bend, but it must be remembered that, so far as the Assam borderland is concerned, the Lhasa hierarchy possesses very little influence in these eastern hills.

From such information as that enterprising traveller and Tibetan scholar, Colonel Waddell, has been able to obtain, it might appear that the actual valley of the Brahmaputra itself affords as little opportunity for road-making as do those of the Indus and Sutlej, where these rivers part the Himalayas to make their way to the plains of India. It may be interesting, therefore, to note what the experiences of our native explorers have been in these same districts, anticipating to a certain extent the record of their great achievements in southern Tibet. The explorer Krishna, whose marvellous adventures in Tibet and Mongolia would fill an entertaining volume of travel, and to whom we owe the only plan of the city of Lhasa which we possessed before the late mission reached that city, once traversed the highlands between Batang and a point on the Lohit River called Rima, which is about one hundred and fifty miles from Sadiya in upper Assam. An enterprising political officer (Mr. Needham) in the winter of 1885–86 explored the Lohit valley route as far as Rima in lower Zayul, and (with his companion Captain Molesworth and three policemen) is the only European who has penetrated far into the Mishmi country. Thus between Krishna and Needham we have the whole route illustrated from Assam to the Chinese frontier. Krishna was himself unable to reach Assam through the one hundred miles of intervening frontier hills from Rima. He was compelled to turn northwest from Rima, and has thus given us another instructive route running parallel to the Brahmaputra, on the eastern side of its southerly bend, and joining the official Junglam route at Shobando, about which place we have heard from Huc. Needham's journey was most adventurous, and fully illustrates the extreme hostility of those tribes which are more immediately contiguous to our own frontier. It is not amongst the more remote peoples, but amongst those who have the most constant and direct communication with us, who trade daily across our borders and know well their own way into British territory, that hostility mostly lies. It is precisely the same thing on the northwestern border, where the Ghilzai povindah, who trades through the passes into India, and traverses the peninsula through the length and breadth of it, is precisely the most determined opponent to any reciprocal movement from the side of India into his own country. Krishna was afraid to venture alone through the Mishmi band of hills, although he was within a week of Assam and had already spent three years of travel in the northern countries. He preferred to go round by Lhasa. However, his route report from Ta-chien-lu and Batang to Rima is most instructive. Between Ta-chien-lu (which he reached from the north by Rockhill's route from Jyekundo through Darge) and Batang he was on the regular post road, and his route survey sufficiently illustrates its difficult character. He followed this road to the crossing of the Chiamdo (Mekong) River, and then struck southwards through Dayul to the next great river, the Giama Nu Chu or Salwin. Crossing by a rope bridge (7,160 feet above sea) he then zigzagged his way, first up a small affluent of the Giama Nu Chu, over a divide by the Tila pass (16,100 feet), and finally down an affluent of the Zayul or Lohit, till he reached Rima without much difficulty. We thus possess the certain information that between the head of the Assam valley and the Salwin there is but one pass (16,100 feet); another between the Salwin and Mekong, which is probably about the same height; and a third between the Mekong and the Chinese post road near Batang, which is certainly lower. The route is full of villages and population. The valleys are narrow but well cultivated, bridges are maintained at intervals across the rivers, and the whole route passes through a fairly prosperous country. Not less remarkable is the result of his journey northwest from Rima to the post road at Shobando. Here we have the same evidences of great prosperity and agricultural wealth extending first up a subsidiary valley of the Lohit, and then along a line of high elevation crossing the upper spurs of the formidable snowy range which here forms the backbone of the Himalayas enclosing the Brahmaputra basin. This main water-shed dividing the Lohit from the Giama Nu Chu is crossed by a pass about sixteen thousand feet high. The passes which are involved by crossing successive spurs of the snowy range as the route keeps high up the mountain side till it reaches Shobando are about six in number, but probably not very much above the general altitude of the route.

There are in the world of geography certain links between well known and much traversed systems of communication as yet unopened, and even unexplored, which in the course of time, as the commercial world develops and the necessities of international communication become too pressing to be longer set aside in favour of political inaction, will inevitably become links in the world's highways. One such certainly appears to exist at the present time in the Dihong, or Brahmaputra, valley, which links together two great commercial highways, *i. e.*, the Tsanpo, or upper Brahmaputra, and Assam, or lower Brahmaputra. It is only lately (comparatively lately) that it has been proved that the two valleys contain sections of one and the same river, and the record of how this fact was ascertained is certainly one of the most interesting in geographical story. The Tsanpo has been followed down from its source eastward through the central valley of southern Tibet by various explorers of the Indian survey, although I do not know that any European has actually followed its banks to the point where it first loops itself northward and then strikes south through the mountains to the head of the Assam valley. Some forty miles to the southeast of Lhasa there stands the great Samye monastery, near the river, and the road thereto is a much traversed route. Ten miles further is a ferry across the river near the town of Chetang, at eleven thousand five hundred feet above sea level. Chetang is important, for there is a trade route due southward from Chetang across eastern Bhutan to Tawang (a frontier market town not far from the Assam border) which might appear to be a most convenient route for reaching India. It is not so, however. Between Chetang and Tawang are at least four considerable passes. and Tawang itself is one of those trade marts which it is impossible to reach from India on account of the fierce hostility of its barbarous guardians. I have already told how Krishna, in descending from the Zayul country down the Lohit River, encountered obstacles at Rima near the Indian border, which prevented him from reaching Assam by that route, and turned him back to Lhasa. Tawang is much nearer to India than is Rima, but it is equally impossible to the ordinary traveller. A third trade market of much more geographical significance than either Tawang in southern Bhutan, or Rima in the Mishmi country, is Miri Padam, in the hills of the Abor tribe. Miri Padam is actually within two days' reach of the Assam valley,—thirty-five miles fairly easy route. It is near, if not on, the Brahmaputra River. It is a central market town for dealers from the northwest, northeast, and south, and yet it is even more unreachable than either Tawang or Rima. The old pundit Nain Sing traversed the route between Tawang and Assam. The plucky political officer Needham reached Rima at the risk of his life, but no explorer, either native or European, has ever crossed that thirty-five miles of intervening hills which part Miri Padam from the Assam frontier. Miri Padam is the key to the whole valley of the Brahmaputra from its great bend in meridian 94 east longitude to its debouchment into Assam. Between Chetang, on the Tsanpo, fifty miles southeast of Lhasa, and Miri Padam, we know all about the river, although we have no exacter survey of it than could be made under most difficult circumstances by one of the native employees of the Indian survey. His tale belongs rightly to the chapter on Indian exploration in Tibet; but as we are dealing now with eastern Tibet and the ways thither, we must include this (the probable highway of the future) amongst them. It is certainly a remarkable testimony to the extreme caution with which the Indian government approaches any question of transfrontier exploitation that through all the years of our occupation of Assam no determined effort should have been made to place the independent tribes people of the Assam border in a position which admitted our right to visit their country as equal to their own right to visit ours for purposes of trade. Russian officers are rather fond of saying that were England in Russia's place she would have had a warm weather port for her navy a century ago. It is probably true; but it is certainly equally true that had Russia been in England's position in India, there would have been a right of way, if not a railway, up the Brahmaputra valley long ere this.

K.P. (or Kinthup) was a native of Sikkim, who had been trained in the Indian survey department as an explorer, and who had already done a good deal of useful work for his government, when he was selected in 1880 by Captain Harman, R.E. (one of the foremost of Indian frontier geographers) to accompany a Chinese lama into Tibet, and make his way from Lhasa to the Brahmaputra bend, with the object of dropping certain marked logs of wood into the stream, which Harman himself was to watch for as they drifted into the Assamese plains. Had K.P. been instructed in the history of the Abbé Huc's travels, and studied the opinions of that worthy Jesuit, he would never have trusted a Chinese lama, and it was certainly a doubtful policy on the part of the survey authorities to have made such a selection for their trusted agent. The lama and K.P. made their way to Lhasa by the ordinary route, and then visited the Samye monastery and Chetang. From Chetang they followed more or less the footsteps of previous explorers along the river banks to the point (Gyala Sindong) where the Brahmaputra has already been turned from a northeasterly into a southeasterly channel. So far no great difficulties present themselves. The river bends and slides first eastward and then northeastward; and there are villages and "Jongs" at intervals, with fairly wide spaces for cultivation. The greater part of this route is on the southern, or right, bank of the river. With the bend, however, there comes a narrowing of the valley, caused by the enclosing mountains; these grip the river some five-and-twenty miles below the bend, and produce a series of rapids and falls. It is, however, possible to follow the left bank of the river pretty closely to a point about five miles above the principal fall (Sindi Chogyal), whilst from a point two miles below them there is a well-trodden route passing from village to village to the market town of Miri Padam. On the right, or southern, bank of the river there are also tracks, some following the river pretty closely through a series of large villages, of which one, Pema Koichung, just above the falls, is the capital of the district, and others striking inland to hill settlements and monasteries. But on the right bank there appears to be no practicable route past the falls any more than on the left. The road on the left crosses to the right bank by a bridge below the falls, and from that point it runs through cultivation and villages at intervals for at least another forty miles. But we have no record of its further connection with Miri Padam, which is approached apparently from the right bank only. Kinthup's description of the valley, its cultivation (which included rice, cotton, and fruit), its monasteries and sacred places, and the wild and savage people inhabiting the Abor country, is deeply interesting. The roads are apparently such as are to be found throughout Bhutan, or the eastern Himalayas, — mere tracks rising over successive spurs, and dropping again into the flats on the river border, precisely as do the majority of native tracks in all mountain regions. The region of the falls below Gyala Sindong appears to present the chief break in their continuity. The falls are very sacred, and the bourne of many a devout pilgrimage. Clouds of misty spray rise into the clear atmosphere above them, and it is said that a rainbow ever spans the valley. Those who have seen the valleys of Bhutan (the Tista and the Monás) can well imagine the wild magnificence of Brahmaputra valley scenery where the river rounds the Himalayas on the east. A dense sub-tropical jungle, rich with every variety of tree fern and bamboo, stretches up the hillsides to the limits of more open spacing, and a more stunted growth of rhododendron and oak. Towering above all are the eternal snows and the everlasting silence of the ice fields. But there is nothing formidable (so far as we can tell) in this route. The grades seem to be easy, and the villages on the flats have often a mile of valley between themselves and the stream. There are no high passes to surmount. It is a gradual rise from the plains of Assam (500 feet) to the highlands of Lhasa (11,600 feet), and in those good times when the last relics of savage barbarism shall give place to that interchange of commercial rights which is, after all, the best guarantee of international peace (a guarantee founded on mutual interest), it will be realised that this is the natural highway from India to Tibet and western China, and we shall have a Tibetan branch of the Assam railway, and a spacious hotel for sightseers and sportsmen at the falls. This prospect is not more visionary than twenty-five years ago was that of a modern hotel at the Victoria Falls of the Zambesi; or the splendid establishments which will soon overlook the falls of Iguazu on the Paraná, in South America. But the people of the Old World move slowly, and it may be long yet ere we can extend our route from India to the highlands of eastern Asia.

Meanwhile we have only to record our ignorance. Perhaps not one geographer in twenty has ever heard of this approach to Tibet, and even now we have no accurate survey of it. Kinthup could not make one for reasons which will be explained. I have said that the tightest place of all in the valley is undoubtedly that which narrows to the falls a few miles below Sindong. Beyond the monastery of Pema Koi Chung Kinthup and his companion could not proceed on the right bank, so they retraced their steps in order to strike the river on the left bank below the falls; a considerable detour had to be made, which passed through the provincial town of Tongjuk jong, some fifteen miles to the northeast of the point of the river bend. Here was a Jongpen, a Tibetan official of some dignity, and here was Kinthup sold (literally sold) by the Chinese lama, who returned to his own country, selling the Indian survey department at the same time as Kinthup.

On the 24th of May, 1881, the lama left Kinthup in this strange plight, and it was not till the 7th of March, 1882, that the latter succeeded in making his escape from domestic drudgery, which was little suited to his fancy. Constantly crossing and re-crossing the river, sometimes on one bank and sometimes on the other, the explorer (who had lost most of his instruments) continued his journey southward. Such bridges as exist are described as composed of a single rope with a loop suspended therefrom. The traveller who crosses hauls himself across whilst lying suspended in the loop with his legs twisted over the rope. It is a crude method, and with the exception of the late General Woodthorpe (who left no travelling artifice untried), I know of no European who has experimented with it. At a monastery (where "fifteen nuns and thirty priests were allowed to live together") Kinthup heard that he was being hunted by his former master, the Jongpen. He "ran to the monastery, and bowed thrice at the foot of the great lama, and told him all that had happened and the cause of his flight from the Jongpen." In reply the lama asked where he was going, and whether he had parents living. Kinthup said "he was on a pilgrimage, and had no parents. He begged the lama not to hand him over to his pursuers." The end of it all was that the lama paid fifty rupees for him and he was a slave once again. After four or five months, however, he obtained leave for a pilgrimage. About twelve miles down the river he hid his things (compass, etc., such as he had managed to retain) in the jungle, and then set about executing the commission which had been entrusted to him by Captain Harman, *i. e.*, the floating of logs down the stream. He prepared five hundred logs and hid them in a cave, carrying them there on his back, and returned to the lama at Marpung.

From Marpung, which is fifty miles below the Brahmaputra bend, Kinthup (on the plea of another pilgrimage) made a remarkable journey to Lhasa via

Tsari. Tsari is the chief town of a district south of the Brahmaputra and not far from Chetang on that river. It was important, because it proved that there is a direct route from the Brahmaputra valley at Marpung to Lhasa without following the river. He returned once more from Lhasa by another route. Following the China route to Giambo, he struck off southeast through the Kongbu valley (where he found a rich soil and big villages) to the Brahmaputra, and again made his way to his old friend the lama at Pema Koichen. For nearly a year more he continued in service, and was then set free by his master, who complimented him on his devoutness as a good pilgrim. Making his way to Bepung he found his logs, and at last started them floating down the stream; but alas, too late. The gallant Harman had died meanwhile (literally worn out by his own unresting energy), and the logs floated unmarked and unowned into the broad bosom of the great river of Assam. But the purpose they were to serve was attained in another way. With almost pathetic devotion to his work, the explorer turned southward to see if he could not reach India himself by the river route. All that we know of the valley has been gleaned from his remarkable experiences. He reached a place called Ohlet, not far from Miri Padam, and there his career was stopped by the obstinate and pigheaded persistence of local savage officials who allow no strange tracks to be made over their road to India. There was no special difficulty in reaching this point, but he was now beyond the indefinite boundary of Tibet, in the land of semi-naked savages, albeit these same savages knew very well how to trade with India. There is no open door where they are concerned. Just as Krishna had been turned back from Rima, so was Kinthup turned from Miri Padam. Once again had he to retrace his steps to Lhasa *en route* for Darjiling, where he finally arrived after further vicissitudes in November, 1884, — four years after he set out on his quest. This is but one instance out of many of the strange persistency with which the native explorer will stick to his work. Time is nothing to him, and the same characteristic of dogged obstinacy which distinguishes the Mongolian character in general, and the Tibetan in particular, has been turned to most excellent account by those who train explorers for Asiatic research in India. With the exception of the thirty-five miles or so intervening between Assam and the central mart (a very considerable one) of Miri Padam, the course of the Brahmaputra has been traced from its source to India, and as far as the great bend southwards it is known not to one but to several Indian surveyors. It is impossible to follow their experiences in detail. We can but take an instance or two here and there of the unravelment of some specially complicated geographical knot.

So far we have been dealing with eastern Tibet; we will now take a cursory glance at the course of those explorations beyond the Himalayas which occupied much of the latter end of the nineteenth century, and which have resulted in the map of Tibet as it is now presented to us. This map (usually attributed to General Walker, R. E., Surveyor-General of India) has been corrected up to 1899, and although far from perfect, there is very little indeed that could be added to it since that date. It will be apparent at a glance that we know a great deal more of southern Tibet (that part of Tibet which it is most useful that we should know) than we know of the central and northern Chang-tang. But the blank spaces of the map to a certain extent indicate blank spaces in nature. There is really little that is important that we can know about the northern Chang-tang. It is, in a sense, one of the best explored parts of Tibet. A whole company of distinguished European explorers (as will be hereafter narrated) have struck into that blank space from the west and the north, and one reason why it is not filled up with topographical details is the want of such details, at any rate the want of features sufficiently marked to render them important in a map on so small a scale.

On the other hand, in the south, where we find a fairly good show of topography, not a single European has ventured far since the days of Huc to the date of the Younghusband mission. The mapping, as we have it, is almost entirely the result of native exploration in geographical interests. About the middle of last century the work of trans-Himalayan exploration was taken seriously in hand. General Walker, Basevi, Montgomerie, Trotter, Tanner, Woodthorpe, and Harman are a few of the names of those who supported this work with all the scientific energy that a life of enterprise and devotion to geographical pursuits had fostered in them. When we read the marvellous records (till lately branded as "strictly confidential" by the government of India) of those patient, painstaking, unresting native explorers who had been trained to use certain simple instruments to perfection, we must always remember who was behind them. They were the agents, but theirs was not the plan. They form (together with another most useful band who have given us most of what we know of the northwestern frontier, and of the hinterland of India even to the border of Russia) a very remarkable group of Indian employees, — a staff of "intelligence" workmen such as probably no other country in the world possesses. They have been as useful in Africa almost as in Asia. Skilful, faithful, persistent, and *cheap*, there is nowhere that they will not venture, and no physical difficulty of mountain or desert that they will not face. Although northern Tibet and Mongolia have been traversed by some of them, — notably by Krishna, whose marvellous record of five years of adventure in these northern lands ere he descended into eastern Tibet is one continued story of persistent effort and final success (except that he was unable to bridge the short interval between Rima and Assam), inasmuch as he preserved his instruments and his records and produced a capital map of the route he followed, — still southern Tibet has been their special field of action, and it is to these men that we owed such knowledge of the Brahmaputra valley as we possessed before the late mission. No European has assisted them excepting so far as the surveyors of the Himalayas have fixed for them by triangulation a number of the remote peaks (even including points in the Kuen Lun north of Tibet) which have been their guiding points in the field, and references by means of which the final record of their own surveys has been pieced together. Various have been the artifices whereby these explorers have effected their purpose. Instruments have been concealed beneath the false bottoms of boxes containing merchandise and tea. Their daily records of distance and bearings have been written in verse, and recited as a Buddhist poem. Then clothes have been made useful by a dozen different devices, and in their hands these pious pilgrims have carried their Buddhist rosaries, counting their paces and dropping a bead as every one hundred or one thousand has been completed. For Himalayan work they have been mostly men of the hills, Gurkhas, Tibetans, lamas of Sikkim or Bhutan. Elsewhere on the frontiers of India they have been less of explorers and more of survey specialists, good topographers, drawn (often) from the ranks of the Indian army, but always specially adapted by their nationality for the region which they have been instructed to map. It is quite a mistake to suppose that we know nothing about Tibet and Lhasa. We knew almost as much as could be told by any traveller many years ago, and there is nothing new in some of the tales which we have recently heard. One excep-

Shigatze, from the Fort looking East

tion, however, must be made to the rule that natives who have visited Lhasa in our interests (and Lhasa has been visited countless times) are men of the hills. The exception is in favour of a Bengali babu,— Sarat Chandra Das,—who accompanied a Tibetan lama of the Indian Survey to Lhasa, and, being himself an advanced Tibetan scholar, a student of Buddhism, and a writer, has given us information which is of special value. But the Bengali was not a geographer. He has added nothing to our map knowledge of the country. He did not even know for certain by what pass he entered Tibet, till it was pointed out to him by Mr. Douglas Freshfield lately; and he cannot rank with the systematic explorers and map makers of the country. He is, however, a living witness to the fact that a certain amount of enterprise (combined with much learning) is to be found in the ranks of the Bengalis. As a rule, the best explorers have been men of action rather than of the pen. It has sometimes been difficult to extract information from them which, having been absorbed in the course of daily routine, does not appear to them to possess much significance. They cannot quite grasp the spirit of curiosity which prompts the European to seek after truth in such unlovely regions as lie north of the Himalayas or west of the Indian frontier.

To a certain extent it is necessary to associate the west of Tibet (the Indus districts adjoining Ladak) with the Brahmaputra valley, as much of the best exploration surveys have started from the west rather than from Himalayan stations.

One of the earliest was also one of the best, for it opened up to us a new era in trans-Himalayan knowledge. It revealed for the first time something of the nature of that central watershed which separates the rivers of the north, the upper Indus, and the upper Brahmaputra, from each other, or rather from the intervening lake land which gives birth to the Sutlej.

Pundit Nain Sing was a schoolmaster in Kumaou when he first mastered the rudiments of exploratory surveying, and no explorer who ever lived made better use of his knowledge. His first Tibetan venture was as early as 1865, and his point of departure was Khatmandu, the capital of Nepal. The frontier town of Nepal, on the direct route to Tibet, is Kirong, a town where there is always jealous guard kept on the Tibetan road by Chinese officials. The governor of Kirong detected weak points in the story told by the pundit, and absolutely declined to let him pass. Other routes across the Himalayas to the Manasarawar lakes were tried, and found to be impracticable. The pundit changed his disguise, — added a pigtail and adopted the role of a Ladaki, — and then made friends with a merchant who borrowed money of him and failed to keep his promise to see him across the border. But by luck the merchant's relations proved better men than the merchant himself. The pundit (Nain Sing, to call him by his right name) managed to persuade them that he was an honest trader, and escaping the inquisitive scrutiny of the Governor of Kirong, he finally succeeded (in August, 1865) in crossing the boundary, and reached Tadam on the Brahmaputra. Tadam is a well known halting place on the great road (the same Junglam which we have followed east of Lhasa) between Ladak and China, where there is a great monastery. Here he feigned sickness, and stayed behind his party, for he was travelling in the wrong direction for Lhasa, and here he had the good luck to fall in with a *bona fide* Ladaki merchant from Kashmir, who took him with him eastwards to the town of Janglache. From this point to Shigatze (eighty-five miles) the great river is navigable for the Tibetan wicker-and-skin craft which they call boats, and it is usually by river rather than by road that this part of the journey is accomplished. This method of progression, however, would not suit a route survey, and Nain Sing stuck to the road. From the end of October to the 22d of December the party remained at Shigatze, where Nain Sing interviewed the Grand Lama of the Tashilunpo monastery, which lies about half a mile to the southwest of the city. It is worth recording that the Lama, in 1865, was a boy of eleven, who did not evince any extra intelligence. From Shigatze the Junglam ceases to follow the river, but runs south to Gyangtse, which place is therefore on the Chinese highroad.

In the middle of December they crossed the Kharola mountains and passed by the Yamdokcho (or Scorpion) Lake, where Nain Sing nearly finished his career at the hands of robbers. This was the first view that was ever obtained of the topography of that lake and its surroundings.[1] Nain Sing naturally, from his point of view, supported the Chinese legend of a large island in the centre, with hills rising to two thousand or three thousand feet above the lake level. We know now that it is not an island but a peninsula connected on the southwest of the lake with the mainland. For some years after Nain Sing's visit to Lhasa the theory of the central island was maintained, although Captain Montgomerie (Nain Sing's instructor) was always sceptical on the subject. Crossing the Khambalá mountain pass, Nain Sing descended rapidly into the valley of the Brahmaputra at Khambabarche. Thence by boat to Chusul village, and from Chusul, following the Kyichu, he reached Lhasa on the 10th of January, 1866. This first modern journey of a British subject to Lhasa was performed in the middle of winter, and it is remarkable in many ways. Nain Sing's description of Lhasa is full of interest, nor have any very essential additions ever been made to it by subsequent native visitors. At Lhasa, however, his disguise was penetrated by two Kashmiris, — who kept his secret well, — and he had the additional bad luck to encounter the Governor of Kirong. He was in great straits, too, for money, and altogether he was thankful when his merchant friends were ready to return to Ladak in April. They received him as a member of their company with much cordiality. The pundit was a favourite wherever he

[1] All this country has now been scientifically mapped by the surveyors of the late mission.

went. His popularity carried him far. In this instance he had his expenses paid over the return journey to Manasarawar (Darshan), where he encountered a friend who advanced him money. After some further adventures he recrossed the Himalayas by one of the western passes, and reached the headquarters of the Indian Survey in October, after an absence of eighteen months.

This journey was an invaluable incentive to enterprise on the part of later explorers. It opened out a possibility not only of reaching Tibet, but of mapping that country on scientific principles. It showed what was wanting in the technical arrangements for the work of an explorer, and led to new devices and new methods. Tibetans always make use of a rosary and a prayer-wheel (mani chuskor), which latter consists of a hollow cylindrical copper box, which revolves round a spindle, one end of which forms the handle. The cylinder is turned by means of a piece of copper attached to a string. A slight twist of the hand makes the cylinder revolve, and each revolution represents one repetition of the prayer (Om mane padme hum), which is written on a scroll inside, or engraved on the copper outside. It was clear that these ritualistic instruments might (with a little adaptation) be turned to useful account. The pundit carried both. His prayer-wheel had within it long strips of paper on which to record his bearings and distances, and the rosary was made up with one hundred beads (instead of one hundred and eight, which is the correct number), with each tenth bead a little larger than the others. The prayer-wheel was made to cover observations with the prismatic compass for bearings, whilst the rosary checked off the paces by hundreds as he went. Latitudes were taken with a sextant, and presented some difficulty. The artificial horizon was made with mercury placed in the ordinary wooden bowl, which every Tibetan carries. These bowls are made of very hard wood (not grown in Tibet), and sometimes are highly ornamented, and fetch large sums. The prayer-wheel was found to be exempt from examination by custom-house or other officials. This immunity led to the introduction of a special form of prayer-wheel (containing a compass) as an item of proper survey equipment under circumstances where prayer-wheels were recognised. There were gradually adopted other devices also, which all tended to simplify the work of the trans-Himalayan explorer, if not to aid his devotions. This first trip over the Tibetan border resulted in a route survey of twelve hundred miles, defining the mountain route from Khatmandu to Tadum, and the great China road from Gartok (on the Indus) to Lhasa, and fixing the course of the Brahmaputra from its source to its junction with the Kyichu. It is a notable record in the annals of Tibetan exploration, for the work done was excellent throughout. The subsequent survey by Major Ryder confirms its general accuracy.

The Southern Watershed of the Brahmaputra

On the Brahmaputra

CHAPTER XI

Nain Sing's Surveys in Southern Tibet — Krishna — Ugyen — The Explorer G. M. N. — The Gold Fields of Thok Jalung — The Source of the Indus and Brahmaputra

IT is often a little difficult to obtain a really graphic and intelligible account of the country explored from the native surveyors who explore it. They become so engrossed with the details of their work that they forget to use their eyes and make those general observations on the people and the scenery about them which is a most important objective of their journeyings. Nain Sing, however, is an exception to the general rule, and from him we have obtained a very fairly comprehensive view of the valley of the upper Brahmaputra and the great China road which follows it. As has already been pointed out, the Brahmaputra and the Indus start from nearly the same point, the intervening watershed between their sources being called the Mariám La, in about east longitude 82°, not very far east of the Manasarawar Lake. The great road from the crossing of the Mariám La does not closely follow the river at first, but is never more than ten miles or so north of it. The upper reaches of the river are hedged in on the south by a gigantic glacier-streaked range which for the first fifty miles of it evidently furnishes the chief water supply. All this upper part of the river (above the junction of the Charta Tsanpo) is known to the people of Nari and Ladak as Tamjan Khamba (horse's mouth), and the first point where road and river meet is at the Tamjan stage. Here, on 7th June, Nain Sing found the river was much swollen, its current rapid, and its waters turbid. The surroundings were wild and desolate. Only small patches of cultivation existed in the immediate neighbourhood of the successive stages. There is nothing attractive or promising about this part of the valley. Two or three great affluents swirl down from the central lake district on the north, between Tamjan and the Charta Tsanpo junction, which is eighty miles below the great Tadum monastery, a well known halting place on the river. All these northern tributaries bring down clear water with them, and some of them are of considerable size. For another hundred miles or so the road and the river separate, touching again near Janglache, a large market town 13,800 feet above sea. From Janglache to Shigatze (eighty miles) the river is navigable. Near Janglache (about twenty miles below it) an enormous tributary flows in from the north called Raka Tsanpo, which is not shown on the map, but of which the course has been traced for a considerable distance.[1] Judging from the great size of these northern tributaries, and the number of them, there certainly

[1] Major Ryder's survey shows this river to rise close to the Brahmaputra, and to flow for about a hundred and fifty miles parallel to it.

seems good reason for supposing that part of the central lake district lies within the Brahmaputra basin. There is no other way of accounting for their volume. The southern tributaries from the Himalayan glacier are comparatively insignificant. The Charta Tsanpo from the north, to which we have referred, was two hundred paces wide in the month of May, at which time of the year it was but very slightly frozen, with ice clinging to its edges. Nain Sing continued his survey by road from Janglache to Shigatze, crossing a fair-sized southern tributary. At Shigatze the river and road meet again. Here is the junction with the Nyangchu from Gyangtse, the river which has been followed by the late expedition from the Tibetan frontier to Gyangtse. As already explained, the post road leaves the river at Shigatze, passing southward through Gyangtse over the intervening mountains to Khambabarche, Chushul, and Lhasa. Between Shigatze and Khambabarche the Tibetans say that the river is too rapid for boats, and indeed navigation with Tibetan craft seems to be rather perilous anywhere. Captain Montgomerie reckons from Nain Sing's measurements that the Brahmaputra at Tadum [1] (just below the junction of its first great tributary) must be one half wider than the Ganges at Hardwar. The main river below this point is never fordable, nor are the tributaries from the north during summer. There is not a single wooden bridge over the upper Brahmaputra, and no twig, rope, or cane bridge either.

[1] Tradum in Ryder's map.

Iron suspension bridges have been made at Janglache and elsewhere, but they are all dangerous to use and the Tibetans prefer boats. Navigation at 13,500 feet above sea is unique, and must be regarded as a record for the world. Lake Titicaca, on the borders of Peru and Bolivia, which is systematically navigated, is only 12,500 feet above sea, but there navigation is well developed. Montgomerie, after a very careful estimate of the volume of the many affluents, and a comparison of Nain Sing's observations with those of Turner, reckons the discharge of the river just below its junction with the Lhasa River (Kyi-chu) to be about 35,000 cubic feet per second in the low season, or about seven times that of the Ganges at Hardwar (where the river leaves the Himalayas) under similar conditions. Practically, then, it is to Nain Sing that we must accord the credit of proving that the Brahmaputra of Tibet is the same river as the Brahmaputra of Assam, for no other river channel issuing southwards, to the east of the Himalayas, contains this amount of water. Taking it for all in all the valley of the Brahmaputra above Shigatze affords fairly easy opportunity for travelling between Kashmir and Lhasa. The great rolling stone-dusted plains, in which the road often loses itself, present no great physical obstacle. There are no passes east of the Mariám La till after passing Gyangtse; but there is a lamentable want of grass or forage for animals. There are a few large towns, about which a very fair spread of agriculture is maintained; but the large towns (strikingly picturesque, with dominat-

Alung Gangri Mountains

ing monasteries and white lines of stone-built dwellings climbing the slopes of hills) are at long intervals, and the ordinary post towns on the great trunk road are not equal to any greater demand than that of a passing caravan. Nevertheless a considerable amount of traffic yearly passes along that road, and it is one to be reckoned amongst the world's great trade highways. The altitude is nowhere excessive; it is often subject to unpleasant warmth as well as rigorous cold. We shall have to refer to Nain Sing's journeys again; but meanwhile it will be well to turn our attention to the western end of this China road (the Janglam) within that part of Tibet which is watered by the upper Indus, and which is not really of much less importance than is the long lateral valley of the Brahmaputra. Nearly coincident with the despatch of Nain Sing on the Brahmaputra quest was that of other explorers to the upper Indus, who left with instructions to seek out the source of the river, and to report on the gold mines. A glance at the map at once reveals the main features of southwestern Tibet.

From the remarkable hydrographic centre which is indicated by the Manasarawar lake system, and the great group of sacred peaks to the northwest dominated by Kailás, the Indus starts westward to Ladak; the Sutlej starts southwest to join the Indus in the plains of India; and one of the largest affluents of the Ganges starts southeastward for the Bay of Bengal. The bleak and desolate district of Nari Khorsum, through which flows the Sutlej, as well as the eastern branches of the Indus, were not known to us fifty years ago. The veteran explorer, Richard Strachey (afterwards president of the Royal Geographical Society), and his brother Henry were the first actually to demonstrate the physical characteristics of the country surrounding Manasarawar, although Moorcroft and Hydar Hearsey had crossed the Himalayas in 1812, whilst other surveyors (notably Godwin Austen) first approached the Tibetan frontier from the Kashmir dependency of Ladak, and, after fixing the position of the great Kailás with many other peaks to the north, mapped the region of the Pangong Lake on the Tibetan border. Traders passed to and fro across the Kumaon group of passes to Gartok on the Indus, and Totling on the Sutlej, or else made their way by Shipki to Nari Khorsum, but nothing like systematic exploration of these regions was attempted until Montgomerie took the matter in hand with his gallant band of trans-Himalayan explorers. The pundit Nain Sing and his companions had already visited the trading centre, Gartok, in 1867, when he was detailed with two other explorers to work northward into the upper Indus valleys, in order to connect Gartok with the regular Ladak surveys, and to explore the region of the gold and salt mines. In June, 1867, they started from Badrinath and made their way by the Mana pass (18,570 feet), north of that place, into the Sutlej valley. The Chinese officials on the frontier had given the usual amount of trouble. From their lofty elevation in the Himalayas they had looked down on the

The late Nain Sing, C. I. E., Survey of India

plains of Hindustan, and had condescended to admit that the country was fit to trade with. They declared the pass open, and they set about searching the baggage of all traders as they passed to make certain of their *bona fide* character. However, in this instance they missed the explorers' instruments, and the little band got over safely. At Totling they crossed the Sutlej by a remarkable iron bridge of seventy-six feet span suspended forty feet above the water, and then passed over the watershed between the Sutlej and the Indus by the Bogolá (19,200 feet), continuing over the Gugtilá (19,500 feet) to a vast desolate plateau, the home of antelope and multitudinous wild-fowl. Yet another pass had to be negotiated before they dropped into an eastern affluent of the Indus and encountered a Tibetan camp. Here they nearly came to grief. The head man not only disbelieved their story, which represented them to be harmless Bisahari traders, but he actually pointed out with great accuracy who they really were! Nain Sing, however, was equal to the occasion. He was a man of extraordinary nerve as well as of great powers of persuasion. Bribery helped him through the difficulty, and with his smooth tongue and an open hand he managed to get leave for himself to proceed, and at the same time detached one of his survey companions on a separate exploration. The third pundit had had enough of it, and he was left behind.

Making a long march to avoid further complications, Nain Sing found himself at the foot of the

Chomorang la (18,600 feet), the last pass which separated him from the gold-fields; but the snow fell so heavily (even in August) that it was three or four days before he could push his way across and descend upon those historic diggings which have proved such a source of wealth through untold ages. Here at last was Thok Jalung. The miners' camp was pitched in a broad, desolate, red plain, and the sound of singing came from the midst of it to greet the pundit as he approached. The miners and their families in those days (the Thok Jalung mines have since been deserted) were a happy-hearted people. The head of the mines was, however, most suspicious, and not even a letter of introduction which the wily pundit had extracted from the last suspicious head man, or a present of the best Indian tobacco, soothed his objections, until coral ornaments were displayed to his wife. These were irresistible, and although the pundit had to drive a very bad bargain in his rôle as trader with these Lhasa officials in the matter of ladies' outfit, he succeeded in winning his way with them, and establishing himself as the friend of the family. Never was his power of ingratiation shown to such advantage, for the result is a graphic description of these remarkable Tibetan mines such as no other explorer has ever been capable of attaining. In a wide expanse of red-brown upland the black tents of the Tibetan miners were massed without order or arrangement. Around the plain were bare and desolate mountains, with snow on their summits at the time of the pundit's visit, and not a vestige of a green thing in the whole dreary landscape. The altitude of the camp was about 16,330 feet above sea. The tent of the head man was made of black yak's hair. In it were bales of wool for shawl-making (pushm), leather, packages of tea, strings of dried yak beef, dried fruit, and domestic utensils. On the poles were hung ancient matchlocks and a sword. From the fact that this chief wore the red lama robe (with a brown felt hat), Nain Sing was inclined to believe that he was a lama, and his suspicions were strengthened by observing images, brass bells, books, pictures painted on cloth, and other ritualistic property piled up behind his seat. But he never ascertained the fact for certain. The chief's time was mostly passed in the congenial occupations of smoking a silver-mounted Nepalese hookah, and in drinking tea or "chung" (whisky). At the door of the tent was tied one of those gigantic black Lhasa dogs, of a breed which Nain Sing at once recognised by his deep jowl and white chest mark. These Tibetan mastiffs are unpleasantly savage. Sudak Mingmar (the miner chief) was a shrewd observer. It is doubtful whether he ever believed in the pundit. He examined his box with great care, and asked how it was that he came to have such a good box; but he was not sharp enough to detect the secret compartment which contained the sextant.

Gold was worked from the alluvial soil by digging shallow trenches (about ten feet deep — as deep as the Tibetan workmen could get with their long-handled spades) and throwing out the earth to either side. A small stream was introduced into the gold pit (diverted from the neighbouring hills) and used for washing. The water was dammed up with a sloping channel of escape. A cloth was spread at the bottom of the channel, and kept in position by a number of stones, which made the bottom lumpy and uneven. One man sprinkled earth over the channel, whilst a second drove down the water by means of a leather bag. The lighter soil was carried away, but the gold sediment remained deposited in the uneven places, collected in the cloth. The yield of gold was large and the finds occasionally heavy. The pundit saw one nugget which he estimated to be about two pounds weight. The diggers maintained that they could always tell at once when the soil contained gold. All round Thok Jalung (indeed all the way to Lhasa across the Chang) are the remnants of ancient gold mines now disused and abandoned. Thok Jalung itself is now exhausted. The gold industry in that part of Tibet seems to have been incapable of surviving the enormous taxes imposed by the Chinese. Most of the miners hail from the Chung province around Shigatze. In spite of the intense cold the diggers preferred the winter for work, as the excavations stood so much better under the action of frost. The cold is much intensified by wind, and the tents of the diggers were generally pitched seven or eight feet below the ground level for shelter. Throughout these elevated regions the nomad inhabitants usually sleep whilst resting on their knees and elbows, with all the clothes they can get piled on to their backs; and in some parts of western Tibet they have been observed to work at their digging, scratching up the soil into heaps, in much the same attitude. It was this, and the probable use that they made of antelope horns as instruments for scratching the soil, that originated the ancient fable of gold-digging ants protected by dogs to which Herodotus alludes.

The gold-digging industry must be inconceivably ancient in the western part of Tibet. Ancient mines exist in numbers to the east of Thok Jalung and throughout the Chang; to the northeast of the Aru Tso (lake) there are many square miles of alluvial diggings, which are worked even now. The gold of the Jalung mines was conveyed to Pekin by regular official caravans which visited the fields every year for this purpose until the mines were abandoned. These particular mines may have lasted some twenty-five years, or possibly rather more, before they were definitely left as unprofitable. The climate and altitude proved no obstacle to working them.

In spite of the desolate nature of the surrounding hills there is a great deal of coarse grass to be found, and enormous troops of wild animals, but no wood or timber. Water, too, is not very abundant. It is more probable that the mines were closed on account of the heavy imports levied on the miners than for any other reason. There is quartz in the neighbourhood; the surrounding hills are decorated with the mystic sentence "Om-mane-padme-hum," picked out in white quartz stones and repeated on every point of vantage in the landscape. At the time of Nain Sing's visit (1867) gold was worth thirty rupees per ounce in the camp. This visit to the gold workings of Thok Jalung was most useful, for we get therefrom the only authentic account of Tibetan processes of gold-working which we possess. The methods employed at Thok Jalung are the methods employed throughout the Tibetan highlands, and we see at once how very elementary they are. The gold which from time immemorial has enriched the Pekin treasury, and which, in smaller quantities, has found its way to India and to Kashgar, is all obtained from alluvial soil. There is no deep mining (*i. e.*, no shaft sinking) to be found in any of the thousands of disused workings which are scattered over the surface of the Chang. The gold has all been taken from alluvial, or surface, soil, and it has all been washed out by the very crudest of washing processes. At a moderate computation there must have been as much gold left behind on the surface of the land as has ever been put into the market, and it can only require the application of scientific methods to make it available. But it is impossible without scientific examination to decide whether it is there in paying quantities, estimated by the cost of working in such a country and such a climate. The Tibetan miner represents cheap labour. It is notorious that he never grows rich, — in fact he often starves; but that again is no criterion of the value of his labour to his employers. So far as the mining districts of Jalung are concerned, the difficulty of reaching them is not to be estimated by the pundit's account of his own experiences.

There are other ways of getting to them, and to the borax fields which lie east of them. The Tibetan frontier town of Rudok, at the eastern end of the Pangong Lake, is (as we shall see presently) on one of the highroads from Leh to Lhasa and not 150 miles from our frontier. From Rudok to Jalung is, perhaps, another 150 miles of route, involving but one considerable pass; and from Jalung onwards the pundit ascertained that there was a fairly open road by the Ghalaring Cho to the Brahmaputra valley, following one of the great northern affluents of that river.

One of the best of Nain Sing's performances was his first exploration of Central Tibet (the lake region) from the west to Lhasa, — a route survey which gives us most that we know of that remarkable region. Bower, Littledale, Deasy, and Rawling have also added much to our knowledge of the Chang, but their sphere of Tibetan exploration belongs to another chapter, and we must turn again to the west and south.

On the pundit's return from the gold-fields he fell in with his survey companions who had exploited the upper Indus and mapped its upper branches, meeting with no special opposition (when once over the border) but running considerable risks from the bands of robbers who infested the country. Fortunately

"Pundit No. 2" was a tall and powerfully built man, and he was well able to defend himself; otherwise, on one occasion at least, he would have been murdered on the banks of the Indus. So far we are indebted to these plucky agents of Montgomerie for all we know of the districts of Majin, Bongthol, and for most of Nari Khorsum.

Between Sikkim and Lhasa, and northward to the Tengri Nor Lake, it will be apparent from the map that we have more complete topography than we possess elsewhere to fill up the map of Tibet, and for this we are indebted to a large number of native explorers. Lhasa has been frequently visited. The best map which we possess of it is that made by that grand explorer, Krishna (A. K.), whose performances fully equal those of the pundit Nain Sing, and who carried his route surveys so far afield that he anticipated nearly all the subsequent efforts of European adventurers. He traversed much of the ground which has been more recently (and perhaps more fully) illustrated by Prjevalski, Rockhill, and others, and a full examination of his work is unnecessary here. We have already referred to a small section of it in south-eastern Tibet. Perhaps the most useful additions to our knowledge of this (by far the most important) region to us have been from the work of the explorer "G. M. N.," who mapped the Brahmaputra from the meridian of Lhasa to its great bend; and of the lama U. G. (or Ugyen), who worked with the Bengali Chandra Das between the passes north of Sikkim and

Lhasa. Chandra Das (as I have pointed out) is himself no surveyor, but the lama Ugyen not only completed a very large amount of useful work on an independent excursion, but has added a good deal of interesting detail to the accounts of Lhasa given by Nain Sing in the first instance, and by Krishna and Chandra Das subsequently. As I compiled his reports for him, I do not hesitate to say that there is much valuable material in them which has never yet seen the light. The lama (like Chandra Das) was an employee of the Bengal educational department, but he joined the headquarters of the Indian Survey for technical instruction under Colonel Tanner. He entered Tibet by the Donkhya la, west of the Tangla (the pass used by the late expedition in the summer of 1883), and first travelled westward to Khamba jong, now well known as the first advanced post of the Tibetan mission, in order to secure his footing with the local officials.

During this journey he was accompanied by his wife, and he found that it was much easier to maintain his rôle of a pilgrim under such conditions. From Khamba jong he retraced his steps to the Tha sang monastery (south of Bamtso), and then struck out northwest for Gyangtse. This part of his journey is interesting, as it illustrates a second route from the Sikkim frontier to Gyangtse, parallel to that taken by our force following the valley of the Nyangchu, but separated therefrom by an intervening watershed to the east. In some respects it appears to be a better route, more thickly inhabited, and very full of local interest in the matter of monasteries and rock-cut caves, about which Ugyen has many curious and childish legends to relate, — legends, however, which are not at all more childish than those which may be heard any day in more civilised centres. Open gravelly plains and a fair amount of barley cultivation are the chief features of this new route, which includes the crossing of three minor spurs from the watershed on the east, and finally of the pass across the watershed itself, from whence Gyangtse may be seen surrounded by orchards and gardens across an intervening waste of gravel plain. The pass is the Pongong La (16,200 feet), and is described as very difficult. Crossing the Nyangchu by a stone-built bridge three hundred paces in length, Ugyen visited the old temple of Gyangtse. It is nine storeys high and octagonal in shape. On each storey in succession he found eight chapels or sacred places, corresponding to the sides of the building. At the top there were images or "cylindrical figures." The roof is covered with plates of mixed copper and gold, and from it are suspended bells attached to chains. From here he could overlook the market-place with its busy crowds. Gyangtse has now been made familiar to us in the pages of our illustrated journals.

On the 24th of August he left Gyangtse and followed the course of the Nyangchu towards Shigatze. This part of his journey lies through a valley already described; but Ugyen adds more positive information about the extent of cultivation in it. Continuous villages, gardens, and barley fields formed the chief features of the route, which, combined with the stupendous mountains on either side, and the blue waters of the Nyangchu meandering gently near his path, impressed even this unimpressionable Tibetan with its beauty. The river is fed by innumerable streams, and the whole wide expanse of plain is cultivated up to Shigatze. Tashilumpo (described by Bogle and Turner) is, according to Ugyen, an enclosed position, forming a sort of outwork to Shigatze itself. Nain Sing calls it "a well-built monastery surrounded by a wall, enclosing numerous houses and temples, about a mile in circumference." There are upwards of three thousand priests in residence. The Panchen Lama (co-equal in dignity, or nearly so, with the Dalai Lama of Lhasa) in Nain Sing's time was a boy of eleven years of age. Bogle's account of the cheery, hospitable individual, about forty years old, who represented this high authority in his days, will be fresh on the reader's memory. But this was not Ugyen's first visit to Tashilumpo. He had been there in the winter of 1881 with the Babu Chandra Das. On the early morning of the 3d of December, 1881, in intense cold, with a light wind blowing, the two weary travellers approached the Jong. Chandra Das records that he was "in high spirits," but "not so Ugyen: he was ill and fretted fearfully; his appearance was repulsive, and his language to the Tang lung men, whose ponies we rode, was most abusive,[1] but they bore

[1] Journey to Lhasa and Central Tibet, p. 43.

patiently with him." The lama (Ugyen) was the harassed and hard-working surveyor; the Babu the light-hearted observer. Of the two the lama went furthest. But we owe much to the Babu for his description of the social life and customs of the people. He describes a "black-hat" dance which took place at Tashilumpo in presence of the Grand Lama with much more graphic power than he describes the place itself. We are, however, on well trodden ground at Tashilumpo and Shigatze, and we must move farther. In August, 1883, the lama continued his surveys along the southern banks of the Brahmaputra, passing through well-cultivated and well-populated country, with sweet valleys reaching from the southern mountains down to the river banks, to Tagh-tu-ka, where there is a ferry and where the river valley road practically ceases. At the junction of the Rongchu he struck off southwest and followed that river to the great Yamdok tso, or Palki lake. In the Rongchu valley he found many celebrated monasteries, of which the Rong cham chen is perhaps the chief. It is a cultivated and well-peopled valley, — one of the "oases" of Tibet. Nothing in the story of Tibetan exploration appeals more strongly to the imagination than his subsequent account of his survey of the Yamdok tso. The weather was unpropitious; thick mists enveloped the mountain sides and hung over the surface of the water; from the western shores of this vast lake a mountainous peninsula projects northeastward into it, connected with the mainland by two arms which themselves enclose a second and smaller lake called the Duma tso. One of these arms is a precipitous mountain ridge called the Tag La, the sloping sides of which descend so sharply to the water's edge as to bar all access to the peninsula. The other arm forms an accessible link between the grass lands about Nagartse and the towering mountains which are the central feature of the projecting mass. They are margined, however, with a cultivated border dotted with fishing villages, fringing the purple sides of the hills with green, and dividing them from the deep, blue waters of the lake. Hidden in the dark recesses of the mountains is the secret hermitage of Padna Sambhava. Ugyen made his way right round the peninsula, meeting with hospitality from the people after much questioning and a boisterous reception on the part of the huge Tibetan dogs. Footsore and weary, he reached Samding on the 29th of August, after losing his way and risking his life amongst the rocky passages which overhung the Duma tso. The Duma tso impressed him mightily; its deep, still waters embosomed amongst terrific cliffs and precipices; the silence which hung over the stupendous crags encircling it, broken only by the rush and roar of falling masses which ever and anon thundered down the mountain sides into the depths of the lake; the legends of the demons and genii who inhabited the lake, and whose good will was daily propitiated by the people living around, — all these things reduced him to a condition of superstitious awe and reverence to which his usually phlegmatic nature was a stranger. The level of the Duma tso is five hundred feet higher than that of the Yamdok tso (13,800 feet), and it is said to be gradually rising. There is no apparent outlet, and the landslips to which Ugyen refers must in time sensibly affect the lake level, so there is a probability of truth in the suggestion. The superstitious inhabitants believe in an eventual overflow which will destroy all human life; hence their dread of the lake and their constant endeavours to live on good terms with its presiding demons. The belief in the change of lake levels seems to pervade all Tibet, and is combined with strange legends of their shifting character. There can be no doubt that the level varies considerably in the course of years, and that Lob Nor is not the only lake which will eventually be proved to shift its position as the ages pass.

From the Yamdok tso Ugyen struck off southwards to explore another lake, — the Pho Mo Chang Tang tso, — which presented a strong contrast to the gloomy grandeur of the Yamdok tso. To the south-east he could see (from the Yeh La) the snowy peaks of Kulha Kangri and Menda piercing "the vault of heaven like the dazzling spires of crystal chhortens" (a chhorten being a solid masonry building of pagoda form, frequently embellished with a gilt ball and crescent at the top, enclosing certain religious books and stone engraved prayers which are placed in a recess in the interior) "whilst the lake was surrounded by an array of magnificent peaks such as my eyes never before beheld." "There is a belt of gentle slopes

A Typical Tibetan Valley

round the lake, dotted with Dokpa tents; a spacious plateau extends to the northeast of it, along which the road to Manda La lay." The name Pho mo (male and female) is derived from two islands near the north-eastern shores. The people about here are of Mongolian race (Hor dokpa and Sog dokpa), but they are comparatively civilised. Crossing the Manda La (17,450 feet) after leaving the lake, from the province of U he passed into the Lhobrak country. The upper Lhobrak valley is well cultivated. Barley, peas, mustard, wheat, and rape crops were all abundant. Here, too, are great monasteries and the shrine of a saintly Guru built upon the ancient model of the Nalendra Monastery in Magadha. The shrine is surrounded by groves of poplar, and contains important relics, "amongst others a stuffed horse of great sanctity"; but the lama's story about the horse must be left (with many of his inimitable folklore tales) to another historian.

Ugyen was now on the borders of Bhutan, and he has much to say about the trade routes between that country and Lhasa. Crossing the Tum La pass (after leaving the Lhobrak valley by a southern affluent) he reached the grassy plateau which embosoms the sacred cave of Tong tso Pama ling. He describes this as "a beautiful flat country which gently sloped up to the foot of the mountains, carpeted with exquisite verdure and lovely flowers and bushes of different shrubs." At the head of the lake is the great monastery from which, looking to the southeast the view embraced "the crystal surface of the thrice holy lake flanked by a range of billowy mountains, overtopped in the distance by the lofty snows of Kulha Kangri," which "with their snow-clad peaks standing in picturesque array, resemble (to compare great things with small) the Buddhist prayer-offering called Torma. To the north of Kulha Kangri is the dome-like peak called Kulhas Cham, — that is, his wife; on her sides stand exalted the sublime peaks Chenrezi, Lonchen, Lathoi Kar (the hoary-headed minister) as also Gartoi, Namgyal, and others. In her front is the pinnacle of Dsam balairi." Who shall say that the Mongol mind has lost its mediæval capacity for poetic impression? The couplets with which the Emperor Babar interlines his inimitable "Memoirs," or those which enliven the pages of his cousin Mirza Haidar, are not a bit more poetic in their imaginings than the similes which the Lama Ugyen draws from the abundant sources of nature. Descending again into the Lhobrak valley, he followed it to its junction with a large affluent from the northeast called the Tamshul. Near the junction is the great monastery of Lha Kang jong (9800 feet). In this part of his journey he speaks of spacious flats and beautiful parterres adjoining the river; of large villages, monasteries, stone bridges over the river, and terraced cultivation. The valley is reckoned "the most populated and fertile valley in Tibet." It was harvest time when the lama passed along it, and the air was full of the song of the reapers. He crossed both the Lhobrak and the Tamshul by magnificent stone bridges. At the latter bridge he found a guard house. A large bell was suspended to the top of the narrow gateway of this house, which he struck, when the door opened and on either side a fierce Tibetan mastiff was found chained to guard the passage. The use of these magnificent dogs as guards is often referred to by Ugyen. They are quite as large as the English mastiff, rough-coated, shaggy, and untamably fierce. At Lhakang jong he found himself in difficulties. During his absence from the house his baggage was examined. His wife managed to hide his instruments, but there was quite enough evidence left to prove him to be a British spy. The Tibetan officials seem to have behaved with remarkable moderation. They burnt his note-book, but they restored all the rest of his property,and gave him a free pass onward. Possibly a few judicious bribes and his own tact in replying to his cross-examiners saved the situation. Anyhow he proceeded unmolested up the Tamshul bank again to Tibetan territory.

The Tamshul valley possesses all those attractions which we usually associate with Sikkim rather than Tibet. Villages, cultivation, rich monasteries (about which the lama has much to say), stone bridges, and all the accessories of a rich country with a fine climate. But beyond the head of the Tamshul the wide gravel plains surrounding the Tigu tso (about which Ugyen says very little) are typically Tibetan. Between the head of the Tamshul and the sources of the Yarlung he had many a rough experience, and often literally did not know where to lay his head. The Yarlung valley is famous throughout Tibet. A rich damp soil, with abundant crops, flower gardens around the monasteries, temples, and "Mendongs," must have been in pleasant contrast to the sterility of the Tigu tso plateau; but the lāma tells us little about the nature of the cultivation or of the architectural beauties of the Yarlung valley, and only dwells on the richness and importance of one temple at Kha Chung Na, which was built as a protection against the ghosts of certain men who were murdered there many years ago, and which decline to leave the neighbourhood. The valley of the Yarlung must be very rich and abundantly fruitful, or it could hardly support the number of monasteries which Ugyen found there, the legends and traditions of which he is never weary of relating. The copper and gilt images with which they are filled struck him forcibly. Here again are traditions of severe floods which have depopulated and laid waste the valley. At Chetang he was on well trodden ground, but he adds a few details about the places which are interesting. Wheat and meat soup are sold in Mahommedan shops here. Pork is especially cheap, three annas being the price of a pig's head. Radishes, carrots, and yak's flesh is also abundant. The Mahommedans inter-marry with the Tibetans, but the form of marriage is, I suspect, wanting in ritual. From Chetang to Lhasa the lama worked his way systematically, hiding his instruments at night, but making on the whole a very effective survey. He was constantly on Krishna's tracks, and on those of other explorers, so that we have several authorities for all this part of our Tibetan mapping. Incidentally in his narrative are many quaint stories of Tibetan manners and customs which show the freedom accorded to women in Tibet. He was constantly indebted to the kindness of the gentler sex for shelter and food, and he relates on one occasion that, having experienced an undignified repulse from a Tibetan gentleman, he accidentally met the man's daughter-in-law soon afterwards and related the occurrence to her with a good many uncomplimentary remarks about her relative. The girl laughed, and took him straight back to the house, and treated him with marked respect and consideration. She was very fair, and Ugyen records his impression that a fair skin always covers a soft heart.

Working along the northern bank of the Brahmaputra to the great Samye monastery (most celebrated of all in Tibet), he tells of scenery that must rival that of Kashmir, — woods and gardens and, above all, excellent roads "like the roads of Darjiling." The eighth book of his adventures is full of queer legends about the Sangri Kha Ma monastery, and about Dansa Til, which is overshadowed by a hill covered with cypress trees, every one of which sprung from the hair of a saint. The monastery of Ngaritatsang also attracted his attention, with its surroundings of houses and gardens, streams and trees, now tinted and brightened with the touch of early October. The Samye monastery is literally enveloped in legends — some of

17

which as touching the rise and early progress of Buddhism are interesting. Here there is a large image of Sakya Muni in gold and brass, ten feet high, and many sacred treasures. The legends and stories related by the lama are of course of varied character; some are but the record of childish superstitions; some are fairly authentic history; and some are very remarkable repetitions of old-world tales and folk-lore gathered in Lhasa, which are of much more than passing interest — for they clearly indicate the possibility that many of the Eastern fables (such, for instance, as the Arabian Nights stories) may have had their origin in the farther East — in Tibet, Mongolia, or China — rather than in Arabia. No one yet has made any use of them, or even properly examined them. Samye is about 11,500 feet above sea. A wall of 1,700 paces encloses the religious edifices (including a temple) and four large monasteries besides small ones. The roof of the temple is gold and copper and its construction regarded as "miraculous." "In all Tibet," says the lama, "there is no place so celebrated as Samye, and throughout Tibet and Sikkim there is not a man who does not worship Samye Gyalpo, the great god enshrined in its temple."

The lama experienced some difficulty in re-entering Lhasa. A solitary wayfarer on foot runs no little risk from the number of savage dogs which prowl around the city-walls feeding on offal and human corpses. He had to supply himself with bones and delicacies such as dogs love in order to win his way amongst them. His residence of several months at Lhasa was chequered by his being recognised by a Darjiling coolie. He had to go into hiding, taking refuge in the house of a Chinese soldier, where he gathered together his quaint collection of Tibetan and Chinese stories. He managed to effect a fair amount of surveying in spite of the hampering precautions which such work rendered necessary, but his maps and plans of Lhasa are not on the whole so good as those of the distinguished explorer Krishna.

He has, however, much to say about Lhasa; but the story of Lhasa must be told subsequently. From Lhasa he finally made his way to Darjiling and India by a route which is important as the most direct and shortest route between our frontier and the capital of Tibet. The late mission to Tibet traversed the usual route via Gyangtse, which is by no means direct. That of the lama Ugyen is considerably shorter, but his account of it would not lead one to prefer it. The route from Lhasa to the southwest of the Yamdok tso (Nagartse Jong) is the same, but from that point, instead of striking westward over the Kharola pass to Gyangtse, it reaches out southward over the Dug pass (16,900) into the basin of the Pho Mo Chang Lake, skirting its western extremity, and then making straight for the head of the Chumbi valley over the successive spurs of the great water divide to the east of the Nyangchu — the river of Gyangtse. The passes over these spurs are not high, but there are at least three of them averaging about 16,000 feet, with no great ascent or descent, but still presenting difficulties which are not to be found in the valley of the Nyangchu below them. A part of the district traversed is reckoned to be the coldest in Tibet, and in October the lama suffered considerably from the intense fierce winds and the biting frosts of the bleak bare plains. There is, however, a fair amount of grass to be found in the upland valleys to the east of the Nyangchu, although there are periods when the passes remain snow-bound for weeks together. It can in no sense be reckoned a better military route between Lhasa and our frontier than the circuitous road which passes through Gyangtse, but at certain seasons of the year it might prove to be a useful alternative. The Horpa herdsmen of this part of Tibet claim a Mongolian origin and consider themselves superior to the Tibetan.

With the lama's return via Chumbi to Darjiling there closed one of the most useful and one of the best records of Tibetan travel ever made by an agent of the Indian Survey. The short description of it herein given by no means includes the full extent of it, and to the greater mass of information obtained it is hardly possible even to refer. It is through the lama, and men like the lama, that we have obtained our knowledge of western and southern Tibet; that is to say, we owe to them all that we know of that part of Tibet which it most concerns us that we should know — as being not only contiguous to our frontier, but beyond any comparison the richest and most valuable part of the country. For this reason I have given some space to these explorations — and for another reason also. These men do not write for themselves. They send in useful reports, it is true; but their reports get no further than the docket stage. It is unfortunate in the interests of the public which concerns itself about Tibet (a very small public indeed) that the best and most important of all the stirring records of that remarkable country have never yet seen the light of publication. The one native who has written on his own account (the Bengali, Chandra Das) has nothing to say about the country at large. He confines himself to Lhasa and its neighbourhood, and even there he is on well trodden ground.

CHAPTER XII

Western and Northern Tibet — European Explorers — Deasy-Stein — The Kuen Lun and Chang Tang — Wellby — Bower — Littledale — Bonvalot — Sven Hedin — Comparison of Routes from West and North

THERE is a useful geographical corner of Tibet to be studied which lies just beyond the wall of the Himalayas, stretching northwest and southeast from the central lakes of Manasarawar (Tso Mobang and Tso Lagang). On to this narrow stretch of highland known as Nari Khorsum, or Hundes, which includes the valley of the Sutlej flowing northwest, and the valley of the Karnáli (afterwards the Gogra) flowing southeast,[1] there converges a whole series of Himalayan passes, of which the Shipki from Simla, the Niti at the head of the Alaknanda (a Ganges affluent), and the Milam at the head of the Sarda, are perhaps the best known. They all attain great altitudes, and none of them are open for more than a few months of the year (15th of June to 15th of October). Nevertheless, over these heights there passes to and fro a considerable amount of trade between

[1] Neither of these rivers takes its source from the Manasarawar Lakes. The former channel of the Sutlej River from Tso Lagang (Rakas Tal) is now dry.

India and the elevated valleys beyond. The pasturage about the Manasarawar lakes is excellent, and the shawl wool (or pushm) grown in this part of Tibet is of especially fine quality. A great deal of it is traded into India, and with it a certain amount of gold dust and borax. Most of the trade is effected by the use of sheep as transport animals, but a hybrid between the yak and the cow (known as the jibu) is also commonly used over the rough paths which lie beyond the crest of the Himalayas. Up to the crest roads have here and there been engineered from the Indian side, and are passably good, but beyond the line they are little more than a series of narrow steps hollowed from the face of rugged cliffs. Men of Hundes (Hunias), Bhotias (of Kumaon and Garwhal), and Bisaharis (the recognised trans-frontier traders) are continually to be met with in the Himalayan frontier markets between Ladak and Almorah, and these are the people with whom we are most familiar on the Tibetan border. North of the great lakes is the sacred mountain of Kailás, the paradise of the Hindoos of northern India. Shaped roughly like a Hindu temple with a part of the conical top knocked off, Kailás is a strikingly remarkable peak. From its immense bulk and height it is probably one of the most impressive amongst trans-Himalayan peaks, but its altitude is less than that of Gurla Mandhata (25,860 feet), from which it is separated by the lake region of Manasarawar. This mountain also has its legend. It is said to be the transformation of the body of a Raja of

Banares, who died on the banks of the lake some thousands of years ago.

The trading town of Gartok, now open by treaty to foreign trade, on the upper Indus, to which we have already alluded, is the chief town of a lengthy province which extends from Rudok on the Pangong Lake to the sources of the Brahmaputra and Karnáli. Wild and apparently desolate as this region is, it is by no means destitute of wealth.

The Hunias are of Tartar origin, with many of the leading characteristics of that race. They are not prepossessing in appearance. The life they lead on those sublime heights has wrinkled them exceedingly, the old people being especially hideous. But they are all rich after their fashion, owning large flocks of sheep and herds of cattle and goats, which latter are the celebrated breed known as shawl goats. The gold which finds its way to India was once brought chiefly from the Thok Jalung fields and is still found in the Sutlej valley, and on the edges of the Manaṣaṛawar lakes. Borax and salt are abundant, but borax has become lately almost a drug in the market. Pushm is the chief export now, and (curiously enough) tea, which comes from Lhasa, and is carried into India even as far as Amritsar. There is a strong prejudice against Indian tea amongst the natives of the Tibetan border, which is of course carefully kept alive by the Chinese officials. Much of all this Himalayan hinterland has been surveyed by European officers of the Indian Survey department, working from Himalayan stations, and explorations further north have been pushed through by Montgomerie's staff of native explorers. Rawling and Ryder have lately completed a valuable geographical survey of all this country, from Gartok on the Indus to the sources of the Brahmaputra, and from those sources to the city of Lhasa. British explorers have passed into Tibet eastward from Leh frequently, but till lately they have kept north of the Brahmaputra valley. It is with the experiences of some of these that we now have to deal. They must be dealt with shortly, chiefly from want of space, but also because the great central and northern theatre of their researches is not nearly so important to British interests as is the southern ground of Tibet. Bower, Littledale, Wellby, and Sven Hedin all have reached far into Tibet, sometimes crossing each other's tracks, sometimes wandering in the footsteps of the native explorers; and all have made splendid additions to our knowledge of the great Chang Tang. Deasy and Stein have worked in the north and northwest, and these two gentlemen (with Bower) have added thoroughly sound and scientific geography to our mapping, working on scientific methods and employing native surveyors on their staff. It cannot be too strongly urged that the employment of professional assistance is the real way to amass consistent and homogeneous map information. No traveller responsible for the welfare of a mixed caravan of Europeans and natives can possibly spare the necessary time for the patient drudgery of survey duty (if he would make the most of his opportunities) in addition to those of his command. The work of such a scientific observer as the great traveller, Sven Hedin, stands perhaps unrivalled in the annals of geographical research, but it may be surmised that even this great explorer would have been thankful enough to have been spared some of the more or less mechanical drudgery of constant observations and records by the employment of a trustworthy and well trained assistant.

Leh has always been a favourite position for the first take off into the wild regions of Tibet. At Leh there is a permanent political resident, for it is the farthest outpost of the Kashmir state; and there is a good bazaar and fair opportunity for careful equipment. But immediately beyond Leh the traveller faces a formidable mountain barrier and must accept the difficulties of a snow-bound pass at the very outset of his travels. The Chang la has, however, never presented such physical obstacles to advance as has the careful watch of the Chinese outposts on the frontier; and the difficulties of the pass have never been greatly dwelt on by explorers. Once over the Chang the Pangong Lake depression opens out into a long southeasterly plain, with the Tibetan market town of Rudok at its south-eastern extremity picturesquely clinging to the mountain sides and dominated by an imposing red and white monastery. Many travellers and sportsmen have been to Rudok, but few succeed in penetrating further. An alternative route on to the elevated Chang Tang of Central Tibet avoids Rudok and passes over some

Captain H. H. P. Deasy

Captain Wellby

difficult ground at the northern end of the lake, whence it emerges straight on to the wide wilderness of the north central highlands, crossing the Kashmir frontier at the Lanak la and skirting the southern borders of that inexpressibly dreary region the Aksai Chin. By this route, turning northwards, the head of the Keria River can be reached, and the Polu route to Chinese Turkestan. It was opened up by the explorations of Deasy. Avoiding the northerly bend, and proceeding straight eastward, we have the route of Wellby to Tsaidam and Koko Nor, and between it and the Kuen Lun, some of the many Tibetan detours of Sven Hedin, which, with Stein's useful topography, gives us a very fair idea of that long strip of northern Chang Tang, which for desolate sterility and general unproductiveness is probably unmatched in the world by any other region which is not actual desert. It is, however, exceedingly interesting to us to know the quality of these Tibetan uplands which lie between the lowlands of Chinese Turkestan and the comparatively depressed basin of the Brahmaputra. They form the great obstacle to advance from the north, and the records of those travellers who have visited them is our guarantee for its impracticable character.

Captain Deasy was a cavalry officer of the British Army who combined in his own person many of the most essential qualifications of a good explorer. Animated by the true spirit of adventure, possessed of great determination, excellent physique, and a thorough appreciation of scientific methods of working, he has always, whether traversing Tibetan wilds or making motor records in more civilised countries, been completely successful in carrying through the programme laid out for accomplishment. He was in the northwest of Tibet and on the plateau of Aksai Chin in the summer of 1896 (finding the Lanak La at 18,000 feet free from snow in June), accompanied by Mr. Arnold Pike. On this occasion he succeeded in surveying about 24,000 miles of Tibetan territory, and in connecting his work by triangulation with the Indian surveys. Captain Deasy attached a native surveyor to his party as topographer. The general characteristics of this northwestern corner of Tibet are those of dreary desolate plains intersected with ranges of hills which, without rising much above the plains, are of great absolute altitude. The country is by no means entirely destitute of either grass or water, but long weary days were passed without finding either. Nomads were frequently met with, and they were invariably useless as guides. Great obstruction was caused by the Rudok officials. In spite of the physical difficulties encountered, — intense cold, want of water, terrific wind, and general desolation, — the country would not have been impracticable for travelling but for the obstructiveness of the people encountered. They were all instructed from Lhasa, and it was impossible to obtain either guides or information. Nevertheless, a very remarkably accurate addition was made to our knowledge of Chang topography, although Deasy's caravan of sixty-six mules and ponies was reduced to six ere he returned to Leh at the close of the year.

Once again, early in 1898, Captain Deasy attacked the Tibetan Chang, but on this occasion he worked southwards from Yarkand, which place he reached on January 20. Official obstruction on the north is just as great as it is on the west, and Deasy found that in spite of Chinese passports and proper credentials, he was unable to pass Polu on the Kiria River, leading from the plains of Turkestan to the Tibetan plateau. The Polu route is perhaps the most direct and the best available — if, indeed, it has not been finally destroyed under official orders from Lhasa. Deasy made use of a route further to the east, which he found to be fairly easy, and struck the plateau at the head of the Kiria south of Polu. We owe to him a survey of the sources of this river as well as those of the Khotan, both important lines of connection with the northern plains. Once again he traversed this wild northwestern region between the Kiria sources and Rudok, and made a most excellent map of it. It is a district of mountain ridges enclosing salt lakes with no central line of drainage. It appears to be the confused and wrinkled surface of a vast upheaval disturbed by the superincumbent weight of long ages of ice cap, with the lake remnants of its departed snows and ice-fields now gradually desiccating and disappearing. Deasy's map of the district lying southeast of the Aksai Chin is a very remarkable illustration of the general conformation of the Chang. All northern Tibet is much the same, —

a broad, soft, alluvial wilderness of hill and valley relieved by the drab green of the stunted burtsá scrub, with gravel plains interspersed; an occasional spread of good grazing (and the grass, like that of the Pamirs, is of excellent quality when it does occur), and starred all over its surface with the blue mirrors of innumerable salt lakes, each lake being a space of water surrounded by an intensely saline border of soft mud. Vast herds of wild antelope, kyang, and yak (with camels farther east) roam through these plains, and their droppings are the salvation of travellers in the matter of fuel.

Deasy finally returned to Leh by the route he had previously followed; but before bidding adieu to the wild scenery of the northern borderlands, he made a most successful exploration of the upper Yarkand River, and linked in his surveys with those of the Pamirs, executed during the Russo-Afghan boundary settlement in those altitudes. Here he was assisted by Ram Singh, who had proved his quality as an exploratory surveyor with Bower previously.

Dr. Stein's work in the north of Tibet is comparatively recent. His original quest was the discovery of certain ancient town sites which have long been buried in the sands of the Takla Makan desert north of Tibet; but incidentally he has given us most valuable additional topographical information about the Kuen Lun mountains, carrying out a systematic survey of a portion of that range to the east of Deasy's work, and basing his maps (with the assistance of a native surveyor) on a scientific series of initial observations.

These two British explorers have done a great deal to clear away some of the mists which overhung those far northern mountains. The physical conformation of them is accurately defined in so many parts that we can well conjecture what the structure of the whole may be. The magnificent work of Dr. Sven Hedin yet still more recently will add further detail when published *in extenso;* so that we now have a very fair idea of the nature of the flanking wall of the Tibetan highland which faces the northern plains even as the Himalayas face India on the south.

It is clear that the Kuen Lun may be crossed at frequent points in its length. The narrow valleys leading up from the Turkestan lowlands appear to slope upwards with comparatively gentle grades to the crest; and the latter presents depressions in its long, sinuous line, involving far less of precipitous ascent through rugged defiles than is common on the Indian frontier, or the Himalayan backbone. Sven Hedin's researches, together with those of Bonvalot and Littledale (who have both crossed the Kuen Lun from north to south), have confirmed our impressions of the general geographical character of the borderland to the northeast of Tibet, as now represented in our maps. The main water-parting, or divide, of the Kuen Lun extends east and west, closely hugging the parallel of 36° north latitude from east longitude 78°, through 20 degrees, till it merges into the long ridge and valley system of the Chinese borderland. But it does not face the Gobi depression (or Chinese Turkestan) farther than about

84° east longitude, where a broad plateau of somewhat less elevation than the Chang opens out northward of it, gradually widening towards the east; and this plateau is itself bounded by mountain ranges (Altyn Tagh, Nan Shan, etc.), which face the Gobi depression, hedging in the gigantic upland between themselves and the extension of the Kuen Lun. In this lower steppe are the wind-swept basins of the Achik Kul, Prjevalski's "valley of the winds," the vast desert of Tsaidam, and other subordinate lake basins, amongst which we may reckon the Koko Nor depression.

This is not recognised as a political part of Tibet, but it would be difficult to assign it to any other government. It is a land which owns no law, and is the home of the Golok (or Kolo) robber bands. Besides Prjevalski and Rockhill (to whom we have already referred), as authorities of this singularly unattractive corner of the elevated world, we have the records of Sven Hedin, and further evidence from Littledale and Bonvalot. Sven Hedin has crossed the mountain regions between the Chinese Turkestan depression and the elevated Chang Tang oftener than any other traveller of whom we have record, and he has illustrated the conformation of the eastern extension of the Kuen Lun with much accuracy of detail. In one of his earlier wanderings in the northern Tibetan borderland, he crossed the Kuen Lun divide south of the Tsaidam steppes, and once again south of Cherchen at the eastern end of the Takla Makan desert of

Chinese Turkestan, his intermediate route being approximately parallel to the great divide and south of it. Between the meridians of 86° and 92° east longitude he proves the Kuen Lun to be a continuous range of high, rugged, and snow-clad mountains, to which he gives the name of Akka Tagh, dividing the great plateau of Tibet from the subordinate table-land on the north whence flow the infant sources of the Cherchen River northwards, and wherein lie the lake depressions of Achik Kul and Aiag Kum Kul. The ranges which again divide this plateau land from the Turkestan lowlands (the Altyn Tagh, Chimin Tagh, etc.,) lie in a broad system of approximately parallel ridges, forming a wrinkled and folding edge to the uplands. They broaden eastwards to a total width which nearly equals that of the Himalayas, but westwards, at the head of the Kiria River, the width of the Kuen Lun is not much more than fifty miles. The transverse routes and passes are hardly Himalayan in character on the east. The valleys are less steep, and the general altitude of the main waterparting is considerably lower. It is the desolation and the cold, with the terrific force of the wind currents bearing icy blasts from the west, that prove the greatest obstacle to exploration. The storms which sweep across these northern steppes recur with almost diurnal frequency at certain seasons of the year. The burán of the highlands is not less to be dreaded than the black storms of the Turkestan lowlands.

A very remarkable journey across the northern

Chang Tang from west to east was made by Captain Wellby and Lieutenant Malcolm in 1896. They crossed the Lanak La, working eastwards from Leh, in the month of May, and, in spite of the initial difficulties and obstructions of the Rudok officials, they continued their journey (keeping approximately between 35° and 36° of north latitude, till they finally emerged from Tibet at the Koko Nor and the Chinese frontier town of Sining. This is the only record we have of a direct east and west route through what has generally been reckoned the worst part of the Chang Tang. A native surveyor accompanied them, so that we have a certain amount of topographical detail of their route. It was an almost desperate adventure. Their guides deserted them at the outset; the district they traversed was barren, grassless, and waterless. Salt lakes innumerable were found, but very little fresh water. Nearly every day for two months water had to be found by digging at the end of the day's march. By the end of June only sixteen out of thirty-nine of their transport animals were left, and they had to march on foot. It is a little remarkable that they should complain of the great heat by day, but the summer mid-day heat is referred to by many travellers in Tibet. With the thermometer reading 105° Fahrenheit in the sun by day, there were sometimes 18° or 20° of frost at night. On the 2d of August all their men deserted except their body servants, taking with them the last twenty pounds of flour. The deserters, however, turned up again at the end of two

Dr. Sven Hedin

Colonel Bower

days' march. They were too faint-hearted or too ignorant to find their way to Lhasa. Only a few, however, were re-engaged. There was not food for more. With the exception of three mules, all their animals died (poisoned by some noxious weed) and the travellers were reduced to feeding on wild onions. Game became scarce in September, and the rain and snow season set in. Finally they struck an encampment of Chinese merchants on the road between Koko Nor and Lhasa, where it crosses the upper Yangtse, and with them they turned northwards into the Mongol country. It was a most extraordinary feat to perform in the way of exploration. Captain Wellby subsequently distinguished himself in exploration in northern Africa, and finally met a soldier's death on the veldt of the south during the Boer war.

The geographical results of this expedition were chiefly confirmation of previous accounts of the utterly sterile and barren nature of northern Tibet. Wellby's route, however, illustrates the prevailing characteristic of long and comparatively low folds and anticlinals (striking transversely to the meridian) as the prevailing orographical feature. He was considerably south of Sven Hedin's route, and must have been well within sight of the latter's Mount Oscar, which is no doubt a peak on a lateral extension westward of the Koko Shili range.

No geographical evidence which has ever been adduced is more conclusive as regards the physical characteristics of northern Tibet than that of the gallant Wellby. Sun-baked and storm-swept, frozen and roasted by turns, we have all the usual climatic conditions of Asiatic plateau land from the Pamirs to Baluchistan; whilst the general distribution of the wide treeless plains, and the monotony of an endless ridge and furrow system leaves little to describe and is almost a weariness to the imagination.

We will now take a cursory glance at the results of four exploratory expeditions, all of which had one great objective before them, viz., the holy Buddhist city of Lhasa. Bower, Littledale, Sven Hedin, and Bonvalot (in addition to Rockhill, to whom we have already referred) all started on the same quest, all arrived within a short measurable distance of their goal, and were all beaten finally, not by the physical difficulties of the desolate regions which they traversed, but by the pig-headed obstinacy of the Tibetan official. Captain Bower, like Deasy and Wellby, was a cavalry officer. He was attached to an Indian regiment when he first formulated his programme for reaching Lhasa from Leh. Possessed of great determination and magnificent physique, he had further the advantages of a most unusual experience in the rough travelling of the northern hinterland of India. It was Bower who ran to earth the murderer of Dalgleish. It was Bower who first astonished the world of Oriental scholars with the birch-bark manuscript dug out of the Turkestan desert near Kashgar, which proved to be one of the most ancient manuscripts in the world, and has set scientists exploring and working in the same direction ever since. He took with him a companion (Dr. Thorold) and a native surveyor — the same Ram Singh who subsequently did good service with Deasy, but who was then in his infancy as a trained topographer. Nevertheless he did promising work even in those early days. The party left Leh in 1891, crossed the Lanak La on July 3, and succeeded in avoiding the Rudok officials. Keeping east, they crossed another pass (Mangtza, 18,020 feet), which presented little difficulty, and continued at a high altitude (Bower reckoned this to be the highest part of the Chang) till they reached the Horpa Cho, which lake is probably the highest in the world (17,900 feet). From there for many weeks Bower maintained a southeasterly trek through the Khampa country, inhabited by the Tibetan Dokpa, or nomads.

Bower was well to the north of the route which had been followed between Leh and Lhasa by the pundit Nain Sing in 1874 (to which I have made no reference, since it was subsequently traversed by Littledale), as it was his intention to explore the northern regions, rather than the lake district which borders the Brahmaputra basin. Like other travellers he found lakes innumerable, but almost invariably salt, and obviously desiccating and contracting. Fresh water was scarce, but the party never failed to find it on the surface as they proceeded (without guides and with recurrent arguments with the Dokpas) to make their way Lhasawards. There is a refreshing contrast in Bower's narrative to the monotonous tale of wild, barren sterility which Wellby relates. Wild animals existed in incredible numbers. The indigo-blue lakes were often fringed with grass. Wild-fowl, gulls, bar-headed geese, and brahmini ducks (sheldrake) were abundant wherever a fresh-water affluent occurred, and wild yak, Tibetan antelope, kyang, and gazelle were always in sight during that part of their march which centred in Aru Cho. For weeks they passed through a country where the valleys were "wide and open," the hills "rounded," with snow peaks showing beyond them to the south. It was by no means a deserted or naturally an inhospitable country until they approached the enormous lake which figures on our map as Zilling (? Sining) tso. Constant collisions occurred wth the nomads *en route,* but on no occasion was it necessary to resort to actual physical force. We have, on the whole, a not unpleasing vision of these Hor uplands presented to us by Bower. He tells his story with soldierly brevity, but it is not difficult to distinguish, between the record of long weary and thirsty marches, a country which presents a favourable contrast to the blank sterility of the more northern plains. It is obviously greener, with more frequent grass oases, more of the interest of human occupation, more of a sportsman's country, and, in spite of its great altitude, a country which in summer must be attractive. The deep-blue lakes set like jewels in the depressions of nature's swelling downs and rounded hills, the far-away lines of snow-capped mountains, and the constant presence of the black tents of the Dokpa herdsmen, their yaks and sheep scattered over the plains, must be a very close repetition of the northern Kashmir and Pamir scenery farther west, from which Tibet can hardly be dissociated geographically. South of the Zilling tso, and northwest of the Great Tengri Nor Lake, Bower's journey Lhasa-wards came to an end. There he was met by the usual array of Tibetan officials swelling with enormous dignity, and the usual request that he would retrace his steps and return the way he came. This may be regarded as the normal request of Tibetan officialdom whether addressed to a solitary traveller or to a responsible agent fully accredited by the government of India, and it is not confined to Lhasa officialdom. The same request was made to Bower that was made to Huc and Rockhill at Chiamdo farther east, when making his way via Ta-chien-lu to China. It is made everywhere, regardless of the geographical position of the place where it is advanced relatively to the starting-point of the traveller. However, Bower was not the sort of explorer to be easily stopped. He turned north, rapidly reaching more sterile and inhospitable regions, and then made his way eastwards to Chiamdo and Ta-chien-lu by a route which was new at the time, but which from Amdo eastwards closely coincides with that of Rockhill subsequently. He was the first of modern English explorers to illustrate this part of Tibet, and to him we still owe all that is known of the geography of the central Chang north of Nain Sing's mapping.

Littledale and Bonvalot are two other distinguished explorers who from the north have made gallant attempts to reach Lhasa, and who have indeed succeeded in penetrating farther south than any other traveller. Both of them reached the Tengri Nor, and Littledale must have been well within sight of the hills which immediately enclose the sacred city. Littledale crossed the Altyn Tagh, and the northern mountains by the opening of the Cherchen River. Bonvalot traversed the same mountain band farther east, from a point east of the Lob Nor lake system in Chinese Turkestan, and made tracks southward which cannot be very far removed from those of Sven Hedin during his last great journey. But there has always been a little difficulty about placing Bonvalot's route in its right position. He was not alone (for he was accompanied by that distinguished Anglophobe, Prince Henri d'Orléans, one of the most enterprising of Eastern explorers), yet there was not the accuracy of observation which is necessary to secure really valuable geographical results in these days, such, for instance, as distinguishes the topographical work of Bonvalot's ill-starred compatriot Dutreuil de Rhins, or the splendid achievements of Sven Hedin. However, Bonvalot has added valuable descriptive accounts of the northern Chang to those of Littledale and Sven Hedin. It will be enough, however, if we refer in short detail to the descriptions of Littledale, and (subsequently) of Sven Hedin, to prove, if proof be needed, the absolute waste and sterility of those bleak, wind-swept highlands

G. Bonvalot

St. George Littledale

which separate all of Tibet that is useful to us from the great plains of Chinese Turkestan.

In one particular Littledale's records differ in a most surprising way from those of other Tibetan travellers. He took his wife with him on his journeyings, and his wife was more or less of an invalid. The pure, fresh air of the Tibetan highlands restored her to health. It is worth recording, therefore, that an English lady approached Lhasa more nearly than any other European (saving her husband) from the days of Huc to those of Younghusband. In the year 1893 Littledale had made a most useful reconnaissance, and a route survey between the Chinese frontier town of Saitu (or Sachu) on the east of the Lob Nor region and the Koko Nor, as a link in a journey which extended from Constantinople to Pekin. So he was well acquainted with the general features of the northern edge of Tibet, and quite *au fait* with Central Asian methods of travel. In the spring of 1895 he found himself once again in the same neighbourhood (rather more to the west) with his wife and Mr. Fletcher (a noted Oxford athlete), and on the 15th of May the party crossed the Akka Tagh, after surviving a bitter experience of incessant mountain climbing as they twisted their way through the narrow passes and over the ridges of the Altyn Tagh and the Tokus Davan. This part of their journey was distinctly the most difficult, and involved the greatest hardships. They were faced perpetually by transverse ridges which had to be surmounted at an enormous altitude, and in face of blinding snow.

They did not even know when they had reached the Akka Tagh. The unutterably barren desolation of this country is its prominent characteristic. Baggage animals began rapidly to succumb before the Tibetan Chang was reached. Even south of the Akka Tagh there is the same monotonous tale of the perpetual crossing of comparatively low ridges, which proved to be more than the weakened animals could surmount. It is the frightful scarcity of water and grass in these salt-impregnated regions which invariably proves the greatest difficulty. The repetition of the ridge and furrow conformation of Tibet in this region which is evidenced by the repetition of low passes, seems to point to a surface orography in that part of the Chang differing from that of the western regions (Aksai Chin) surveyed by Deasy. The successive folds appear to be in approximate parallelism to the main chains of the Akka Tagh and Altyn Tagh. This is indeed precisely what we should expect to find. Littledale's observations on the class of country here encountered are most interesting. The pass of the Akka Tagh was steep and long, and then "we found ourselves at last on the Tibetan plateau, having lakes and low mountains to the south as far as could be seen, and to the north the high ranges of the Akka Tagh, with fine glaciers and snow-fields." Some of the Akka Tagh peaks hereabouts were estimated to be 25,000 feet high. "This great upshoot of the earth's surface, which from its elevation and size deserves, in its central part, far more than the Pamirs, the name 'Roof of the world,' may be considered to commence in the west with the Pamirs, where, however, its physical character differs in some parts from the central or Tibetan portion, which again bears little resemblance to its eastern continuation on the confines of China. On the Pamirs we find a high mountainous country where the rivers are fairly large and rapid, the valleys are precipitous; in other parts where the streams are unimportant, the country is more undulating in character, and the lakes are, with some notable exceptions, fresh. The Tibetan plateau proper, which probably has an average of quite 2,000 feet in excess of the Pamirs, has, in its northern parts especially, a very small rainfall; and in the absence of rivers the drainage of the country finds its way into one or other of the innumerable lakes, which, having no outlet, are salt. Except in the volcanic country, the valleys are broad and open."

This, then, explains the general character of the northern Chang, which gradually improves southward till it reaches a point where the southwest monsoon is felt, and where the greater rainfall induces more grass and a warmer climate. Between 36° 50′ and 33° 50′ north latitude the path of these adventurers ran through a volcanic country, numerous undoubted volcanoes being visible, but in spite of the constant succession of short ridges which they encountered "we never saw one single continuous mountain range till we came south of the Tengri Nor." After leaving Cherchen in April, it was not till June that men were met with, when they struck the first Tibetan encampment of nomad herdsmen. With infinite precaution and trouble they succeeded in evading detection for many days. They passed the Zilling tso (Garing tso of Bower) on the east, and, hitting off a line of excellent grass country, they gradually restored the condition of the exhausted remnants of their transport. Nearing the Tengri Nor, they finally collided with the Tibetans, and their onward movements subsequently were impeded by every device known to Tibetan obstructiveness. Entreaties and threats on the part of the Lhasa officials were of no avail. The party held on at great risk to themselves till they reached the magnificent range of Ninchen Tangla, south of Tengri Nor — "a succession of snow-clad peaks and glaciers partially hidden in clouds and vapour, which added to their size and grandeur, while above all towered the great peak of Charemani, 24,150 feet" (probably identical with the Chimuran of the "lama" survey map of 1733). It seems possible that the determination to proceed which was shown by these travellers would after all have ended in Lhasa but for the alarming illness of Mrs. Littledale. They were perforce obliged to make their way back to the British frontier as rapidly as possible. They were probably within fifty miles of the holy city when they turned. The route over the central Chang to Ladak was practically the same as that traversed earlier by our old friend Nain Sing, south of Bower's route, and probably near the northern rim of the Brahmaputra basin.

The notable feature about it is that there is not a pass nor a water-parting of any significance to be crossed. It is a route which follows the general strike of the folds and ridges on the surface of the plateau which on either side of it extend in lines approximately parallel to the course of the Brahmaputra. The fact that no large rivers are crossed seems certainly to indicate that it is here, or near here, a little to the south, that the northern water-shed of India is to be found. From some of the innumerable lakes (the desiccating remains of ancient snow-fields which border it on the south) it is probable that those big affluents of the Brahmaputra noted by Nain Sing must take their rise; but intermediate to this long line of route through the central Chang and that of the Brahmaputra River no traveller has yet contributed the necessary topography to enable us to decide with certainty. We can only conjecture that the basin of the great river extending from its banks to the main water divide (wherever it may be) is warmer, more favourable to pasturage, more thickly populated by Dokpa herdsmen than any of the districts farther north. From Sven Hedin we get further glimpses of this central plateau region which are of the very greatest interest. Sven Hedin, in his last great journey in 1890, crossed the Altyn Tagh on his way from Lob Nor southwards to Tibet in July, near the meridian of 90° east, which cannot be far from the point where Bonvalot crossed previously. A notable feature in this remarkable journey was the employment of camels for transport — a sufficient indication of the difference in the nature of the mountain barriers of the north from those of the Himalayas. He crossed a subsidiary range called the Akato Tagh, to the northwest of the Gass Lake, by "an easy double pass," and he describes the southern flank of this range as a repetition, in point of orographical relief, of the northern flank of the Altyn Tagh, pointing to the inference that it is the southern edge of a width of plateau between these two bounding ranges, and he thus disposes of that connecting range running northeastwards from the eastern end of the Chaman Tagh of Walker's map (the Illvo Tjimen of Sven Hedin), which is obviously conjectural, and out of line with the true topographical configuration of this borderland. No great difficulty beset him so far. The pest of flies and mosquitoes, which are in this part of Asia a terrible drawback to the comfort of travelling, and the cutting force of the driving whirlwinds of drift-sand were the special plagues of the season. Gravelly formations alternated with "Kavir" — deposits of argillaceous mud — which must be a very fair equivalent for the "Kavir" of Persia. Near Lake Gass (8,900 feet), where there is tamarisk jungle and water, Sven Hedin established a sort of depot for his subsequent operations, and from that centre conducted his explorations in Tibet.

Leaving Temerlik and the salt lake of Gaz Kul, and striking southeast, he passed from the zone of vegetation over hard, barren, gravelly ground with patches of reeds and rushes near the fresh-water pools. Approaching the Tjimen Tagh (the Tsaidam range of Walker's map) they passed through a "transverse breach in the northern face of that range, deeply trenched between gravel and shingle terraces twenty-five feet high." Later they encountered granite. Slowly making their way upward over the broad flanks of the Tjimen Tagh (" Chimen " in the letterpress and " Tjimen " in his map), Sven Hedin encountered snow in July when camped near the summit, and a temperature of 23° Fahrenheit at night. The Chimen (Tsaidam of Walker) differs from the northern parallel ranges of the Altyn Tagh system in its conditions of climate and conformation. It is Alpine in character, moist, and full of vegetation (instead of being bare and barren), with rounded, weather-beaten features. Two other parallel ranges (the Ara Tagh and the Kalta-alagan), with broad latitudinal valleys intervening, were crossed before Sven Hedin reached the basin of the Ajig Kum Kul. These valleys (Kayir) are but successive steps on the staircase which leads to the Tibetan plateau. North of Chimen Tagh the plain level is less than 10,000 feet above sea. The Kayir is 13,700 feet, the pass over the Ara Tagh being only 14,350 feet. Another high valley separates the Ara Tagh from the Kalta Alagan which rises to 15,700 feet. Stretches of sand characterised the plain at the southern foot of the Kalta Alagan, at an altitude of 12,000 feet, and here were kulans (wild asses), marmots, and hares. Gnats again abounded, and the temperature rose to 68° Fahrenheit. Far off in the southeast were gigantic mountain masses covered with snow — evidently the peaks of the Arka (Akka) Tagh, or Kuen Lun. Leaving the Ajig Kum Kul lake system on the west, Sven Hedin trekked due south over the intervening plateau wilderness to the Arka Tagh, meeting with granite ridges and secondary passes *en route* with varying vicissitudes of rain, snow, and sunshine. Here they met the orongo antelope, and on the night of the 2d of August the thermometer fell to 22° Fahrenheit.

Like Littledale, Sven Hedin found it a weary process of ascent and descent to reach the true backbone of the Arka Tagh. He finally crossed it almost on the 90° east longitude meridian by a flattened saddle with a slow gradual ascent strewn with black, slaty debris leading to the summit at 17,000 feet. In his map he gives the name Koko Shili to this part of the Arka Tagh; Walker places the Koko Shili far to the south. Sven Hedin was now on the same part of the Tibetan plateau that he had previously visited, but he did not penetrate on this occasion much farther south. There is nothing very attractive about this part of Tibet, but the spirit of the explorer was within him: "Although we led the lives of dogs in this country, which was as desolate as the moon is supposed to be, yet we reaped more than an equivalent reward in the discoveries and observations which we made from day to day. It was a delicious feeling to know that we were the first human beings to tread these mountains, where there existed no path, where there never had been a path, and where there was not a footprint visible except those made by the hoof of yak, antelope, or kulan. It was a no-man's land; rivers, lakes, and mountains were all nameless; their shores, banks, and snow-fields had never been seen by any traveller's eye but mine; they were mine own kingdom for a day."

Quagmires and swamps at 15,000 feet of elevation — the action of melting snow on spongy soil — were the leading features of the next step in the journey. "One gigantic morass of yellow, plastic mud." "Truly, an accursed land." "It was like the muddy bottom of a lake just after the water had been drained out of it."

Farther south matters improved, and by the 22d of August they had reached a group of lakes about the parallel of 34° north latitude, which Sven Hedin proceeded to explore. "The bottom of the lake was covered throughout with a layer of salt from ¾ to 1½ inches thick." The salt rested on a layer of red mud. The maximum depth was 7½ feet. Here in this wild, barren lake region many interesting observations were made; but the eternal solitudes and vast steppes surrounding it would have been deadly in their weird monotony but for the ever-changing vicissitudes of storm and sunshine. "What a wonderful, what an utterly God-forsaken, region this was! The ground seemed to be thin as the air; the very mountains themselves soft as pumice stones. Everything was in a state of disintegration in some places; although the ground did bear, it nevertheless quaked under the horses' feet, and undulated before them as though it were an india-rubber sheet."

From this region of lakes and morass which have all the characteristics of a land which has only recently emerged from under an ice cap, Sven Hedin turned northward and retraced his way with many vicissitudes and the loss of one of his party to Temerlik, by a route which lay about two degrees west of the one he had taken on their southern journey. Arriving late in October, he immediately laid his plans for further explorations, which resulted in his magnificent success as the exponent of the ancient topography of the Lob Nor region, and of the physical and social conditions of life that must have existed during mediæval ages in the desert regions adjoining.

It was not till April, 1901, that he found himself at Charklik facing the Altyn Tagh again, with arrangements complete for a more southern extension of his previous reconnaissance in the hope of reaching Lhasa. He assumed the disguise of a lama for the purpose, and he took with his company a Tibetan lama of the "red" sect. Following up the Charklik River into the gorges of the mountains, by an exceedingly rough and difficult way, Sven Hedin crossed the Altyn Tagh in May, and reached the western end of the Ajig Kum Kul about the beginning of June. The water-parting of the Altyn Tagh at the head of the Charklik was 13,380 feet, and the pass was "quite easy and gentle." At the Kum Kul Sven Hedin was joined by his camel caravan, which had not followed the trail through the gorges of the Charklik. From the lake he struck southward, making fresh tracks as far as possible, eastward of his own return route of the previous year, and of the routes of Littledale and Dutreuil de Rhins, and westward of that of Bonvalot. Then follows the old record of wading through the muddy flats of the Kum basin, and the frightful toil of pushing through the swampy glens and valleys leading up to the crests of the transverse ridges, a conformation which is in many respects remarkably similar to that of the salt "shor" by-paths in the glens of the Turkestan Chol. We need not follow Sven Hedin in detail through the weary wilderness which lay south of the Arka Tagh till he reached the Zilling tso, which the reader will recollect was the terminus of Bower's route Lhasa-wards. The character of it may well be gathered from what we have already written. Gradually improving southwards, where the widely scattered tents of the nomads become more frequent, it is never in this part of the Chang absolutely destitute of sustenance. "Generally speaking, the region was perfectly barren, except for a few small patches of hard, sharp, yellow blades, one or two inches high. This was called grass. I would not advise any one who was wearing summer clothing to fling himself down on grass of that description for a siesta, for it was as hard as whalebone, and pierced like a needle through even thick clothes." Even at midsummer the low hills about the Arka Tagh are sheeted with ice. The general level of the plateau is between 16,000 and 18,000 feet.

Long before Sven Hedin (who had assumed the rôle and the dress of a Mongolian pilgrim) reached the Zilling tso, news of his coming reached Lhasa. He was given away probably by the Mongolian pilgrims who left Charklik a little later than himself, or by the first yak hunters he encountered south of the Arka Tagh. It does not matter which. Southeast of the great lake and about half way between that lake and the Tengri Nor he was brought to a stand by the armed opposition of a Tibetan crowd, and a final interview with Kamba Bombo the governor of Nagchu decided his fate. He was sent back under an escort to the Kashmir frontier at Ladak, over what was practically the same route as that of Littledale and Nain Sing. The Nagchu governor was a man of about forty, small and pale, and his dress was tasteful and elegant. After removing a red Spanish cloak, he "stood forth, arrayed in a suit of yellow silk, with wide arms, and a little, blue Chinese skull cap. His feet were encased in Mongolian boots of green velvet. In a word, he was magnificent." He was decided, however, and he made it abundantly clear that there was nothing for it but to return. His Tibetan escort were almost equally magnificent with himself. "They carried their swords in handsome silver-mounted scabbards decorated with corals and turquoises; silver 'gavos' or cases for 'burkhans,' that is, little images of Buddha; bracelets and rosaries; and in the long plaits of their hair various parti-coloured ornaments, — in a word, they were decked out in the handsomest finery they possessed. The more distinguished among them wore big hats with plumes in them; others had scarves round their heads, while the rank and file were bareheaded." The Kamba Bombo insisted on it that Sven Hedin was an Englishman from India. This was the great offence, and back to India he must go. No "sahib" will ever reach Lhasa but with an armed escort.

Sven Hedin's return across the central Chang gave us little that was actually geographically new, and he was too well looked after by his Tibetan escort to move far afield from the direct route. Is not the story of it written in one of the most delightful books of modern travel? To him we owe a most valuable record of careful observations in the wild highlands of northern Tibet, and his records alone would be sufficient, without the confirmation of other explorers, to convince us that there is no royal road from the north to Lhasa, west of Huc's route from Koko Nor. Nor can even that be considered as a route to be reckoned with for aggressive demonstrations towards India. It is a pilgrim route, and a commercial route, but practicable for no travellers unless they be Chinese or Japs. As a practicable military road, or even as a road for useful commercial purposes, it is absurd to talk of any approach to Lhasa which crosses the Kuen Lun from Chinese Turkestan to the west of it.

CHAPTER XIII

Recent Expedition to Tibet—The Reconnaissance of the Upper Brahmaputra by Ryder, and the Exploration of a Part of Western Tibet by Rawling

THE record of the Tibetan expedition to Lhasa under Colonel Younghusband, which practically commenced in the autumn of 1903 and lasted more than a year, can hardly be included in a work which deals with the adventures and vicissitudes of exploration. Volumes have been written about it, and some of the charming and instructive chapters which have illustrated Lhasa have made that sacred city almost as familiar to the public as any continental town. But such works are intended to appeal to the popular imagination, and deal more with the outward and passing presentation of their subject than with historical detail or social institutions. It is very satisfactory to find that on the whole the impressions produced by previous explorers have been confirmed by these later experiences. The way to Lhasa from Darjiling is but a short way and touches but a small fraction of the vast regions of Tibet. Explorers' work, whether as studies on topography, history, or social economics, has been amplified and corrected in many details over this restricted area by the observers

Major C. H. D. Ryder, D. S. O., R. E

and writers of the expedition; and we have learnt that, on the whole, our previous map knowledge was fairly accurate, and previous records and descriptions of the city of mystery were reasonably truthful — facts which are most gratifying to those who have spent months of official labour in sifting and sorting the mass of uncertain material which has come to hand from native sources. Inasmuch as these earlier records contain much information, patiently acquired from local authorities, which is wanting in the later journalistic accounts of Lhasa and its surroundings, we need not apologise for continuing the story of exploration rather as told by the original explorer than by the latter-day journalist. We now have a scientifically constructed map of the city of Lhasa, but so far as this book is concerned it is useful only as an illustration of the success which attended earlier efforts made under most difficult circumstances. The Tibetan expedition indeed furnishes a striking commentary on the work of long years of native exploration, and, on the whole, our explorers come splendidly out of the ordeal of comparison. If, however, we have gained little that can be called absolutely new geographical information, we can point at least to one feature of that now historic mission which redeems it from the charge of being a geographical disappointment.

The reconnaissance carried out by Captains Rawling and Ryder from Gyangtse to Simla via Gartok was of the nature of scientific exploration, such as is new to Tibet, and such as we may yet hope to see extended farther and farther from the edge of the Indian borderland into the cold wilderness of the north. It was a grand opportunity for unravelling certain geographical problems on scientific principles which could hardly be solved by the restricted methods of the weary single-handed native explorer making his cold and cheerless way from point to point of the Tibetan hinterland, always in uncertainty and often in danger. If Captain Ryder had proved nothing more than that there are no higher peaks than Mt. Everest to the north of Nepal, that alone would have been well worth the journey; but he has gone far towards answering several questions which arise when the northern water-parting — the great divide — between India and central Tibet is under discussion. It seems unlikely that he has established the position of that dividing line between the central lake region and the Brahmaputra basin, one of the most important geographical features in Asia, and he has certainly set at rest the controversy as to the connection of the twin lakes of Manasarawar, proving that the connection existed even as Strachey maintained, and that these lakes are no longer the source of the Sutlej River. This expedition (which included Captain Wood and Lieutenant Bailey) was sufficiently strong to make a complete examination of all those alternative routes following the Brahmaputra valley from its source to Shigatze which constitute a link in the Janglám or great trade route from Leh to China. Starting from Shigatze on the 7th of September, the party reached

The Gorges of the Brahmaputra above Lhatse (Rawling)

Gartok on the Indus (now established by treaty as an open trade mart for India) on the 9th of December. "We were unanimous in looking on it as one of the most dreary inhabited places we had struck on our journey — a long broad plain, absolutely bare, with a dozen wretched hovels in the middle, constitutes at this time of the year what is in summer the chief trading centre of western Tibet; but in summer traders are said to collect in large numbers, living in tents." Crossing the Ayi La (18,700 feet), the party dropped into the Sutlej valley at Totling and thence took the Shipki trade route to Simla, surmounting a series of passes (of which the Shipki La is the chief) as they followed the Sutlej valley traversing the mighty axis of the central Himalayan ranges. They reached Simla on January 11. It was a notable achievement successfully carried through in the depth of winter.

To one of the party, Captain Rawling, must be credited a most valuable geographical reconnaissance of a considerable area of the central lake region of Tibet, forming a useful extension of Captain Deasy's surveys in the western regions of the plateau. Captain Rawling, with another officer of his regiment, Lieutenant Hargreaves, reached the Tibetan plateau in the summer of 1903, and together they explored and mapped the highlands at an average elevation of over sixteen thousand feet above sea level as far east as the eighty-fourth meridian, working on strictly scientific principles with theodolite and plane table, and making full use of the data furnished by Deasy's work, as well as of the provisions which that officer had thoughtfully left behind him for the benefit of future explorers. It was a very notable performance. Captain Rawling's excellent map illustrates a country of vast elevation, seamed as to its surface with an irregular formation of comparatively low ridges (some 2,000 to 3,000 feet above the valleys) enclosing narrow spaces forming a confused system of self-contained drainage areas. One of the most remarkable features in this vast scene of dreary desolation was the extensive area of gold mines which they encountered. There was abundant evidence of a gold-mining industry still in existence which must have employed large numbers of people; the shallow pits stretched for miles, and the "water runs and dams were clear and sharp."

Indeed at every step almost of this eventful journey the explorer acquired fresh evidence of the extraordinary richness of the alluvial soil of the plateau in gold and borax. Nor was the country that they traversed during the summer months absolutely devoid of charm. Rich soil and abundant grass were frequently a feature which gladdened their eyes; game was extraordinarily abundant, and the scenery possessed the varied features of wide-spread lake and overshadowing mountain peak, an association which always lends beauty to a landscape. The lakes were obviously diminishing in volume, and in one case at least there seemed to be evidence that a lake once salt

Lhasa. Plan of the City

had gradually become sweet. Few more valuable records of Tibetan exploration exist than this of Captain Rawling. To him and to Deasy, Stein, and Ryder is due the credit of having introduced scientific methods of exploration into Tibet. It is for future explorers to follow their system, which includes a frame-work of points fixed by triangulation — and the spread of topography based thereon by the employment of trained native topographers of the Indian Survey.

CHAPTER XIV

The Approaches to Lhasa — The Dalai Lama and High State Officials — Feasts and Customs — Temples and Palaces — Folk Lore — A Tibetan Story

NOW that our mission to Tibet has returned to the Indian border we know (if we did not know before) how very little there is in Lhasa to justify that mystic fascination which has somehow or other exercised so powerful an influence on European minds. The veil has been torn aside and the naked city has been revealed in all its weird barbarity. It is in truth a scattered, unkempt, and ill regulated town, full of impurities, infested with savage dogs, obscene pigs, and night prowlers, revelling in many most unholy institutions. But there is a singularity about its barbarous ways; a quaint inconsequence in many of its most sacred functions (bringing them perilously close to the realm of pantomime) which exhibit Lhasa as a most extraordinary feature in the study of Asiatic developments, — one quite apart from anything that we can recognise elsewhere. The policy of the Tibetan hierarchy is inscrutable. Beyond a pigheaded determination to ignore the inevitable, and to admit no Englishman within the walls of the sacred city, it is difficult to discern any settled plan of political action. From

Lhasa itself we get no sign, and with the departure of the mission the gates of Lhasa are closed again as fast as ever. No voice will reach us across the Himalayan wall. We shall hardly know how the disturbed relations between Tibet and China will readjust themselves; nor can we tell whether the mild influence which we have left behind us will really out-balance the more dominant overshadowing of Russia or not. In short, we have left no representative in Lhasa, and no information which we can obtain through local channels will be in any way trustworthy.

But for the purpose of framing an idea of its appearance as a city and of its functions as the centre of a vast religious institution we have plenty of material.

Approaching Lhasa from the west over the wide gravelly plains which border the Kyichu, the first view of the town seems to be striking enough. Chandra Das describes his sensations when the city first greeted his eyes. He had passed Cheri (the great slaughter-house beyond the city-walls) and the wooded hill whereon stands the Debung monastery with its 7700 priests, and he had left behind him a "dark red temple of Chinese design with gilt spire which is known as Nachung-chos-Kyong," when at a turn of the road "the whole city stood displayed before us at the end of an avenue of gnarled trees, the rays of the setting sun falling on its gilded domes. It was a superb sight the like of which I have never seen. On our left was Potala with its lofty buildings and gilt roof; before us, surrounded by a green meadow, lay the town with its tower-like whitewashed houses and Chinese buildings with roofs of blue glazed tiles. Long festoons of inscribed and painted rags hung from one building to another waving in the breeze." Beyond Daru (at the foot of the Debung monastery hill) the road had run for a while "through a marsh overgrown with rank grass, numerous ditches drained the water into the river, and at the northeast end of the marsh we could distinguish the famous monastery of Sera. Beyond a high sand embankment on our left was the park and palace of Norbu linga, and the beautiful grove of Kemai tsal, in the midst of which stands the palace of Lhalu, the father of the last Dalai lama." A reference to the plan of Lhasa which was made by the explorer Krishna (on which Colonel Waddell has introduced further information derived from native sources) will show the general disposition of the city and its surroundings. The potala, or hill, on which stands the Dalai Lama's palace is a very remarkable feature when viewed from the west against the background of grey distant hills, with irregular masses of whitewashed Tibetan buildings clustering around its foot. The main body of the city, however, is at some distance east of the palace. A very effective photograph of the Potala was obtained by a member of one of the late Nepalese missions to Pekin passing through Lhasa, and it illustrates the curious lines of Tibeto-Chinese architecture very clearly.

The explorers Nain Sing and Ugyen were obliged both of them to exercise considerable caution in approaching Lhasa, and neither of them seems to have been much fascinated by his first acquaintance with the town. "The city of Lhasa is circular," says Nain Sing, "with a circumference of two and a half miles. In the centre of the city stands a very large temple called by various names." This is the Jo (or Jovo) Khang of the map, the true "Lhasa, or place of the Gods." "The idols in it are richly inlaid with gold and precious stones. This temple is surrounded by bazaars and shops." "At the northern end of the city are two monasteries called Muru and Ramoché; at the northwest corner the Chumuling monastery; at the west end the Tankyaling monastery; the monastery called Kontyaling is about one mile west of the city." Nain Sing observes that several of these monasteries are likewise residences of Tibetan government officials.[1]

Nain Sing paid the usual homage to the Dalai Lama, then (1865) a "handsome boy of about thirteen years of age," whom he designates Gewaring boche (Great lama of Tibet), who was attended by the Raja Gyalbo Khuro-Gyágo, the prime minister, who is, in effect, the real governor of Lhasa. According to this authority the government of Lhasa is conducted by the Raja, or Gyalpo, with the assistance of four ministers; the resident Chinese Amban having "the power of reporting against either the raja or the four

[1] It is impossible to reconcile the different forms of spelling place names adopted by native explorers, so they are given as they occur in their reports.

ministers to the Emperor of China, and if necessary he can have them removed from office." Such authority, if it remains valid, certainly gives China an effective control over Lhasa. The process of selecting the infant who represents the reincarnation of a deceased Dalai Lama is said by Nain Sing to be kept a secret from the people of Lhasa, but his account does not differ materially from that which other writers narrate. Until 1860 (according to Chandra Das) the rightful reincarnation of the defunct lama was determined by the use of the "golden jar," in which were placed the names of infants born about the time (within a month, according to Nain Sing) of the death of the Dalai Lama, and the choice of his successor determined by lot. It was only after reaching years of discretion that the ceremony took place of selecting the property of the late Lama from amongst an assortment of articles of all descriptions placed before him. But in 1875 (according to Rockhill and Ugyen) a new method was introduced after consulting the Nachung chos gyong oracle. The discovery of the reincarnation was to be entrusted to a monk of the purest morals; and only the oracle could discover such a monk. After a monk of sufficient saintliness had been discovered by the oracle, he was instructed to seek for the reincarnation near Khong-po, a little to the east of Lhasa. A vision and a voice directed him to the lake of Choskhor, and on the crystal surface of that lake he saw the future grand lama seated as a babe on his mother's lap. On his way back from the lake to Khong-po he encountered "in the house of a respectable and wealthy family" the realisation of his vision. The infant whom he recognised as having been thus revealed in the lake was taken to Lhasa and there he is now installed as the "Lord of speech, the mighty ocean of wisdom," — the Dalai Lama. This newer system seems to have been due to some misgivings on the part of the priestly hierarchy at Lhasa as to the sentiments entertained by a late Dalai lama towards his advisory council. It was feared that his spirit might influence the drawing of the lot which was to indicate his successor, and that the selection might prove unpropitious. Whether the new system of selection is to remain a permanent institution and to be regarded hereafter as constitutional remains to be seen.

So much has been written about Lhasa that it will perhaps be better to adhere to the general description of the place which is given by the later explorer Ugyen, and which generally confirms the records of the earlier explorer Nain Sing. Ugyen, it will be remembered, accompanied Chandra Das on his expedition, but he also visited Lhasa on his own account subsequently, and has added many unpublished details to those which have been previously collected and collated. His description at least possesses the merit of absolute originality. After his explorations of the Bhutan borderland (when he returned by the Yalung valley to that of the Tsanpo), Ugyen passed much of his time in visiting monasteries and in squaring matters with his conscience for acting as a British explorer in the land of the lamas. He finally crossed the Tsanpo (Brahmaputra) near the mouth of the Theb valley and visited the monastery at Dorjethag. At this point the river is about 800 yards wide and "very full of fish." From Dorjethag there is a road northward leading to Lhasa over the Tungo la, and this road the lama (forgetful of the promises made when a prisoner at Lhas Kang Jong) determined to follow. The road was good enough as far as Phurin; then open gravel plains covered with thorny bush supervened. He crossed the Tungo la at 16,330 feet, where was a flattish open grass plain at the summit; beyond the plain was a secondary pass, from which the city of Lhasa can be seen "as in a looking-glass." The descent on the northern side was steep for some distance, after which the grade becomes easy. Ugyen crossed the Kyichu on the 9th of October (1883) where the river is 500 yards broad, by a ferry under the guidance of boatmen who were so drunk as nearly to upset the boat. From the north bank he made his way through marshy ground till he reached the outer circular road of the city. It was here that it was so necessary to move circumspectly on account of the gangs of savage corpse-eating dogs which infest the purlieus of Lhasa. After a chequered night's experience he found refuge, and an old friend, in the Daphung monastery. In his search for lodgings he encountered a Chinese sergeant, who suspected him and gave information which led to his property being searched. However his Mongolian friend the Dingpon

Tibetan Natives. (Littledale)

stood by him, and finally introduced him to the Nepalese agent in Lhasa, who received him with courtesy and attention, but greeted him with the significant query "How do you do?" in English! However, Ugyen established his position in Lhasa, and commenced a systematic survey of the town "under cover of an umbrella." We may as well add that the results were not so successful as those of Krishna, whose map we give. It is well to note that in all these proceedings (as in subsequent preparations of his reports) Ugyen was much assisted by his wife. Ugyen confirms the accuracy of Chandra Das' statements about the formation of the Tibetan government. He states that the Desi Gyalpo, the regent or King of Tibet, who ranks as second only to the Dalai Lama at Lhasa, may be elected from amongst the grand lamas of one of the four great "lings" or monasteries, *i. e.*, Tsechok ling, Chenmoi ling, Kundul ling, and Tengal ling. These spiritual chiefs (for the institution of Desi as the secular ruler of Tibet apparently lapsed as long ago as the year 1680, when the Mongolians retired from interference with the government) are all incarnations of one or other of the previous rulers of Tibetan history, and are apparently embodiments of both secular and religious wisdom. The regent in Ugyen's time was from Kundul ling, and is described as "young, pious, and generous-minded," and as being "kind to the people." His periodic tours in the country were always notable for the evidences of his popularity which they led to. A previous regent (of whom the grand lama of Chen-moi ling was an incarnation) was a poor settler in Tibet who became a monk on the Sera monastery by the lucky accident of a dream which led him on the right way to promotion. This is the regent to whom the Tibetans still ascribe the regeneration of Lhasa morals by processes which one cannot describe. According to Ugyen every part of a Tibetan woman's dress, her striped petticoat, her headdress, even the discolouration of her face, is a significant reminder of the pains and penalties attending any lapse from the path of virtue. He says that the Chinese Amban is under the authority of the Regent, and that under the Amban are four Shapchi; under them again are seventy-three Tsidungs, and several Kahdungs (secretaries) who work in court under the Shapchi lama. Chandra Das gives a somewhat different account of the administrative staff. He places the council of five Kahlons next to the Regent assisted by one Kahdung only and one 'Tsipon.' The Jongpons, or district officers, and Depons, or military chiefs, rank next; whilst seventy-three pundits are retained at the principal monastery of the Dalai lama to pray for the prosperity of the kingdom and the long life of the Gyalpo. No state undertakings can be initiated without consulting the Nechung-Chos-Kyong — the great oracle of Mongolian origin — all of whose utterances are inspired.

On the second day of the first month of each year this oracle prophesies the events of the year to come. His consulting fee is about five rupees, and as private adviser as well as public functionary his time is well occupied. Much superstitious reverence surrounds him; no one is permitted to look on him as he approaches Lhasa, and the atmosphere of mysticism in which he is enveloped is strictly maintained by the authority of the State, which surrounds him with a staff of seventy lamas and burns incense before him.

Ugyen adds some interesting details regarding the Molan holiday at the commencement of the New Year to those which had previously been given by Nain Sing; but there are certain rather confusing discrepancies as regards the exact dates of the various functions. According to Ugyen the Nachung-chos-Kyong is the only oracle consulted at this feast, the second oracle (Kasmasha-chos-Kyong) mentioned by Chandra Das not being then permitted to inspire men. During the continuance of the feast the chief magisterial power is assumed by a lama of the Dapung monastery, the only monastery which can be called upon to produce this temporary representative of the law. This lama is called Shalngo by Ugyen (and Jalno by Nain Sing), and he purchases his privileges for six weeks, dating from the third day of the first month (Nain Sing). During this period he rules all Lhasa at his own discretion, appropriating all fines, and making the best he can of his bargains with government. The Dalai Lama and the Regent only are beyond his control. The Nachung-cho-Kyong oracle issues decrees which are read out to the public by assembled monks perhaps as often as 10,000 times in succession. The object of the repetition is indicated by the fact that the monks receive a reward for their exertions at the rate of eight annas per volume. Both authorities agree that the ground procession and display of idols before the Machindranath temple takes place on the 15th day of the New Year. On the 29th day of the first month a strange ceremony takes place, for an analogy to which one must turn to Jewish history. On that day a man is selected who is called the Logon gyalpo (or carrier of one year's ill luck) who becomes a sort of scapegoat for the sins of the people, and is hunted through the streets and market-place of Lhasa into the desert country towards the Samye monastery. For a week previously he perambulates Lhasa as a sort of clown with his face painted half black and half white, and is permitted extraordinary license. He helps himself to what he wants at purely nominal prices, and as he wanders through the streets he shakes a black yak's tail over the heads of the people, thus transferring from them to himself the full measure of their ill luck. Nain Sing says that this ceremony takes place at the end of the second month, and further states that the Jalno's authority, after lapsing for twenty-four days at the end of the first twenty-three days of anarchy (for that is what his rule represents), is then resumed for ten days more, and that this ceremony ends it. Ugyen also maintains that the expulsion of the Logon scapegoat from the city concludes these strange proceedings, but makes the Jalno's authority last for one and a half months. It is tolerably clear that for at least six weeks Lhasa is very much in the hands of the mob. Previously to his expulsion from the town the Logon plays an apparent game of chance by throwing dice with the Jalno (according to Nain Sing). Officially it is an open question which of the two is to undergo exile. Practically the matter is settled by the fact (according to Ugyen) that the Jalno's dice carry nothing but sixes on all their faces, whilst the Logon is supplied with ordinary cubes. Anyhow the Logon invariably loses on the throw, after a pompous official announcement that if he wins he and the Jalno will change places. Ugyen maintains that the Jalno does not appear in this ceremony and that the game is played between the Logon and the Grand Lama of the Chang-chup-ling. It is not a matter of much consequence. The Logon remains the scapegoat. Then he receives certain presents from the government — a white horse, a white dog, a white bird, with other smaller gifts of provisions and offerings from the people. Finally he is hunted out of the town amidst the yells of the mob towards the Samye monastery, where he may (if he survives his treatment at the hands of the people) be accommodated in the Lhakang, or dead house. He is privileged to remain in this sanctuary for seven days. He then retreats for another week to Chethang. Again he moves on to Lhoka, where he remains for five or six months. He lives as an outcast and outlaw, but he is privileged to commit any crime. He may murder or rob without punishment. I believe that, as a matter of fact, the wretched scapegoat seldom survives long enough to exercise his privileges. Amongst all the weird customs of Lhasa — devil dances, incantations, and the general atmosphere of religious pantomime — this appears to be the most strange. It would be interesting to trace its derivation.

Every temple, every building of note in Lhasa has been described by Indian explorers, but there is a monotony in the repetition of temple properties and the magnificence of idols and their decorations which is hardly worth imitating. The customs and fashions of the people (which are far more interesting) are only alluded to casually, even in the pages of Chandra Das' narrative; for the native mind always experiences some difficulty in realising that that which is familiar to itself is precisely that which requires most careful illustration for the enlightenment of the European public. We really know very little either of Tibetan ethnography or of those social surroundings of the various communities which are the distinctive characteristic of the various nationalities represented amongst the people of the great plateau land. Methods of disposing of the dead (probably from the repulsive prominence which is given to them) are, however, generally referred to. There are two burial-places in Lhasa. The larger of the two is to the northeast of the town called Raga and the other is near a temple within the walls of Lhasa. Dead bodies are laid on a large flat stone, on which places for the limbs have been roughly hollowed out, with their faces to the sky and their limbs stretched out. "A smoke is then sent to the sky" (Ugyen), and two vultures appear. If these vultures in their flight wheel to the right, then the soul is happy "in heaven," otherwise the vultures either turn to the left or disappear altogether. The body is finally torn to pieces and devoured by these birds. This is the only ceremony alluded to by Ugyen. But it is not the only method of disposing of the dead. The bodies are cut to pieces by the "ragyabas," or scavengers (who form a sort of guild in Lhasa into which is received any outcast or criminal who cannot be otherwise disposed of), and is then distributed amongst the city dogs. Burial is also resorted to under certain circumstances. The "ragyabas" are a specially offensive class of the lowest type of Tibetan humanity, who enjoy privileges of their own, one of which appears to be insulting all whom they meet who do not respond to their demand for alms. They are not allowed to build houses or to live otherwise than in huts constituted of mud and the horns of animals. These "ragyaba" huts appear to form a prominent feature in the entourage of Lhasa. All writers refer to them, and to the crowd of mangy savage dogs which feed on the dismembered corpses of defunct Tibetans.

The great temple of Ramoché, erected by a princess of the house of Tai tsung and wife of the Tibetan King Srong-btsan gambo, is described by Chandra Das as a flat-roofed edifice, three storeys high, by no means fulfilling the expectations he had formed of its magnificence from all that he had heard about the famous shrine. "Heaps of relics" and "a few holy images" shut in behind an iron lattice were all that the temple contained of special interest, and a small gilt dome built in Chinese style was the only expression of the form of architecture which generally leads to such magnificent effects. The ideal splendour of the temples and monasteries of Tibet is no doubt much exaggerated by Buddhist pilgrims, owing to the religious impressions produced in their minds as they wander on pilgrimages from one temple to another, amidst scenes of unusual sterility and wildness. The devotee gradually forgets what he has seen elsewhere, whilst he is ever endeavouring to realise the impressions acquired in his infancy of the glories of his ancient faith. But it is not quite the same thing with the sceptical Bengali, who measures the magnificence of these outward and visible signs of a faith which does not appeal to him from a standard which is more nearly European.

Our special pilgrim, Ugyen, visited all the holy places in Lhasa, but he was in constant peril of detection and did not move about freely. Chandra Das was able to devote much more leisure and more careful attention on the details of the principal points of interest, and is consequently a better authority even than the Buddhist lama. The Jo Kang, however, the great central temple or cathedral, which forms such a prominent feature in the view of the city as seen from the neighbourhood of the Potala, did certainly appeal to

Chandra Das. He calls it magnificent; and it is not difficult to conceive that with its dominance over the surrounding town, the height of its massive walls and the constant shimmer and movement of the banners with which it is encompassed make it impressive. "In front of it is a tall flag-pole, at the base of which hang two yak-tails, some inscriptions, and a number of yaks' and sheep's horns. In the propylon of the chief temple, the heavy wooden pillars of which are three to four feet in circumference, and about twelve feet high, upwards of a hundred monks were making prostrations before the image of the Lord (Jovo) on a throne facing the west, when Chandra Das was there. This famous image of the Buddha, known as Jovo rinpoche is said to have been made in Magadha during the lifetime of the great teacher. Visvakarma is supposed to have made it under the guidance of the god Indra, of an alloy of the five precious substances, god, silver, zinc, iron, and copper, and the "five precious celestial substances," probably diamonds, rubies, lapis-lazuli, emeralds, and "*indranila*." When the Princess Konjo, a relative of the Emperor Taitsung, was given in marriage to the King of Tibet, she brought this image with her. "The image is life size and exquisitely modelled, and represents a handsome young prince. The crown on its head is said to be the gift of Tsong Khapa, the great reformer." "On the four sides of it were gilt pillars with dragons turned round them, supporting a canopy. On one side of the image of Buddha is that of Matreya, and on the other that of Dipin Kara Buddha. Behind this again is the image of the Buddha Gang Chang Wogyal, and to the right and left of the latter those of the chief disciples of the Buddha." Then follows an enumeration of other statues, a catalogue of relics, and a tale of quaint legends connected with them. There can be no doubt that the Jovo Kang is the central religious institution of Lhasa, and that, as such, it occupies the place which the temple of Solomon held at Jerusalem in the veneration of the ancient Jews. Of the Potala (the palace of the Dalai Lama) Chandra Das also gives us the best description of any native visitor from India. The Nepalese photograph well illustrates the nature of the approach to the residence of the Dalai Lama which cost Chandra Das such an effort to surmount. "Arrived at the eastern entrance of the Potala," says Chandra Das, "we dismounted and walked through a long hall, on either side of which were rows of prayer-wheels which every passer-by put in motion. Then ascending three long flights of stone steps we left our ponies in care of a by-stander, — for no one may ride further, — and proceeded towards the palace, under the guidance of a young monk. We had to climb up five ladders before we reached the ground floor of the Phodang marpo, or the red palace, thus called from the exterior walls being of a dark red colour. Then we had half a dozen more ladders to climb up, and we found ourselves at the top of Potala (there are nine storeys to this building), where we saw a number of monks awaiting an audience. The view from here was beautiful beyond compare, — the broad valley of the Kyi-chu, in the centre of which stands the great city, surrounded by green groves; the gilt spires of Jo Kang and other temples of Lhasa, and farther away the great monasteries of Sera and Dabung, beyond which rose the dark blue mountains." "Walking very softly, we came to the middle of the reception hall, the roof of which is supported by three rows of pillars, four in each row, and where light is admitted by a sky-light. The furniture was that generally seen in lamaserais, but the hangings were of the richest brocades and cloth of gold; the church utensils were of gold; and the frescoes on the walls of exquisite fineness. Behind the throne were beautiful tapestries and satin hangings forming a great canopy. The floor was beautifully smooth and glossy, but the doors and windows, which were painted red, were of the rough description common throughout the country. An attendant approached, who took our presentation 'Khatag,'" and "we then took our seats on rugs, of which there were eight rows; ours were in the third, and about ten feet from the Grand Lama's throne. The Grand Lama is a child of eight (1882), with bright and fair complexion and rosy cheeks. His eyes are large and penetrating, the shape of his face remarkably Aryan, though somewhat marred by the obliquity of his eyes. The thinness of his person was probably due to the fatigue of the court ceremonies and to the religious duties and ascetic observances of his estate. A yellow mitre covered his head and its pendent lappets hid his ears; a yellow mantle draped his person, and he sat cross-legged with joined palms. The throne on which he sat was supported by carved lions, and covered with silk scarves. It was about four feet high, six feet long, and four feet broad. The state officers moved about with becoming gravity; there was the Kuchar Khanpo, with a bowl of holy water, coloured yellow with saffron; the censer carrier, with the golden censer with three chains; the Solpon Chenpo, with a golden teapot; and other household officials. Two gold lamps made in the shape of flower vases burnt on either side the throne." We cannot, however, follow further the graphic narrative of Chandra Das, as our business is rather with the processes of Tibetan exploration than with the incidents of Lhasa.

Ugyen, whilst hiding from the too inquisitive regard of old acquaintances at Darjiling, collected some very curious old-world legends and folk-lore which might well be worth scholarly investigation. It is impossible to do more here than reproduce one of these tales shortly as a sample of their nature. The story is apropos of the introduction of music (symbolised by the harp, or guitar, or some instrument of a similar nature) into Tibet from China by a Chinese princess named Gyara.

"Once upon a time," says the story, the King of Tibet was warned by his oracle that unless he married a Chinese princess the Buddhist religion would decline. He finally (after much difficulty) selected one Lompogara as his ambassador on the delicate mission of securing the hand of the Emperor of China's only daughter. But Lompogara on his arrival in China (after adventures too numerous to recount) found three or four competitors in the field, amongst whom were the King of Persia and the King of India. Miraculous feats of strength and of arms were set by the emperor to the representatives of these different suitors to perform; in all of which Lompogara was triumphantly successful through the strength granted him by his Tibetan gods. Amongst other marvellous performances he claimed the princess by his success in recognising her amidst two thousand of the most beautiful girls in China. Advised by an old woman with whom he lodged, he boldly selected the ugliest. Now this is a distinct departure from the ordinary course of Eastern story and indicates originality. Such details of the story as those which represent the princess as consulting her own looking-glass in order to obtain a vision of the bridegroom have a more familiar ring. The glass first told a flattering tale, but when it finally presented her suitor as an ugly old man she broke it to pieces. Mention is made too of a book which was once the great Chinese oracle, called Kabtsi thamo. "All that we do or say is found out in that book. In that book even the lice that are on the body of a man" (surely this is quite Tibetan!) "and the leaves and fruits of trees are also found out in that book," says the lama in his quaint English. But the book could not tell the king by what magic art Lompogara had divined the identity of the princess. He accordingly threw it into the fire. Throughout these Tibetan tales there is a curious contempt expressed (or at least intimated) for household oracles. At the end of the story the princess (who had throughout been in communication with her lover by means of a carrier pigeon) stole the household gods, — the image of Sakya Muni and the image of Jitsun Dolma Sungjin, — and went off to Tibet; *not* with the ambassador who had been sent to claim her, but with his assistant. Lompogara was detained for two years in China by the orders of the Chinese emperor, for the purpose of raising up descendants as acute as himself. At last he escaped by means of a subtle device and returned to Tibet. Here he found the princess still waiting for the king (who was more interested in a new Nepalese wife than in any Chinese princess), and it was during this period of waiting and of lamentation that she introduced the harp. By means of her skill as a musician she finally gained the king's attentions. Thus all ends happily, except that the Nepalese wife subsequently disputed the maternity of the child that was born to Gyara, and the king as arbitrator was unable to decide. He left the question to the boy himself to settle, but although the boy gave a strictly impartial decision (for he said that he belonged to both), he had one eye knocked out by the enraged Nepalese woman who claimed entire possession of him, and thus satisfactorily proved that she was not his mother. Students of eastern legends and tales will at once recognise several points of departure in this from the usual sequence of events as recorded in similar literature of the nearer East. The origin is probably Chinese, and much more ancient than that of the "thousand and one nights," or any similar collection of fables. The ugliness of the heroine is in itself an original feature; such a sequel as the domestic quarrel with which the story terminates is a marked departure from the ordinary construction of Turkish or Arabic tales.

CHAPTER XV

General Summary — Significance and Value of Approach to Lhasa from the Northeast — Russia's Position relatively to Tibet and India — The Value of Eastern and Southeastern Tibet — The Promise of Gold — Necessity of Opening up the Valley of the Brahmaputra

THE gradual progress of Tibetan exploration (more especially the researches of the Indian native surveyors) have revealed to us the value of Tibet as regards its political and commercial relationship to India. Politically, this huge mass of elevated hinterland is as much of a guardian buffer to the northern approaches to India as ever it was. No means have been discovered by which the barren, dry, and storm-swept wastes of the northern Chang can be bridged so as to evolve a practicable highroad across them. Their stony desolation, amidst which water is scarcely to be found, and fuel only to be obtained by grace of good luck and much searching, presents a barrier of at least five hundred miles between the inhabited depression of Chinese Turkestan and that of the upper Brahmaputra — five hundred miles of sterility at an elevation where many men would find it impossible to live. Too much stress should not be laid on the obstacle presented by intersecting ridges and ranges, which are not relatively high and which have never proved to be insuperable obstacles to advance, although the whole surface of the Chang is seamed with them. It is the absence of good water and shelter which places the possibility of crossing these wastes with any great company of people beyond the category of human possibility. It has always been so. No Mongolian or Chinese host has ever swept southwards across the Kuen Lun into the comparatively rich and fertile valleys of the Brahmaputra basin by any line of route west of that meridional water-parting from which the Chinese rivers spring.

Similarly from the west. No explorer has yet discovered a route to Lhasa which could by any stretch of imagination be called practicable for military purposes. We know much about the Janglám, the commercial road between Leh and Lhasa, and we know that of two military expeditions which have attempted to follow this road, neither could record any substantial success, although neither met with any substantial opposition. But when we examine the value of Tibet as a buffer from aggression from the northeast and east, we are faced with other possibilities. From the days of Huc to those of Rockhill and De Rhins and Krishna, travellers have made their way with no difficulties greater than those which beset ordinary travel in out-of-the-way places between China and that land of no-man's occupation which lies west of the Koko Nor. The Koko Nor region is indeed but an outlying province of the Chinese Empire, with which intercommunication is habitually maintained. From the Koko Nor region southward it is true that we have still the width of the Chang to cross ere we reach the Brahmaputra — wider and yet more elevated here than it is further west, for we are touching that central divide where the small sources of all the great rivers flowing east are found. Huc's account of his journey is enough to prove that in winter, at any rate, the difficulties of this route must be most formidable. But in spite of such difficulties, it is a well-trodden route on which the feet of thousands of pilgrims press annually, and by which much Chinese trade finds its way to Lhasa. Not only in small companies of two and three do the Mongolians of the northern steppes make their way to Lhasa by this road, they come and go in great companies, and it cannot be set aside as a highway to be ignored, either from the political or commercial point of view, whatever may be its value for military purposes.

From the east again we know that Tibet has been invaded and conquered, and that armies have passed and repassed by a regularly maintained line of route which forms the recognised highway between Lhasa and Pekin. The southern approaches are in our own hands. It is only to the east and northeast that we have to look for any possible scheme of expansion or advance, such as might peril our position in India as the dominant power in this Indian hinterland — the upper Brahmaputra valley. On the direct east lies China. To the northeast is China again, and a wild, irregular border country over which China possesses little control, and in which she has no interest. It is only China with whom we have to deal on the east, and in spite of the marvellous record of Chinese invasion over the passes that lie between Ta-chien-lu and the Brahmaputra valley, we need have little fear of a repetition of such performances, or of serious difficulty in checking them should it be necessary. It is by this route that China still maintains her political influence in Tibet — an influence which, whether great or small, we have always recognised and with which we have no wish to interfere. But on the northeast the political position is not so easy to define. Just as Leh, the capital of Ladak, is the base for all commercial movement from the West, so is Sining fu, flanking the Koko Nor depression, a similar base for northeastern advance. The occupation of this region would undoubtedly lead to the command of political influence in Lhasa, and might even dominate commercial relations with Tibet. It must be remembered that the direct line of communication between Manchuria and the Koko Nor is as much Mongolian as Chinese, and that it is always open. The process of expansion from Manchuria to the Koko Nor region would be simple and rapid. At Urga in northern Mongolia (well within the pale of Russian influence) there dwells the third greatest Buddhist pontiff in the world, ranking only after the Dalai lama and the lama of the Tashilumpo in the Buddhist hierarchy. This great prelate is known as Bogdo, and, although he does not appear to be strictly orthodox, he is, nevertheless, the representative of the Buddhist Church to many millions of Buddhists who dwell around him. Russia is already a great Buddhist power in Asia; and she is geographically nearer to the centre and fountain of the faith which so strongly influences nearly a third of the world's inhabitants than we are in either Burma or Ceylon. Russia in Manchuria would be but the prelude to Russia on the borders of Tibet, holding in her hands those pilgrim avenues to Lhasa which start from the Koko Nor. With Russia firmly established in Manchuria, can we doubt that in a very few years' time we should have all the pastoral waste around Koko Nor (now recognised as no-man's land) permanently occupied?

But Russia, overlooking the northeastern frontier of Tibet, would be almost as far removed from the possibility of active aggression against India as ever. She would no more dream of crossing eastern Tibet than she would of crossing the Chang from the north with any aggressive scheme against the Indian frontier; but she would occupy a very central position indeed in the Buddhist world; she would enormously increase the weight of her political influence in Asia, and she would obviously dominate the Tibetan trade which trends vastly more Chinawards than towards India.

The importance of Tibet as a factor in the great world of commerce is perhaps hardly to be estimated at its exact worth. We can only hazard a guess at it. Our explorers have sufficiently proved that the commercial wealth of the country centres itself in the southern and eastern valleys, and the recent expedition has confirmed their views. In the south we have a small amount of gold, borax, salt, and goat's hair (or pushm) in the upper Indus valley and Nari-Khorsum, which finds its way to Leh, or over the Kumaon passes. From the markets of the Brahmaputra valley (Shigatze, Gyangtse, and Lhasa) an insignificant trade dribbles to Bengal by the Sikkim and Assam routes, which includes silver, musk, wool, horses (or ponies), yaks' tails, etc., in return for piece goods; but taking it for all in all, our trade with Tibet is ridiculously small, and would probably be fairly represented by an estimate of £150,000 per annum. Doubtless it could be increased. Wool, for instance, is capable of large development in Tibet, and it is possible (but not probable) that the opposition of the Chinese officials to the introduction of Indian tea might be overcome; in which case an immense field would at once be opened up to India. At present, however, it is idle to hope for such a radical change in the conservative tastes of the Tibetan people as an appreciation of Indian tea. They like it in bricks, coarse and strong, big-leaved and black, and the Chinese mode of preparation is hardly suitable to the more refined qualities of the Indian growth.

Trade with China, however, — with the provinces of Kansu, Sechuan, and Yunnan, — is on quite another footing. The chief trade depots, or central marts, between China and Tibet are Sining fu, east of Koko Nor, and Ta-chien-lu, on the eastern frontier. The former is the commercial entrepôt for Mongolian trade, and the latter for Sechuan. The position of these towns has already been discussed. Other important trade centres are Li Kiang in the south, on the right bank of the Yang tsi River, and Tali-fu, which distribute Tibetan trade in Yunnan. There are, in fact, innumerable trade marts of more or less significance which deal direct with those valleys of eastern Tibet which (we once again point out) include by far the wealthiest districts of the country. It is in those eastern valleys, of which we know so little, that the centres of Tibetan art and manufacture, as well as the richest agricultural districts, are to be found. Darge and Chiamdo, Zayul and Poyul, with their thousand hidden valleys, are all districts where a comparatively thriving population develops the indigenous produce of the country in peace and contentment. The value of the Tibetan trade with China is not to be estimated by the light of any available statistics — but it cannot be less than several millions. If the enterprises of commerce admit of strategical combinations, then we can clearly indicate Jyekundo on the Dichu River (the upper Yang tsi) as the strategic centre for the dominance of this trade — and Jyekundo is the next step southward from Sining fu and the Koko Nor. These few brief considerations of the geographical distribution of Tibetan trade will be enough to indicate that the channels of Tibetan commerce are far more eastward and northward than southward towards India. In a word, Manchuria (especially Manchuria with a well established Koko Nor connection) might very well rule the best of the Tibetan market if in the hands of competent and enterprising European management.

So far we have looked at Tibetan trade from the ordinary standpoint of commercial exchange; but there is just one consideration which affects Tibet, placing that country apart from the usual category of the world's consumers, or distributors of ordinary trade commodities. Tibet is rich in gold — and it is impossible to suppose that the exceptional position which the great highland country occupies in that respect is altogether absent from the minds of those who would grasp at political influence at Lhasa. Tibet is not only rich in the ordinary acceptance of the term; she must be enormously rich — possibly richer than any country in the world. For thousands of years has gold been washed out of her surface soil by the very crudest of all crude processes and distributed abroad. Some has gone to India via Kashmir or Kumaon, some northward to Kashgar; but most of it undoubtedly has gone to fill the treasuries of Pekin. From every river which has its source in the Tibetan plateau, gold is washed. Every traveller who records his experiences in that country speaks of gold workings, and refers to the vast extent of the abandoned mines — mines which on the Chang Tang appear to be shallow and superficial, from which probably not even one-half of the gold upturned has ever been extracted.

The pundit Nain Sing gives a detailed account of

the gold-mining processes which were in full force at Jhalung, about two hundred miles from the Ladak frontier, twenty-five years ago. He reported that the mines there were seldom more than trenches from twenty-five to thirty feet deep, the gold being roughly washed out of the alluvial soil which was workable with spades. Littledale tells of the remains of many such superficial mines which he found abandoned on the road between Lhasa and Ladak. Rawling found mines extending over many miles of country, which appear to be still worked. Gold is said to be found in quantities near the Manasarawar Lake. Prjevalski records that in the north of Tibet gold is very plentiful, and that the Tungut diggers went no deeper than two or three feet; "nevertheless they shewed us whole handfuls of gold, in lumps as big as peas, and twice or thrice as big." Mr. W. Mesny (R. G. S. Proceedings, Vol. VII. p. 545), however, questions the accuracy of Prjevalski's deductions from what he saw, and maintains that gold in the Koko Nor region is almost invariably found under a pebble bed of twenty feet in thickness, resting in nuggets (varying in size from a turnip seed to a pea) on a bed of hard rock; and that the diggers seen by Prjevalski must have been washing in the old bed of a lake or river. Rockhill refers to the celebrated "Gork" mines south of this region; and there is abundant evidence of the existence of free gold in all the upper valleys of the Chinese rivers within the limits of eastern Tibet and on the borders of the Kam province. Bower notes the extreme cheapness of gold at Litang, near Batang; and, finally there is the certainty that whatever gold may have been extracted from Tibetan soil by such crude processes as explorers have witnessed, there must be at least as much left behind. There can be no doubt that Tibet is a great natural treasure-house of gold; but its mineral wealth is by no means confined to gold. Silver, copper, lead, iron, and mercury are all found (and worked) in southeastern Tibet. Agate, borax, and salt are also amongst its products. Musk, of course, is a prominent feature in Tibetan trade, and there are vast possibilities in the forests of timber which exist in southeastern and eastern Tibet. Thus we see that there is quite enough of material value in Tibet to make it an objective to commercial enterprise.

Tibet possesses great natural resources, and these resources are chiefly developed in the south, in the basins of the Indus and Brahmaputra, and in the east, in the valleys of the great Chinese rivers which rise in the plateau and flow southeastward, skirting India. The entrance to these valleys is in the hands of any strong power settled in the northeastern corner of Tibet, the Koko Nor region, and it is this rather than the doubtful advantage of the pilgrim route to Lhasa which makes the Koko Nor and the adjoining Chinese frontier town of Sining fu significant, if not important.

But Russia is no longer the dominating power in Manchuria. The Japanese have decided that, and the way from Manchuria to Tibet is no longer open to her. It is from the direction of Urga, if from anywhere, that the shadow now falls. We may reasonably hope, however, that for many a long year to come the shadow will be removed. The true geographical hinterland of India beyond the Himalayan snows, the valleys of the Indus and Brahmaputra (our own rivers) are quite near to us, quite reachable, if we choose to make them so, and one of the first and most effective methods of asserting our determination to safeguard the glacis of India's northern barrier of defence is to open up the nearest and readiest approaches across or through the main ramparts.

The road to southern Tibet tapping the most useful commercial avenues is that which has been adopted by our mission under Colonel Younghusband — the route which passes up the valley of Chumbi to Phari, and thence to Gyangtse by the Tang la pass. This we may fairly hope will never be closed again. It is the highroad connecting Darjiling and Bengal with Lhasa. But this is not the only important route into Tibet, — not even the most important if we regard it from the purely commercial point of view.

What we want is an open road through country more promising than Chumbi, encountering no formidable passes, no high altitudes, until the end debouches on to the Tibetan plateau; one which rises by gentle grades over comparatively easy slopes. There is only one such road rendered possible by geographical configuration, and that is the road which follows the course of the Brahmaputra from the valley of Assam to the Kyichu and Lhasa. The routes through Bhutan either by Baxa to Phari, or further east by Tawang more directly to Lhasa, do not realise these conditions, nor do they affect our prospects of direct commerce with the rich districts of Tibet which lie to the south-east at comparatively low altitudes. The one great natural highway into Tibet is indicated by the valley of the Brahmaputra, which may possibly not only lead by easy grades to the plateau, but directly taps such wealthy valleys as may exist in Zayul and Poyul (about which we know little geographically, but have heard much) and points the straightest way to Eastern Tibet. It is impossible on such evidence as we possess to decide on the precise characteristics of this mist-enveloped valley, but probably they do not differ largely from those of other transverse Himalayan valleys through which pass the waters of the Asiatic highlands to the plains of India. The most difficult and most steeply enclosed portion of the valley will probably be found near our frontier, where the strike or axis of the outer edges of the mountain system are transverse to the course of the river. Beyond this outer barrier the main valley will be found to widen for long stretches, the flanking mountains being withdrawn to a distance, and only touching the actual banks of the stream with the foot of their spurs. These are fairly well described by an explorer who found it necessary from time to time to leave the river and cross these spurs by narrow paths. Approaching the great bend the valley obviously closes to something in the nature of a gorge, and the stupendous falls near

Samding can only be outflanked by a turning road involving a considerable detour. Westward of the bend to Lhasa the nature of the valley is sufficiently well known and has been sufficiently described. There is nothing so far which can be reckoned as a formidable obstacle to the engineering of a road unless it be the falls near Samding. On the whole (regarded as a Himalayan road), it would probably prove an easier problem to deal with than is usual in the category of mountain road-making; but a further and more detailed exploration of the valley is urgently required. Nor can we pass over the importance of a thoroughly accurate route survey of the connecting link between Sadya, in Assam, and Ta-chien-lu, the Chinese frontier town on the Tibetan border which dominates the road to the rich province of Sechuan and the Yangtsi valley. Assam is parted from China by about 500 miles of hill country on this line of connection, the direct distance being considered less. Batang in Tibet may be placed at 300 miles from Sadya. From the explorations of Needham and Krishna we know something of the nature of this 300 miles of intervening hills. From a dozen different sources we know all about the route between Batang and Ta-chien-lu; and it is obvious that the chief difficulties of the route are concentrated in the latter section, which is already the great recognised trade route between Lhasa and Pekin; and has been so since the Mahommedan rebellion discounted the value of the route via Koko Nor and Sining.

I am no commercial prophet, but it appears to me

that it would surely open up a splendid vista of future trade activity to India if one at least of her present great commercial highways (the river Brahmaputra) were extended into the heart of the richest corner of Tibet on one side, and to the borders of one of the richest provinces of China on the other. We may set aside our nervousness about Russia here; no military opening could be afforded by the development of such routes as these, excepting to Chinese enterprise; and marvellous as have been the feats of the Chinese in former years, such performances are not likely to be repeated. The extension of Russian influence from a Manchurian base through Mongolia to Tibet, and along the borderland of western China, has been checked by Japan for a time, but we must expect that the pressure induced by the laws of national expansion will still remain, and we must look for a revival of that commercial rivalry in these regions of the far East as soon as Russia can regain her position in Asiatic prestige and influence.

What is it that bars the way to the establishment of a line of commercial traffic both along the Brahmaputra and northeastwards to China? Nothing but our own official indisposition to advance one single step beyond our Indian frontier that can be by any possibility avoided. In order to break through the obstinate determination of the frontier people immediately adjoining our own border, which prevents a stranger (whether native or European) from setting foot in their hills, and impels them to retain in their own hands the monopoly of the route between their trade marts (close to our frontier) and India, we should probably require a small expedition. These tribes who bar the way are neither Tibetan nor Assamese; their origin and ethnographical extraction is conjectural, and they are in social ethics, in manners and customs, amongst the most irreclaimable savages in the world. We have no influence with Abors or Mishmis; Tibetan priesthood does not touch them, or affect them in any way. The Christian missionary cannot reach them. They are but half-clothed aborigines of those jungles which they infest, and which they are determined to keep to themselves. Above all, they are profoundly impressed with the notion that we are afraid of them. Just as the Tibetans laughed aloud at the idea that they could not overwhelm or expel the British mission (even after the affair at Guru) if they chose, so do these savages dance their war dances on their own wild hills and proclaim to the mountains that we dare not cross their frontier. Such action on their part is, of itself, no reason for our interference, but there may be other reasons of which they know nothing which may finally make it imperative that we should move freely through their country, whilst still leaving them as independent as are the Afridis or Swatis who dwell on either side our road to the Khaibar and Chitral. Possibly it will not be long before such action is recognised as essential to the progress of Indian trade.

BIBLIOGRAPHY OF TIBET

Andrada, Antonio de.

Novo Descubrimento de grao catayo ou dos Regnos de Tibet. Lisbon, 1626.

Grueber and Dorville.

Tronnier, R. Die Durchquerung Tibets Seitens der Jesuiten, Johannes Grueber und Albert de Dorville im Jahr 1661. Zeitschrift Gesellschaft für Erdkunde, Berlin, 1904.

Voyage à la Chine des Pères Grueber et d'Orville (in Thevenot's Voyages, Part IV).

Kircher, Athanasius.

China, Monumentis qua Sacris qua Profanis, necnon variis. Naturæ et Artis Spectaculis. Illustrata. Antwerp, 1667.

Della Penna di Billi.

A Short Account of the Great Kingdom of Tibet in 1729 A. D. Journal Buddhist Text and Anthropological Society, V (1897).

Desideri, Ippolito. Puini, Carlo.

Il Tibet (Geografia, Storia, Religione, Costumi) secondo la relazione de Viaggio del P. Ippolito Desideri. (Memorie Societa Geogr. Italiana, 1904, pp. lxiv and 402.)

Turner, Samuel.

Account of an Interview with Teshoo Lama, at the Monastery of Terpaling, 1783. Asiatic Researches, Calcutta, Vol. I, 1788.

Moorcroft, William.

A Journey to Lake Manasarovara in Un-des, a Province of Little Tibet. Asiatic Researches, Calcutta, Vol. XII. Map.

Strachey, Lieut.-Gen. Sir Richard.

Narrative of a Journey to the Lakes Rakas-tal and Manasarawar, in Western Tibet, undertaken in September, 1848. (Geographical Journal, 15, 1900.) Map and illustrations.

Strachey, Capt. H.

Narrative of a journey to the Lakes Cho-Lagan or Rakas Tal, and Cho-Mapan or Manasarowar, and the Valley of Pruang in Tibet, in 1846. Map.

Physical Geography of Western Tibet. (From the Journal of the Royal Geographical Society, Vol. 28. 1853.) Map.

Huc, E. R.

Recollections of a Journey through Tartary, Tibet, and China during 1844-46. 2 vols. 1852.

Prjevalski, Gen. N. M.

Mongolia, the Tangut Country, and the Solitudes of Northern Tibet Translated by E. Delmar Morgan, with Introduction and Notes by Col. Henry Yule. 2 vols. London, 1876.

Markham, Sir C. R.

Narratives of the Mission of George Bogle to Tibet, and of the Journey of Thomas Manning to Lhasa. (Second Edition.) Map and plates. 1879.

Montgomerie, Capt. T. G.

Report of a Route-Survey made by Pundit from Nepal to Lhasa, and thence through the Upper Valley of the Brahmaputra to its Source. (Journal of the Royal Geographical Society, Vol. 38. 1868.) Map.

Report of the Trans-Himalayan Explorations during 1867. (Journal of the Royal Geographical Society, Vol. 39. 1869.)

Narrative of an Exploration of the Namcho, or Tengri Nur Lake, in Great Tibet, made by a Native Explorer, during 1871-72. (Journal of the Royal Geographical Society, Vol. 45. 1875.) Map.

Journey to Shigatze in Tibet and return by Dingri-Maidan into Nepaul in 1871, by the Native Explorer No. 9. (Journal of the Royal Geographical Society, Vol. 45. 1875.) Map.

Extracts from an Explorer's Narrative of his Journey from Pitoragarh, in Kumaon, via Jumla to Tadum and back, along the Kali Gandak to British Territory. (Journal of the Royal Geographical Society, Vol. 45. 1875.)

Report on the Trans-Himalayan Explorations in Connection with the Great Trigonometrical Survey of India during 1871. Folio. Map. Dehra Dun, 1872.

Hennessy, J. B. N.

Report on the Explorations in Great Tibet and Mongolia, made by A.-K., in 1879-82, in connection with the Trigonometrical Branch, Survey of India. Plan. Folio. Dehra Dun, 1884.

Walker, Gen. J. T.

Four Years' Journeyings through Great Tibet, by one of the Trans-Himalayan Explorers (A. K.) of the Survey of India. (Proceedings of the Royal Geographical Society, Vol. 7. 1885.) Map.

Exploration of the Great Sanpo River of Tibet during 1877, in connection with the operations of the Survey of India. (Proceedings of the Asiatic Society of Bengal. 1879.) Map.

Desgodins, C. H.

Le Thibet d'après la Correspondance des Missionaires. (Second Edition.) Map. Paris, 1885.

Report on Explorations in Nepal and Thibet by Explorer M.-H. (Season 1885-86.) Map. Folio. Dehra Dun, 1887.

Chandra Das, Sarat.

Narrative of a Journey to Lhasa in 1881–82. Map. Folio. Calcutta, 1885.

Journey to Lhasa and Central Tibet. Edited by the Hon. W. W. Rockhill. Maps and illustrations. 1902. New edition. 1904.

Report on the Explorations of Lama Serap Gyatsho, 1856–68; Explorer K.-P., 1880–84; Lama U. G., 1883; Explorer R. N., 1885–86; Explorer P. A., 1885–86; in Sikkim, Bhutan, and Tibet. Maps. Folio. Dehra Dun, 1889.

Prjevalski, Gen. N. M.

Fourth Journey to Central Asia, 1883–85. (In Russian.) St. Petersburg, 1888.

Morgan, E. Delmar. Prjevalski's Journeys and Discoveries in Central Asia. (Proceedings R. G. S. April, 1887.)

Roborovski, V.

Progress of the Russian Expedition to Central Asia under Colonel Pievtsoff. (Proceedings R. G. S. N. S. Vols. XII, XIII. 1890–91.)

Bonvalot, G.

De Paris au Tonkin à travers le Tibet inconnu. Map and illustrations. Paris, 1892.

Bower, Capt. H.

Diary of a Journey across Tibet. Maps and illustrations. Calcutta, 1893.

(Pievtsof.) Morgan, E. Delmar.

The Pievtsof Expedition and M. Bogdanovitch's Surveys. (R. G. S. Journal, II. 1893.)

Rockhill, W. W.

The Land of the Lanas: Notes of a Journey through China, Mongolia, and Tibet. Maps and illustrations. 1891.

Diary of a Journey through Mongolia and Tibet in 1891 and 1892. Map and illustrations. Washington, 1894.

Littledale, St. George R.

A Journey across Tibet, from North to South, and West to Ladak. (R. G. S. Journal, vol. 7. 1896.) Maps.

The Central Asian Expedition of Captain Roborovski and Lieutenant Kozloff. (R. G. S. Journal. August, 1896.)

Dutreuil, de Rhins, J.-L.

Mission Scientifique dans la Haute Asie, 1890–95. 3 vols. Maps and plates. Paris, 1897–98.

Wellby, Capt. M. C.

Through Unknown Tibet. Maps and illustrations. 1898.

Deasy, Capt. H. H. P.

In Tibet and Chinese Turkestan. Map and illustrations. 1901.

Beligatti, Cassiano.
Relazione Inedita di un Viaggio al Tibet. (A. Magnaghi.) (Revista Geografica Italiana. VIII, 1901. IX, 1902.)

Rijnhart, Susie Carson.
With the Tibetans in Tent and Temple. Narrative of Four Years' Residence on the Tibetan Border, and of a Journey into the Far Interior. Illustrations. Edinburgh and London, 1901.

Kozloff, Capt. P. K.
The Russian Tibet Expedition, 1899–1901. (R. G. S. XIX.) Map and illustrations. 1902.

Sandberg, Graham.
An Itinerary of the Route from Sikkim to Lhasa, together with a Plan of the Capital of Tibet and a New Map of the Route from Yamdok Lake to Lhasa. Calcutta. 1901.
The Exploration of Tibet. Its History and Particulars from 1623 to 1904. Map and plan. Calcutta, 1904.

Tsybikoff, G. T.
Lhasa and Central Tibet. (Translated from the Russian.) (Smithsonian Report, 1903.)

Grenard, F.
Tibet: The Country and its Inhabitants. Translated by A. Teixeira de Mattos. London, 1904.

Hedin, Sven.
Through Asia. 2 vols. Maps and illustrations. 1898.
Central Asia and Tibet; towards the Holy City of Lassa. 2 vols. Maps and illustrations. 1903.

Stein, M. Aurel.
Sand-buried Ruins of Khotan. Personal Narrative of a Journey of Archæological and Geographical Exploration in Chinese Turkestan. London, 1903.

Launay, Adrien.
Société des Missions, Étrangères. Histoire de la Mission du Tibet. 2 vols. Lille and Paris (1903).

Grenard, F.
Tibet: The Country and its Inhabitants. Map. 1904.

Waddell, L. A.
The Buddhism of Tibet or Lamaism. Illustrations. 1895.

Waddell, Lieut.-Col. L. A.
Lhasa and its Mysteries, with a Record of the Expedition of 1903–1904. Maps and illustrations. 1905.

Younghusband, Sir F.
The Geographical Results of the Tibet Mission. Geographical Journal. Vol. XXV. Map and illustrations. 1905.

Rawling, Capt. C. G.

The Great Plateau, being an account of Exploration in Central Tibet, 1903, and of the Gartok Expedition, 1904-1905. London, 1905.

Crosby, O. T.

Tibet and Turkestan. a Journey through old Lands and a Study of New Conditions. London and New York, 1905.

Ryder, Major C. H. D.

Exploration and Survey with the Tibet Frontier Commission, and from Gyangtse to Simla via Gartok. Geographical Journal, XXVI. Map, plan, and illustrations. 1905.

Candler, E.

The Unveiling of Lhasa. London, 1905.

Landon, Percival.

Lhasa: An Account of the Country and People of Central Tibet, and the Progress of the Mission sent there by the English Government in the Year 1903-1904. London, 1905.

INDEX

C

D

L

M

TIBET
AND
THE SURROUNDING REGIONS
Compiled from the latest information
CHINESE TURKISTAN
TARIM BASIN
DESERT
UNEXPLORED
TIBET
PROVINCE